Pelican Books

NURSERIES NOW

Martin Hughes is Research Fellow in Early Childhood
Education at Edinburgh University, studying the ways
in which nurseries can help children to acquire number
concepts.

Berry Mayall and Pat Petrie have worked as teachers and,
more recently, have researched day-care for children
under three, especially childminding and day nurseries.
Their particular interests have been the quality of
service offered to children and mothers and the situation
of working mothers.

Peter Moss is studying the experiences of men and
women becoming parents for the first time, and is
especially interested in the role of fathers and the
relationship between work and the family.

Jane Perry is a psychology graduate and has worked in
the Ministry of Pensions and as a researcher at Political
and Economic Planning.

Gill Pinkerton is a psychologist and teacher, and has
worked in playgroups and community nurseries. Her
main interest is in nursery curriculum and parent
involvement in nurseries.

Four of the authors have children and all work, or have
worked until recently, at the Thomas Coram Research
Unit, London University Institute of Education.

Nurseries Now

A Fair Deal for Parents and Children

MARTIN HUGHES

BERRY MAYALL

PETER MOSS

JANE PERRY

PAT PETRIE

GILL PINKERTON

Penguin Books

Penguin Books Ltd, Harmondsworth,
Middlesex, England
Penguin Books, 625 Madison Avenue,
New York, New York 10022, U.S.A.
Penguin Books Australia Ltd, Ringwood,
Victoria, Australia
Penguin Books Canada Ltd, 2801 John Street,
Markham, Ontario, Canada L3R 1B4
Penguin Books (N.Z.) Ltd, 182–190 Wairau Road,
Auckland 10, New Zealand

First published 1980

Typeset, printed and bound in Great Britain by
Hazell Watson & Viney Ltd,
Aylesbury, Bucks
Set in Monotype Baskerville

Contents

Introduction

We first discussed writing a book about nurseries in 1976. At the time we were all working on various research projects concerning pre-school children and their families, and in the course of this work we visited a number of nurseries which were attempting to put new ideas into practice. Our initial intention was to write a short book about these nurseries, but the more we talked with each other, the more we realized the importance of discussing other questions about nurseries in general. Why were innovations needed? What were the ideas behind them? How likely was widespread change as opposed to isolated innovations? And, perhaps most basic of all, what was the case for having nurseries at all – why were they needed?

The book continued to evolve as we read and discussed each other's work. It is not easy for six people to write a book collectively, especially when they don't have much experience of working in this way. Each chapter was rewritten several times, sometimes by different people, so as to incorporate everyone's views and comments. We didn't always agree on issues or the relative importance to attach to them, but hours of discussion helped to develop our ideas and usually produced some measure of agreement. Towards the end we changed our way of working. Partly because of our differing styles of writing, we felt the book was disjointed, and one of us, Martin Hughes, took on the arduous task of editing our various contributions into a more coherent whole. The finished product owes a lot to him.

Despite some minor differences of emphasis and view, there are certain ideas and values which we all share and which are continual themes in the book. In particular, we would all like to see some real changes emerging from the recent movement in Britain towards equal opportunities for women. One of the greatest obstacles to women's equality is the prevailing view that women should assume the major responsibility and workload for home and children. We would like to see these responsibilities shared more equally between men, women and the rest of society. Nurseries are one example of how child-care can be more widely shared, but we would also like to see other means, especially greater involvement by fathers with their children. We feel it is important to move away from the belief that there is only one desirable and feasible type of parenthood in our society – a married couple with the mother at home full-time and father at work full-time. Such an arrangement may suit some families, but for others it is the root of much friction, frustration and unhappiness, with many mothers (and perhaps some fathers) dissatisfied with their role. The answer in our view is neither to assume that such dissatisfied parents are deviants or failures nor to put forward one uniform life-style for all parents to aim for, but instead to encourage real choice in how parents organize their lives and the care of their children. Finally we would also like to see children of both sexes given choice about the kind of people they grow up to be instead of being constrained from an early age by stereotyped sex roles, which impose a narrow view of what is appropriate for boys and girls, men and women.

We pay a lot of attention in the book to the opinions, feelings and circumstances of parents, and particularly mothers. This is because we strongly support equal opportunities for women, but it also reflects our concern at the stress and unhappiness that we and others have come across among many women bringing up young children. But we have not neglected the children and devote a considerable part of the book to their needs and experiences. We have aimed at a balance between parents and children, and tried to avoid regarding either as a mere appendage of the other.

Two other ideas have particularly influenced us. First, we are concerned that there must be a closer and more equal relationship between home and nursery, with parents and nursery workers exchanging ideas, information and insights more readily and with parents given a greater say in the running of nurseries. Secondly, that while issues of quantity and organization such as the shortage of nursery places and inflexibility of hours may be the most pressing problems to resolve, the most interesting and significant questions in the long term are those concerning what happens to children at nursery and who decides what goes on.

We have not attempted to cover every issue in the nursery world, but have focused on areas we are particularly concerned about. We start the book by putting forward the case for nurseries, first from the mother's point of view (Chapter 1), and then in terms of what they can offer children (Chapter 2). In Chapter 3 we discuss a number of objections which are often raised to the kind of nursery service we are proposing. Chapter 4 gives descriptions and information about the main forms of service currently available for pre-school children. In Chapter 5 we take a critical look at the present system of services and highlight some of the main problems, and in Chapter 6 we consider some of the ways in which various people are trying to overcome these problems. In Chapters 7 and 8 we focus on the controversial topics of childminding and the role of parents in nurseries, while in Chapter 9 we look at some of the things children do or could do at nurseries. Finally, in Chapter 10 we discuss how nursery services might be provided in the future, and consider the likelihood of change in the present political climate.

A few points about our terminology. As we shall see in

Chapters 4 and 5, the present system of nursery services is a bewildering hotch-potch of day nurseries, nursery schools and classes, childminders and playgroups. To avoid confusion we have used the word 'nursery' to refer to any place where children can spend time outside their own homes with people paid to take care of them; childminders are therefore included in this general description. Where we discuss a specific kind of nursery we use the particular name, for example 'nursery schools', 'day nurseries' or 'playgroups'. In some parts of the book we discuss individual examples of innovatory projects – nearly all are nurseries which we have visited in the past two and a half years. In all cases real names have been used, the only exception being a factory nursery at 'Morgan Electronics'. We have used the word 'parent' where we mean either the mother or father, or both; where we wish to refer to mothers in particular we use 'mother', and similarly with 'father'. Finally a point about how we refer to children. In most writing the child is usually referred to as 'he' as if all children were male. In this book the child is generally referred to as 'she' except in places where this could be confused with the mother; in these cases we have used 'he'.

*

The book was written while we were all on the staff of the Thomas Coram Research Unit. The Unit is part of London University Institute of Education and carries out a wide range of research, particularly on pre-school and handicapped children and their families. In writing this book we have drawn extensively on this research, including projects in which we have been personally involved, and have received much help and encouragement from other members of the Unit. In particular we would like to thank Dr Barbara Tizard, not only for her comments but for allowing us to use an unpublished paper on whether nursery attendance can harm children; this forms the basis for the second part of Chapter 2.

Above all, we owe our gratitude to the late Director of the Unit, Professor Jack Tizard, who offered guidance, criticism and advice at all stages. We are also very grateful for the hard work and patience of Lorraine Wilder in typing endless drafts and corrections. We should stress however that the views in the book are our own, and in no way represent those of the Thomas Coram Research Unit or its members.

Finally, we would like to thank our editor, Julia Vellacott, for her encouragement and many helpful comments, and also the many childminders, nursery workers and parents whom we have visited and interviewed – without the willingness of such people to give up their time and put themselves out, research workers would soon be out of a job!

The book starts with the views of a group of mothers – part of a sample living in Inner London interviewed by members of the Thomas Coram Research Unit. They open the case for nurseries, from the mother's point of view...

1 The case for nurseries – a better deal for mothers . . .

'I'm very happy with the nursery – having spoken to friends who don't live round here, they think I'm very lucky. I get some "free" time, while Neil [aged four and a quarter years] is at nursery. It's not really "free", but I can go to work.'

'While Ben [aged three and a quarter years] is at nursery, I go shopping, do housework. I think of it as a time to do all my jobs in the morning, so I can take him into the park in the afternoon . . . I've benefited from having a couple of hours on my own. "Thank goodness you're going to nursery on Monday" I feel at the weekend. I'd certainly be more grumpy having to get through my housework with them around.'

'I think I'd be "do-lally" if Timmy [aged four years] didn't go to nursery. The children are so restricted here; we've no garden. I'm such a worrier, I won't even let the big one go across the square. If I had the children on top of me all day, I don't think I would have coped. I like having them both here at half-term . . . While Timmy's at nursery, I usually go to the staff room (at the nursery), have coffee till 10. Then I go home and do the housework, then to work from 12 to 1.15. I like to sew and can do that without interruption when the children are away.'

'I find toddlers very boring and exhausting. Even if I didn't work, I'd like Emma [aged three and a half years] to have gone.'

'I was depressed and lonely and the Health Visitor thought it would be a good idea [sending Jackie, aged two and three quarter years, to nursery]. I've definitely benefited, I'd be lost without it. I can't stand being indoors, I must have some free-dom. After all, you are a person, you are not just a mum. I work on and off – it's more off at the moment than on. I can't sit and do nothing.'

'While Alan [aged three and a half years] is at nursery, I do shopping, ironing, preparing the evening meal, things I can't do when he's around. It's given me time to relax, be on my own.'

'Yes, I benefit from the fact I can work, except the benefits to John [aged two and a half years] are greater. It does disrupt my work having to break at 11.30. Actually, the main benefit for me is seeing how much it's done for him.'

These seven mothers live in a small area near the centre of London, and all experience the limitations and inconveniences of family life in a large city. In one respect, however, they are unusually lucky, for their neighbourhood is served by a range of good nurseries* which offer parents – at least of children over eighteen months – real choice of where, when and for how long to send their children.

These mothers differ in many respects and have chosen to use nurseries in a variety of ways, to suit them and their children. But on one thing they are all agreed: they want nurseries, and are convinced that they and their children benefit from using them – a conviction shared by mothers all over the country, in cities and suburbs, towns and villages.

The evidence that mothers want nurseries is by now overwhelming. In 1974 a survey by the Office of Population Censuses and Surveys (referred to throughout this book as the OPCS survey) interviewed the mothers of 2,501 pre-school children throughout the country [1]. Some form of nursery place was wanted for 90 per cent of three- and four-year-olds, as well as for 46 per cent of children under three – a startling rejection of the official view that children under three should be cared for full-time at home. Other surveys carried out in places as

* For the definition of 'nursery' used throughout this book, see page 10 of the Introduction.

diverse as Westminster [2] and Rochdale [3], Greenwich [4] and Fife [5] have all produced very similar findings, and show that there is a substantial desire for nurseries in every part of the country; indeed, there is a high demand for nurseries throughout the whole industrialized world.

This widespread desire for nurseries is in itself one of the strongest arguments for making them generally available. But we must go further, and argue the case for nurseries *which are not only available to all mothers – and fathers – who want them, but which offer parents a real choice as to the age when their children can start and the hours they can attend for each day.*

Most arguments for providing nurseries emphasize the contribution they can make to children's development and welfare, especially for children who are in some way at a 'disadvantage'. These child-centred arguments are important and we return to them in Chapter 2. But in our view, the main reasons for making nurseries generally available are concerned with the frequently unsatisfactory experience of mothers bringing up pre-school children.

For many women, of course, the experience is not unsatisfactory – indeed they thrive on it. They derive great satisfaction from being at home and caring for their children full-time, and for them early motherhood is a supremely happy and fulfilling time. A few of these mothers will reject nurseries altogether; others will only seek them for short periods as their children approach five, and will often do so reluctantly, more for the children's sake than their own. But many mothers do *not* thrive, or do so only very intermittently: for them, early motherhood is all too often a period of stress, tiredness and frustration. This is not because they are bad or inadequate mothers who fail to love their children, but because they suffer the consequences of an inflexible system of child-rearing – a system that places excessive demands on them, and worsens their already unequal position in society. For these women, nurseries can provide a life-line, helping them at least to survive, and at best to improve their quality of life substantially. Nor will these mothers necessarily need or want full-time nursery care; some may, but for many others a few hours a day, when they need it, will be ample.

A mother's work is never done

The demands of caring for young children are met very largely by mothers. What makes this such a heavy burden is both *the nature of the demands* and their *continuity*: in shorter spells they may be coped with, but without a break they can be crushing. Let us look briefly at some of these demands.

Young children are particularly dependent on adults, and require much time and attention if they are to survive unharmed and healthy, to learn and develop, and to gain satisfaction and enjoyment from life. The demands they make are many and varied – they must be fed, clothed, changed, bathed, kept occupied and amused. Much of this work is physically demanding and involves a lot of lifting, bending, pushing and carrying. It also involves a considerable amount of noise: both the exuberant whoops and shrieks when children are having an exciting and happy time, and the whining, crying and squabbling when they are not.

It is easy for people who see children only when they are well behaved, or for short periods of time, to talk about the joys and pleasures of parenthood. These joys are real enough, as any parent can testify, but they are counterbalanced by the many times when young children are tired, cross, upset or crying, when they are feeling miserable or unwell, or when they are simply 'having a bad day'. These are the times when child-care is a wearisome and exhausting business from which there is little or no escape, the days when mothers are totally worn out long before the children's bedtime arrives.

Nor is bedtime necessarily the end of the matter: a surprisingly large number of children wake regularly in the night. A study in Cambridge by Judy Bernal found that 27 per cent of babies still woke regularly at fourteen months [6], while another study in London by Naomi Richman found that 14 per cent of three-year-olds still woke three nights a week or more [7]. Once awake, children often do not go back to sleep for an hour or more. But however briefly they are awake this still means disturbed sleep for parents:

'I've sometimes woken ten times a night and I've felt like chucking Tracey [aged two years]. There's times I've picked her up and instead of putting her down gently, I've been a bit rough. Then I've had to leave and get my husband to see to her. If you've been woken half a dozen times in the night, you're just so tired and weary, you can't cope.'

'Since just before Christmas, Michael [aged sixteen months] has taken a long time to go down after waking. It can be about an hour – it varies tremendously. Then he's awake at 4 or 5 ... he went through a stage about a week ago when he was awake every twenty minutes. I can't work because I get too tired by the evening, even if he does go down. I feel life's ebbing away. I get strange ideas at night! If I've had a good night, I'm much more pleased to see him. I do more then – otherwise, it's just washing up all day.'

Some children cause problems of a different kind. In Naomi Richman's study of three-year-olds, just under a quarter (23 per cent) were judged as having a 'mild', 'moderate' or 'marked' behaviour problem. She describes one child with a 'mild' problem as:

a very active girl, often in difficulties because interfering and touching things, e.g. when shopping, breaks ornaments, spills things in fridge because she can't leave them alone. Can amuse herself and play with others but may spend the whole day walking around and moaning. Very upset if left even with people she knows. Worries if brother or father not there, very scared of strangers even after several meetings, worries about cuts, quite afraid of the dark. Takes over an hour to get to sleep; has to be in father's arms, usually settled about 10.30 p.m. Poor appetite, faddy eater.

Mothers have to combine continuous child-care with other work. Some have outside employment, all have housework to do, and the demands of housework and child-care are often incompatible. The young child's ability to strew toys round the house, walk sand and mud into carpets, empty cupboards, spill things and generally wreak havoc may be as much at odds with keeping a house as the mother's need to prepare meals, go shopping or get the weekly wash done, all by a certain time, may clash with the child's desire to play, explore and experiment. Not surprisingly, many mothers use their 'free time' while children are at nursery to catch up on domestic chores, such as ironing, shopping and window-cleaning, which become major feats of endurance (or ingenuity) when small children are around.

The fact that mothers work very long hours therefore comes as no surprise. One recent study found that mothers spend an average seventy-seven hours a week on housework and child-care, and other studies of housework in Britain, the United States and France show a consistently similar working week [8]. In addition to these hours of actual housework, mothers are usually 'on call' twenty-four hours a day, fifty-two weeks a year, to deal with accidents, nightmares and all the irregular but not infrequent minor crises of childhood.

Because of the nature of the housewife/mother's job, much of this working time must be spent in the home, away from other adults. Bearing most of the responsibility for child-care, she can go out unencumbered, daytime or evening, week-day or weekend, only if someone else can or will care for the children. Going anywhere with young children requires considerable organization and stamina, with definite limits on what can be done – and many mothers soon learn to restrict their worlds to these limits. Many features of modern life are simply not adapted to the reduced pace and mobility of mothers and young children. As public transport gets worse, shops, entertainments and public services are becoming increasingly hard to reach without a car – which most mothers with pre-school children don't have. The OPCS survey found that only 32 per cent of mothers had the use of a car at least once a week, and many of them were limited to weekend use; another study by the Thomas Coram Research Unit of families from three areas of Inner London (referred to below as the TCRU study) found that only 7 per cent of mothers got to drive the 'family' car at some stage in the week and that most of the mothers in car-owning families could not drive[9].

Over and above the physical demands and restrictions that mothers face, there is the added burden for most of feeling continually and ultimately responsible for the health, development and happiness of their children. However much help a mother may get in bringing up her children, she is still likely to feel that she is the person beyond whom there is no recourse or appeal, and who is answerable for whatever happens. 'Once you have children, you realize your life's not your own. You've got to rear them – they're your responsibility.'

Counting the cost

Caring for young children, a home and usually a husband is demanding and unremitting work, and takes a heavy toll of many of the women who do it. *Overtiredness* is common, the product of long hours of work, too little sleep and in some cases the lethargy that may accompany depression. For many women, the early years of motherhood are frequently remembered as the period 'when one constantly yearns for a full night's sleep and a day free of demands'. Then there is the high level of *dissatisfaction* with the job itself.

'I feel very low sometimes, it's the same thing day in, day out. It gets on my nerves. You feed the kids [aged eighteen months and four years], you wash the kids, you make the beds, carpets, curtains, everything. I'll be honest with you, as much as I love my children, I'd give anything to go back to work tomorrow ... being at home all day, it's not what it's made out to be. It's the same thing every day ... you're tied to a routine. It's not as if I can say I'll go to do some shopping, you can't because of the children. And when you've got two kids around you all day, they're all right as long as you keep them occupied, but you can't occupy them and do the housework as well.'

This woman was one of a sample of young mothers interviewed by Susannah Ginsberg, nearly two thirds of whom were dissatisfied with being in the home full-time as housewives and mothers[10]. Other studies have also found high proportions of women who are dissatisfied with their work in the home. Ann Oakley found that a majority of the young mothers in her sample experienced monotony, frustration and pressure of time in their work, more frequently, in fact, than factory workers, including those on assembly lines. While housework did not require the mothers' whole attention, it persistently demanded just enough of their attention to make involvement in anything else impossible[8]. Mary Boulton, in a third study, emphasizes that women can and do derive considerable satisfaction from their children, while at the same time being frustrated by the continuous day-to-day work associated with child-care[11]. This distinction is a crucial one: *for a mother to express dissatisfaction with her lot does not mean she dislikes her children, but rather that her enjoyment of them is marred by poor work conditions and low job satisfaction.* As Jessie Bernard, an American sociologist, says:

The joy of babies is indeed real ... but loving babies and loving motherhood are far from identical. One could love the baby much more if motherhood were structured in a way to make it more comfortable to the needs of both mother and child.[12]

Because the inescapable demands of exclusive continuous responsibility for home and children are sources of irritation and resentment for many women – who nevertheless feel expected to stay at home full-time while their children are small – this gives rise to considerable inner conflict.

'I don't feel I should go to work … it's a matter of conscience really. In one way you think, well, I could do with going to work, not just for money, for my mind's sake. It drives me up the wall sometimes when I'm shut in … then again I think I've had them [two children aged three and five years], they're mine and I should look after them.'

The anxiety and guilt so common among mothers come from other sources too, in particular from the sense of ultimate responsibility for children's health, development and happiness which we have already discussed. With high standards expected of mothers and housewives – often a product of the idealized mother figure propagated by advertising, television and women's magazines – and the intrinsic problems of achieving these standards, it is not surprising that this responsibility can cause so much worry.

Women with young children also suffer particularly high rates of *depression*. The extent of the problem is most clearly shown in a study of depression among London women by George Brown[13]. 18 per cent of women with pre-school children had suffered a definite psychiatric disorder at some time in the three months prior to interview (referred to by George Brown as 'cases'), while a further 15 per cent had had the same symptoms, but in a less severe form (referred to as 'borderlines'). Naomi Richman estimated that at least 30 per cent of her sample of mothers with three-year-old children had been significantly depressed at some time in the preceding twelve months[14]. Depression is particularly common among working-class women in cities. In George Brown's sample, 16 per cent of middle-class mothers with pre-school children were classified as either 'cases' or 'borderlines', compared to a staggering 48 per cent of working-class mothers.

Many depressed mothers remain unknown to the health and welfare authorities, simply because they seek no help. This may reflect growing scepticism of the value of taking such problems to a family doctor. Those mothers who do go are often prescribed valium or a similar drug, which many abandon after a day or two. In the TCRU study, 23 per cent of mothers had been prescribed sedatives, tranquilizers or other medication for their 'nerves' at some point in the preceding year.

George Brown has suggested that low self-esteem may be a major cause of depression, and indeed many mothers experience a loss of self-confidence and sense of adult identity[15]. Many factors contribute to this, such as feelings of dissatisfaction, when fulfilment was anticipated, and of guilt, when unable to attain idealized standards of motherhood. There is also the low status accorded to child-care in our society, emphasized by the lack of attention paid to it by men, and by the financial dependence of most mothers with pre-school children. Now that a majority of women work up to the birth of their first child and return to work when their youngest child goes to school, early motherhood has become the only period of total financial dependence in most women's adult lives. Jessie Bernard points out:

Only those who have themselves experienced the degradation of having no money can understand the humiliation countless homemakers feel when they must ask for or at least account for every penny they spend.[12]

Diminished self-confidence and sense of adult identity can show in several ways. A common symptom is the anxiety and doubt harboured by many mothers about their ability to deal again with the world beyond the confines of young children, home and other mothers – a world from which they have often been abruptly cut off on the birth of a first child. With this often goes increased difficulty in talking about, or even being able to give serious thought to, anything not connected with the daily care of home and children; mothers may achieve excellent communication with their own children but often at the expense of communication with other adults. Low self-esteem goes hand in hand with the sense of isolation and loneliness felt by many young mothers. For some women loneliness is the sheer absence of adult contact, while for others it is the inability to keep in touch with particular friends or relations, or to build up or sustain a circle of friends consisting not just of other mothers; or it may be the desire to see more of a husband working long hours or too involved with his own interests.

These problems, it should be stressed, are neither universal nor necessarily continuous. A third of Susannah Ginsberg's mothers were, after all, satisfied with being full-time mothers and housewives, and many mothers go through good times as well as bad times. It should also be stressed again that because a mother feels dissatisfied it does not mean she rejects her children or gets no enjoyment from them; few mothers would contemplate being without their children, or do not love and deeply care about them, whatever the stresses of parenthood. But despite these qualifications, the evidence still points to the good side of parenthood being too frequently outweighed by the bad, with its demands and restrictions, frustrations and dissatisfactions. Some mothers are genuinely satisfied with their lot, but the overall picture is alarming, with many mothers paying a high price for carrying a disproportionate share of the burdens of raising young children.

Three mothers

Perhaps the figures have a numbing, depersonalizing quality; after all, people don't hurt in percentages. Let us listen to accounts by three mothers of some of their feelings and experiences – unexceptional mothers in many ways, each living in reasonable housing, each with an employed husband, none suffering the extremes of distress that can be found all too readily.

'I must admit I'm tired these days and I have been getting headaches. I think it's these two crying all the time. I'm not prone to headaches, but since I've been home [from hospital for birth of second child], I've had headaches – a lot more than I've ever had. It's probably just the tension and lack of sleep. The baby does seem to cry a lot and I seem to notice John [older child] crying more since the baby's been home.

'I get terribly woe-is-me and terribly depressed, get so terribly sorry for myself. I feel terribly morbid, think "what's the point of everything?" and all that sort of thing. Don't know why. The silliest things can set me off. I can get like that quite often. I tend to be up and down. Being at home with the children [aged three weeks and seventeen months] gives you so much more time to think about things. I get very sensitive about what people say about me. Mostly felt like this being pregnant, and then in those early months [after birth], each time. It got a lot better after John was about three months. Then I got pregnant again. I don't know if it's all tied up with being tired or having a lot to do. It's mostly to do with being pregnant and having them very small.

'I get tensed up if I don't feel I'm getting everything done. Some days you're on top of everything, some days everything's on top of you. I've said I think I ought to get some pills for anti-depression. Husband laughs and says I've got nothing to moan about. My pet thing is that my husband never talks enough. I wait for him to come home and it's "why don't you talk to me?". That starts it off each time – "I'm fed up, I never speak to anyone or see anyone and you can't even be bothered to speak to me." Then I decide he doesn't do enough around, I get fed up with waiting on him, that really is the strain of it most times. I suppose I expect to run a conversation from the moment he comes in. I wait for him to come home, then nag as soon as he gets here. I get on my own nerves, so I don't know what I must be like to my husband. He's very good. I don't know how he puts up with it. He tends to just ignore me. It must get on his nerves.

'I can get very morbid, and think what's the point of going on, what's your life all for – work and work and nothing else. I've often thought how I'd commit suicide. Now I probably think I can't kill myself, I've got the children to look after! It was all so simple before.

'I worked for years, always with people, and suddenly just like that, I don't really know anybody. There aren't any neighbours with children, there's nobody I really know round here. I'm the sort of person, if there's other people around, I'm O.K. I don't know anyone round here that I see in the day. Seeing people comes in spasms – one week you see masses, then you don't see anybody for weeks. I sometimes feel lonely, especially towards the end of the week when there's less to do in the place. It'd just be nice to be able to go for coffee to someone, have a chat, or someone to pop in to you.

'I don't have any personal money, and hate asking. I want to be independent and get very uptight about it. He doesn't see the necessity – says I can have anything I want, just ask. It's one of our big rows.'

*

'I worry about my present situation [feeling depressed], find it disturbing that someone as efficient as myself can't get out of the mental state I'm in. I can't make my husband realize it's critical. A lot of people don't realize how lonely and self-defeating this existence can be. I've felt in pretty much a continuous state of depression for the past several months. I had a miscarriage two weeks ago, but think I was mainly depressed for other reasons. I feel very isolated, very cut off from ideas, because I haven't got any contacts with people. This really began when I completed my last job three months ago – I find I can't think of anything to do.

'I miss contact with reasonably intelligent people. Boredom is the problem. I try not to let it affect Peter [aged fourteen months], but it probably does, though not very much. It affects my relationship with my husband. I feel envious, I dislike the housewife role, though this isn't a problem when I'm working. My depression affects my relations with other people – when depressed I feel I have less to give, so I see them less.

'I haven't actually contemplated walking out, but I realize why people do it. My husband is not very helpful. His attitude is "pull yourself together". His lack of understanding is very frustrating. I haven't been to my GP – I haven't got much confidence in him and I don't want to go on to drugs.

'I've got quite a few friends, most working, most without

children. I only see them at night, reasonably infrequently. I would like to see more people, but my main problem is that I can't work. I feel lonely because I can't work. I had a lot more to offer people when I was happier.

'I'd like to go out to work now. My husband doesn't mind but says I must pay for child-care if I want to work. The problem is to find some child-care at the moment.'

*

'Last year I was very depressed. It's all been since Deborah [two and a quarter] was born. I always had people around me until I came out of hospital with her – just this baby, there's nobody. I would go out shopping and meet people but that's only five or ten minutes in the day. My friends were still working and those with children were back at work. I was lonely, completely lonely, on my own. When I was working before Deborah was born, I used to get fed up and depressed at times, but after the birth it's been a completely different sort of depression. I used to go walking for hours and she'd be crying and I'd come home and nobody to talk to. I'd phone my husband twelve times a day for somebody to talk to.

'My whole personality changed. I was so depressed it was unbelievable. I went to my GP and she gave me vitamins because I was run down. I didn't want to do anything. I thought life wasn't worth living. There just wasn't anybody to talk to, to talk my problem out with and there's things you don't want to talk about with your husband. Before the play-group, life seemed pointless. It was just one misery, I used to sit and smoke all the time.

'I even thought at one time that I hated her [the child] and I was sorry I had her, especially as it was me that wanted her. I did discuss this with one mother who was very depressed. She was taken into hospital. She was worse than me because she admitted to her doctor exactly how she felt, which I didn't do. When I was really bad, I did only what was essential. I got very jealous of my husband going out and seeing people.

'I'm sorry I've had all these problems since Deborah was born. You're pampered before the babe's born – you are something special. As soon as your babe arrives, you're nothing and the baby's everything. All the attention I used to get off him [husband] goes to her. But if I hadn't had her, I'd have missed a lot. My marriage was pointless without a baby.

'I haven't got money problems, but I worry about money in case I may have money problems. My husband jokes about it, says if I don't have anything to worry about, then I'll think of something. When I go to bed, that's the time I worry, every night; my husband's asleep and I lie awake for hours. Worry about "little" things every day. The worrying tires me out and depresses me. I've always worried about something, but since Deborah was born and I've had responsibility, the worrying has increased. I've always felt she's my responsibility, my husband couldn't cope with her.

'I still get low, no more than I would if I'd never had Deborah. I feel low about once a week. I get low for different reasons now. I get fed up with housework, and just leave it and go out. When I feel low, I get irritated with her over the least little thing. He just leaves me alone. I often have a little cry and feel better afterwards. It relieves the tension. When I've had a bad day with her, I'll cry. Lately I cry more because I don't have a break in the day. Sometimes, I never realized you could feel so tired. When I tell him, he says, "What do you do all day?"

'About once a month I get this feeling [that I'd like to walk out and leave it all]. It used to be more often. The thing that really gets me is that I'll have her all day and when he comes in at night she'll still want me. It annoys me. I feel like just going – I'd love to go, but I'd never do it.

'I take to reading if I'm depressed – escape from my world into someone else's. I do talk to my husband [when feeling depressed]. I do confide in my mother, but all she says is "I've had five so you can't tell me". She hasn't got my sort of character – a bomb could fall over her head and her world would still go round. I talk to my sister, she understands. She's six years older and she's been through it – she has helped.

'My husband understands, but he'll say "oh, you've got the hump" and just leaves me alone. Asks if I want a drink. I wish he was the sort I could talk to more. He's very easy-going, the same mood all the time. He doesn't understand.

'I mix pretty well. I've always had friends till I had Deborah. She's altered my life completely. I feel uninteresting as a person. I've nothing to talk about, only about my home. I'd like to work when Deborah's settled in at nursery school, the sort of work where you meet people. I'd have something to talk about, I'd be more interesting.'

Mothers in employment

It is perhaps not surprising, in view of what we have just seen, that many mothers seek a change from being at home full-time, and an increasing number are now going out to work. Between 1961 and 1971, the proportion of mothers with pre-school children who also had a job rose from 12 per cent to 19 per cent and by 1977 it had risen again to 27 per cent[16]. The number of mothers who work for part of their children's first five years is also considerably higher than the number at work at any given point of time: many drop into and out of the labour force on several occasions. In the TCRU study, for instance, 44 per cent of mothers not currently employed had still worked at some time since having their first child. Nationally, there is evidence to suggest that just over half of all mothers have had at least one job before their children reach school age[17].

The trend towards increasing numbers of mothers seeking work is likely to continue. Recent projections anticipate an increase of 189,000 (9 per cent) in the number of employed married women aged twenty to thirty-four in the labour force, between 1976 and 1986 [18]. As we shall see below, many non-employed

Table 1. Employment rates for women with pre-school children in six countries, mid-1970s

	Employment rate for women with child aged:	
	0–2	3–school age
France	43%	44%
Germany – East	80%	80%
West	33%	No information
Hungary	33%	75%
Sweden	58%	64%
USA	35%	48%
Britain	18%	31%

mothers say they would like to work. Moreover, by
international standards, current levels of employment
in Britain are still low, as Table 1 shows in its comparison
with the USA and five European countries[19].

Some see the reason for these increases in simple
economic terms – mothers work to raise family living
standards. This is far too simple: the reasons mothers
work cannot be found or explained away in a single
cause. American studies have identified some of the
factors involved – the growth of real wages for women
(that is to say their time is worth more); the development of labour-saving devices; shifts in employment
favouring growth in sectors where women are well
represented (such as more secretaries, fewer miners);
a shorter working week and increased opportunities for
part-time work; the declining birth-rate; rising educational attainment (mothers with the highest qualifications are most likely to work)[20]. There have also been
changes in attitudes and expectations about the position
and rights of women; and an increasing number of lone
mothers and mothers from ethnic minorities, both
groups with high employment rates.

But the reasons why an individual mother works arise
from her own personal needs and domestic situation.
All, or nearly all, work for money – as do most people.
For some, the money is paramount and essential to
economic survival, and they would probably stop work
altogether if their family income was higher: this
applies particularly to women working the longest
hours in the poorest-quality jobs. But most employed
mothers enjoy being at work and say they would choose
to continue even if their family income increased –
though some, especially among those in full-time jobs,
say they would take the opportunity to reduce or alter
the hours they work. Most mothers give a wide variety
of reasons for wanting to go out to work, over and above
money, and many of these reasons stem from the problems
experienced by home-bound mothers:

'Independence, continuing with something. I'm interested in the work. It's good for me. Also, I'm not in a pigeon hole as "John's mother".'

'Being able to afford to buy clothes for the children; being able to afford a holiday. It's nice to have a life of your own, to meet people. If you're just a housewife, you haven't got much conversation with your husband.'

'Freedom of mind, independence, money, we've all benefited because I'm happier.'

'Not for money, but prestige and interest and to keep contact with professional life.'

'Complete freedom, feeling myself normal again. Stimulation, friendship, proving myself.'

'It's purely financial . . . [but] it does give you something to do. If I was at home all day, I would get bored and depressed and have more financial problems. It's also a chance to meet people.'

'I couldn't bear not to – I adore what I do.'

The reasons why mothers are seeking work in increasing numbers are long-term and probably irreversible – they are in the labour market to stay. But despite this fact, women with young children still remain at a great disadvantage if they want to go out to work. The most obvious form this takes is that many mothers who want to work are unable to do so. Surveys have consistently found that a substantial proportion of non-employed mothers would rather work, especially if satisfactory child-care arrangements were available, and that these mothers considerably outnumber those employed mothers who would prefer to stop working [1, 9, 21]. In the OPCS survey, for instance, there were three times as many non-employed mothers who wanted to work as employed mothers who wanted to stop work.

Most mothers with pre-school children who do have a job work part-time, and part-time women workers are the most disadvantaged sector of the labour force. In

1977, 78 per cent of these women were employed in only four of the country's twenty-seven industrial groups (distributive trades; professional and scientific services including health and education; miscellaneous services such as hotels, catering and laundry; and public administration). The 1974 Family Expenditure Survey (FES) found that 52 per cent of employed married women with a child aged 0–4 were in semi-skilled or unskilled manual occupations, compared to 21 per cent of their husbands and 21 per cent of younger married women with no children (see Figure 1)[23]. The opportunities for training and promotion are equally

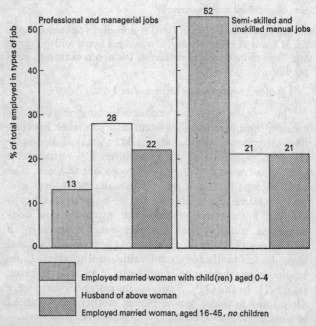

Figure 1. Proportion of employed parents with pre-school children and childless married women in high- and low-status jobs, Britain, 1974

poor. In a recent government study of management attitudes to women by Audrey Hunt, only 13 per cent of firms with part-time women workers were prepared to consider promoting them, and only 27 per cent would consider giving them facilities for further education and training. Part-time workers were also frequently excluded from various occupational benefits, especially pension schemes[24].

Poor earnings are the last part of this grim picture. Figure 2 compares the 1974 FES data on earnings of

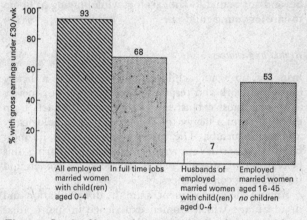

Figure 2. Levels of low earnings among employed parents with pre-school children and childless married women, Britain, 1974

married women with pre-school children; their husbands; and younger, childless married women. The difference between women with and women without children is large, but it is still much less than that between working mothers and fathers; 91 per cent of mothers, including 68 per cent of those working full-time, had gross earnings of under £30.00 a week, compared to only 7 per cent of their husbands.

But the financial and job consequences *for women* of having children do not cease when children are no longer dependent – they are felt through adult life, and beyond into retirement. Recent American research has estimated that the interruption to women's careers caused by parenthood, together with lower levels of education and vocational training due to the anticipation of this interruption, account for up to 50 per cent of the differences in male – female earnings through *all* stages of working life[25]. The long-term career and earnings losses for *all* mothers, because of the child-care responsibilities that they carry, are enormous, and go far beyond any actual loss of earnings while staying at home to care for young children.

Rights and choices

Bringing up young children carries with it a heavy burden of work and responsibility, which in our society is borne almost exclusively by mothers. It exacts from many of them a heavy toll – physically, psychologically and economically. The case for nurseries, at its most basic, is that they provide *one* means of sharing this heavy burden, so reducing the overload on women and its damaging consequences.

Among these consequences are the discrimination and disadvantage which women experience in many areas of life – and especially in employment – as a result of having children: consequences which are rarely suffered by men. Nurseries have thus an essential part to play in changing women's position in society, and in making equal opportunities a reality. In a society which is committed by legislation to ending sex discrimination and promoting equal opportunities, the provision of comprehensive nursery services should be a fundamental social priority.

What would equal opportunities mean in practice? To many people it suggests a grim, uncaring society in which both parents are working such long hours that they see their children only briefly and exhaustedly at the end of each day. This picture is as misleading as it is unattractive. Equal opportunities does *not* mean that women should model themselves on the worst aspects of men's role in society. Rather the fundamental principle is one of *choice*. Parents should not be obliged to fit into the conventional model of family life – a model which so many women find stressful and oppressive – but should instead be able to choose the combination of work and child-care which best suits their particular needs. For some this might mean the conventional set-up in which father works full-time while mother cares for the children, but it could equally mean a reversal in which mother goes out to work while father stays at home; it might mean both parents working full-time outside the home, or both working part-time, or taking it in turns to work, or even sharing the same job. Many people would also be bringing up children outside the standard two-parent pattern, either through choice or through circumstances: lone parents, those living with other partners, or those in a variety of communal set-ups. *It is time we rejected the idea that one model of family life is intrinsically superior, and accepted that there is a wide range of ways in which parents can organize child-care and other aspects of their lives.*

The role of nurseries should therefore be to encourage and support the widest possible range of options for parents. Some parents, for example, might choose to use a nursery for several hours each day, while one or both of them were working in full-time or part-time jobs; other parents might use a nursery for shorter, less regular periods, mainly to give themselves a break from the demands of constant child-care; others might not want to use a nursery at all, or only for brief periods as their child approached the age of five. For this kind of choice to be available, however, requires the general acceptance of two fundamental principles:

- that nurseries should be available for all parents who want to use them

● that parents should be able to choose the age at which their children start attending, and the hours they attend for each day

If nurseries are to achieve their fullest potential for alleviating the stress on mothers, promoting equal opportunities, and giving parents a wide choice in how they organize their lives, then these two principles must be accepted as the basis for providing nurseries. At present, they are *not* widely accepted, either inside or outside the nursery world. Indeed, the very idea of allowing parents greater access to nurseries and control over how they use them strikes at the heart of many people's feelings about the mother's role and the way in which children should be brought up, and gives rise to a number of objections. We will look at these objections more carefully in Chapter 3. Meanwhile, we look at the benefits which nurseries can offer *children*.

2 ... and a better deal for children too

Mother and child

The needs of mothers have taken first place in this book, partly because of their importance, but partly to redress the balance of much other writing on nurseries. All too often mothers' needs are briefly tacked on to those of their children – or else are ignored altogether – and mothers are often advised to play down their own needs and put those of their children uppermost. Yet the needs of mothers and children are *both* important – *if only because they are so closely linked*. A situation which is bad for the mother is likely to be bad for her child: conversely, any improvement in the situation of mothers is likely to have positive effects on their children.

Children's welfare does not depend on insisting that the woman's present role in the family should be maintained. Indeed, the present organization of child-care may often be as disadvantageous to the child as it is to the mother. When the young child has such a close and continuous relationship with only one person, any problems which she experiences – such as tiredness, loneliness, dissatisfaction and depression – are likely to have a bad effect on the child himself. This is shown very clearly in George Brown's study of depression in young London mothers[1]. At the times when these mothers were suffering episodes of depression, the accident rate for their children was *four times higher* than that of children whose mothers were not depressed. Brown adds:

Many mothers report increased irritability, loss of interest in their children, and so on, when depressed or anxious and this can give rise to manifestations of distress in the child [2, 3]. It is unlikely that the link between psychiatric disorder and accidents is explained simply by poor supervision. A change in the behaviour of the child is more likely to be involved.

Naomi Richman's study of three-year-olds also found a link between the state of mother and child: those mothers who were depressed were also most likely to have children with behaviour problems[4].

Nurseries are not a 'cure all' for the range of problems experienced by mothers. But they can make a substantial contribution to mothers' happiness and satisfaction, and in many cases result in a better relationship between mother and child. Of the seven women whose comments began Chapter 1, four explicitly refer to improved relations with their children since going to nursery.

'We get on better. Alan's less dependent. Before, everything was "mummy" – now he seems to get on better with my husband, he shares us.'

'The children are both better tempered. We spend less time together and when we're together, we enjoy it.'

'We form a better relationship. When they've been away from you, you've both got more to talk about.'

'Neil and I probably get on better. He's a very happy but demanding child. Going to nursery tires him out and he's probably happier.'

Complementing the home

If nurseries can indirectly benefit children by helping to reduce the pressures on mothers, they also provide more direct advantages. Again we turn to mothers themselves to describe some of these advantages.

'Children living in flats are very restricted. The only child in a [city] flat really needs the stimulus of other children – he

needs space to run around in. John's made new friends, copes
with different kids, relates to girls more, he's much more
sociable. He also knows more about shapes and puzzles and
his vocabulary has improved dramatically. It's a lovely little
oasis in the middle of the city. He likes the sandpits and pools
and to run around in the big garden.'

'The kids need it. You can't entertain them at home as they
do at the nursery. Jackie definitely benefits, apart from what
she learns. She plays with lots of kids. She can play with clay
and paints and things she doesn't do at home. I'm worried
about what she'll do when she gets to school. She loves the
teachers, they're more friends than teachers really . . . She
loves the nursery. She'd live there if she could. If she's sick she
wants to go. The other day she was feeling ill, but insisted I
take her.'

'I felt I couldn't offer Neil enough. Living here [in a second-
floor flat] is very restricting. He enjoys going, talks about it
happily and openly and is never reluctant to go. He's got a lot
of energy and having the garden at the nursery is very important – he can slosh around in puddles and mud. They can offer
him far more than I can. It's probably made him more sociable,
though he's always been that way.'

'Alan was very shy. That was my main reason for wanting
him to go to nursery. He keeps asking to go – he loves it. He's
much less shy now, mixes well, it's brought him out a lot.
He's very sociable and popular now . . . There's plenty for
them to do, more than I could give at home. Alan loves
climbing, more than anything.'

'Emma is quite happy about going to the nursery. She
doesn't like staying at home. At weekends, she says she'd like
to go. If she was at home with me, she'd have a miserable life.
She's physically able to gain more there.'

'I sent Ben to meet other children. His older brother was
there already. He loves it, every morning asks "am I going?",
also at weekends . . . He's definitely benefited. He's forming
friendships, mixing with other children, learning to share. He
has more interest in things; there he'll paint, but at home they'll
get out the paint and then two minutes later they're finished.
I think it's a marvellous place, maybe more so because living
in flats you have less space.'

'Seventeen months was the right age to start [at nursery]. The other child was not here, so Timmy had no one to play with. It got him in the way to being without me. There's nothing for him to do here, whereas at the nursery he's got everything you can imagine. He's so restricted in the flat . . . He enjoys going, he's full of it when he comes in and sometimes at 3 p.m. he doesn't want to go home. He occasionally objects to going, but we jolly him along . . . I don't send him to be taught. All I'm interested in is his learning to be away from me, learning to cope with things, which he's achieved by going to nursery. It makes the children independent, makes them do things for themselves.'

The benefits mentioned by these mothers are extensive and varied. But underlying this variety is a common theme – *that it is difficult for a mother to meet all her children's needs – especially for play, exploration and companionship.* Let us consider some of these in more detail.

Sometimes children's opportunities to play and explore at home are limited by obvious environmental factors. High-rise flats are the most notorious example. In 1974, 10 per cent of all pre-school children lived in flats above ground-floor level, and 4.5 per cent were on the second floor or higher: in Greater London, the proportions were 28 per cent and 15 per cent[5]. Living in such conditions is rarely easy for families, but sometimes it becomes a nightmare for parents and children.

'The problem is that Sarah [aged three years] never wants to come home, hates the flat, wants to go with milkman, doctor, anyone to get out of the flat. If she can't get out to the park, she whines all afternoon. She has temper tantrums every day [when mother insists she comes home from nursery or park], flings herself down, screams, turns red, won't budge. I have to fight to get her home. Her whole personality changed since we've moved to this flat. She is fine at friends' or at her granny's, but she's difficult and fretful at home.'

There are other unsuitable surroundings for pre-school children. The O P C S study found that 18 per cent of pre-school children were in housing that was over-

crowded or lacked basic amenities, while for a further
11 per cent it included no private outdoor play space[6].
These conditions are heavily concentrated in inner-city
areas. The TCRU study of three areas in Inner London
found that 48 per cent of pre-school families had no
gardens *and* either lived above first-floor level, or were
overcrowded, or had no bath or indoor toilet of their
own[7].

There are further constraints on what a pre-school
child can do at home. His mother must balance what he
wants or needs to do against the demands made of her
by other children, her husband and the housework.
There are limits to the mess and upheaval she can allow
and the amount of supervision and participation she can
offer. Toys and other equipment are often restricted by
lack of space or money.

Being in the care of his mother all day can leave a
young child very dependent on her. He may become very
demanding of her attention and time, and find it hard to
do anything without her constant encouragement and
support. It can also leave him very isolated from other
adults and children. Mothers are usually well aware of
these problems, and the most common reason they give
for wanting nurseries is to enable their children to mix
with other children and develop social competence.
A study by Joyce Watts in Fife found that 71 per cent of
mothers with children at playgroups or nursery education
gave 'getting company' and 'the chance to mix with
other children' as the main reasons for using pre-school
provision. Social aims were the first choice of parents in
all types of provision, but overwhelmingly so among
playgroup parents[8]. In a study of children at nursery
classes by Barbara Tizard, of the Thomas Coram
Research Unit, two thirds of parents reported that their
children had gained in 'getting on with other children',
and this was by far the most commonly reported gain[9].

Parents also value the opportunity for their children
to meet and get used to being with other adults. Children

who are at home all day see a very limited range of adults, and this may well have become more pronounced over the last generation or two. The increasing dispersal of families means less chance for pre-school children to see grandparents, aunts, uncles and cousins. Falling birth-rates and smaller families mean not only fewer relatives per family, but also that young children are now very unlikely to have brothers and sisters in secondary school, college, apprenticeship or work. In addition, more older women are now going out to work while the strong commitment of men to the world of work shows little sign of diminishing. Taken together, these trends point to young children and their mothers becoming more and more isolated from the mainstream of society.

The educational potential of nurseries

To parents, the main benefits of nursery attendance for children are social and recreational: they value the opportunities for their children to mix, play, explore and become independent. Many believe their children can benefit in these ways from a very early age, often well before the officially recommended age of three. The great majority of children also appreciate the opportunities for play and companionship offered by nurseries: like the children described earlier, they enjoy going and are often disappointed when they can't go at weekends or holidays. This is of course a crucial point: whatever else children get from attending nurseries, they should at least get pleasure and enjoyment from going.

But nurseries can offer more. They can provide opportunities for children to learn new skills and generally enhance their development: they have, in short, educational potential. Research studies have shown that attending nurseries can lead to significant improvements in children's language and in performance on intelligence tests, and sometimes these improvements have been very large. In one study, by Rick Heber and Howard Garber in Milwaukee, a group of children attended a full-time nursery with a specific educational programme from three months to six years (the age at which American children start school). By the age of six they had a lead of nearly two years in language development over a 'non-nursery' group, and an average I Q of 123 compared to 94 for the latter group. Differences in language showed as early as fourteen to eighteen months, with the nursery children responding to their educational programme even at this very early age[10]. Other studies, in Britain as well as America, have shown that even part-time nursery attendance at the age of three or four can still produce significant, if more modest, gains in language and I Q [11].

Such findings need qualifying. First, these gains have been found almost entirely in nurseries using special 'structured programmes': that is, where the nursery staff have worked out specific educational objectives for the children and have developed methods to achieve these objectives. Ordinary nursery education, with its emphasis on free play, does not in general produce such gains, and indeed many advocates of 'free play' are highly critical of 'structured' methods. Secondly, the tests used in evaluating these gains can be criticized on the grounds that they involve placing children in artificial situations, with previously unknown testers wanting them to try unusual tasks. What such tests actually measure is open to question. They could be a true indication of the ability or trait under study, or they could merely reflect how children respond to the demands of artificial test situations. Thirdly, most of these studies have concentrated on improving children's language and intellectual development, partly because these abilities are highly valued in the educational system, and partly because tests are readily available which claim to measure these abilities. But language and intelligence are only one part, albeit an important one, of human development and performance: there are also physical, social, emotional, moral and creative sides to any individual, and many parents and nursery workers believe nurseries should be equally concerned with these broader aspects of education. Using the right approaches, and especially the setting of explicit ends and devising of specific methods to achieve them, much can be done to foster these areas of development and to teach pre-school children a wide variety of skills. (A few examples, which only hint at the full range of possibilities, are discussed in Chapter 9.)

What can we conclude from these studies, if we take these qualifications into account? There is probably widespread agreement among psychologists and nursery educators that children in their first five years have a *tremendous potential for learning*, and that nurseries can help them develop and learn skills across a wide range of areas. Projects like Heber and Garber's in Milwaukee show that even very young children can benefit from nursery education. There is much less agreement, however, on *what* children should be learning in nurseries, on what *methods* are appropriate for this, and on *how* – or even *whether* – their progress should be evaluated. Parents, nursery teachers and researchers all have strongly held views on these issues – views which are frequently in conflict.

How should these conflicts be resolved? Who should decide what children learn in nurseries? What are the options open to them? These are clearly fundamental questions in any discussion of nurseries, and we shall return to them more fully in Chapters 8 and 9.

In praise of short-term benefits

Our main concern so far has been with the *short-term* benefits of nurseries – benefits which occur while children are attending and perhaps for a short time afterwards. But many people have hoped for more, seeing the primary case for nurseries in terms of possible *long-term* effects on children's development, especially on their subsequent performance at school. This view was particularly prominent in America in the 1960s, and was one of the main motivating forces behind the massive Headstart Project. As its name implies, this project aimed to give 'disadvantaged' children a flying start to their school careers through attendance at special nurseries, and these children's later school performance was carefully watched. The results were a great disappointment. Although the nurseries had substantial effects on the children *while they were attending* the effects did not persist for very long: after a year or two at school there was virtually no difference between children who had attended the nurseries and others – from the same background – who had not. These findings produced an immediate outcry in the United States: 'Headstart has failed' and 'Nurseries do not work' were the main responses at the time.

Today – with the benefit of hindsight – it seems curiously naive to have expected anything else. A child's performance in infants or junior school depends on so many more immediate factors – such as the quality of her present school, her relationship with her teacher, the influence of her friends and events in her home life – which would all tend to overshadow anything she had learnt three or four years earlier. At the time of Headstart, however, it was widely believed that there was something special about the pre-school years, such that a 'boost' at the age of three or four would have a major and permanent impact on later intellectual development. These beliefs were based – often quite loosely – on the findings of psychologists such as J. McVicker Hunt [12] and Benjamin Bloom [13]: for example, the frequently quoted claim that '50 per cent of adult intelligence is formed by the age of five' is a gross misrepresentation of Bloom's work on the extent to which *variation* in adult IQ can be predicted at an early age. This belief in the critical importance of the early years, however, is being increasingly challenged by an alternative view that the early years, though important, are no more so than later stages of development. According to psychologists Ann and Alan Clarke of Hull University, human development is from this perspective

a slow process of genetic and environmental interactions, with sensitivities (rather than critical periods) for different processes at different times ... There is no implication that infancy or early childhood are unimportant, *only that their long-term role is by itself very limited and the whole of development is important*, not merely the early years. There is as yet no indication that a given stage is clearly more formative than others; in the long term, all may be important.[14]

Nurseries are *not* a short cut to later educational success, and it is unreasonable to judge them in such terms. Most other services for children are concerned in the first place with safeguarding or enhancing the present status or circumstances of the children who use them, and not with their long-term effects. Primary schools are not judged on the proportion of their pupils who go on to pass GCEs or enter university; nor does the value of maternity and infant welfare services lie primarily in their impact on the health and development of the school-age child. Such services would claim that they lay a sound foundation for later progress, but that their main justification and concern is their impact on those children who use them, at the time they use them. Such claims should also form the basis for judging nurseries.

Nurseries and 'disadvantaged' children

A frequently heard argument for nurseries is that they can make an important contribution to the early experience and education of children who are in some way 'disadvantaged'. But, like the issue of long-term gains, the impact of nurseries on 'disadvantaged' children is not central to the case we are making. Clearly, some children and parents may benefit more from nurseries than others – a child in an overcrowded inner-city slum, for example, may well get more from going to a nursery than a child from a roomy suburban detached house. But the need for nurseries and the benefits that can come from them apply to *all* classes and groups in the population. *The role of nurseries should be to help all children attain their full potential and overcome any disadvantages they face.*

'Disadvantaged' is, in any case, a difficult term to define. Does it apply to children from economically and environmentally deprived backgrounds? Or children living in areas where education, health or other services are poor? Or children from homes that fail to provide adequate care, stimulation and experience? Or children who perform below their potential or below the average for their age? Or children from ethnic minorities? Or all or parts of the working class? Where performance rather than background is the criterion, is the main concern with intellectual development, or with all aspects of human development? For instance, is the child who is bright but unable to mix easily disadvantaged, or the child from an intellectually stimulating but emotionally sterile home? It is very easy to talk about 'disadvantage', but a much harder job to define it.

Even if 'disadvantaged' children could be satisfactorily defined and identified, the concept of 'disadvantage' has little to contribute to the planning and organizing of nurseries. Nurseries can benefit *all* children, whether 'disadvantaged' or 'non-disadvantaged', and there is no case for services restricted only to the former group. Nor do we favour the idea of separate nurseries for 'disadvantaged' children (or indeed for any other groups of children), whether that separation is deliberate policy or the unintended consequence of other measures. Separate services for separate groups are socially divisive and can all too easily lead to differing standards. Low standards, inadequate resources and stigma are a recurrent risk in services for the most deprived and powerless groups: services for the poor can all too easily become poor services.

Can nurseries harm young children?

We have been concerned so far with the *benefits* children get from going to nurseries. But much discussion about nurseries has been concerned with their possible *harmful* effects, especially for children under three. This is clearly crucial for our case for nurseries: few people would want to press for nurseries if there was convincing evidence that they harmed young children. In the next few pages, we take a careful look at the current state of knowledge on this important issue.

The idea of mothers leaving children under three at nurseries makes many people emotional and moralistic. The point of view of many doctors, psychologists and nursery staff is that children should spend virtually all their first three years with their mothers, and that their needs are best met at home. This view has been accepted by successive governments. In May 1945 for instance:

The Ministers concerned accept the view of medical and other authority that, in the interest of the health and development of the child no less than for the benefit of the mother, the proper place for a child under two is at home with his mother . . .[15]

Similarly in 1968, the government still held that nursery provision

must be looked at in relation to the view of medical and other authority that early and prolonged separation from the mother is detrimental to the child, [and] that wherever possible the younger pre-school child should be at home with his mother . . .[16]

But are these 'experts' right in believing that separation of mothers and young children is harmful? Let us look at the evidence.*

The notion that any separation of mothers and young children is bound to be harmful first became prominent in the fifties. The major exponent of this view was John Bowlby, and for over twenty years his writings have had a tremendous impact on public opinion and policy. Bowlby argued that it is essential for mental health that an infant or young child should experience a warm, intimate and continuous relationship with her mother or permanent mother-substitute. According to Bowlby, a child who does not have this relationship experiences 'maternal deprivation', and in later life is liable to become delinquent, psychopathic or at least to suffer from grave personality damage[17].

Bowlby's evidence for these statements came largely from studies of children who had grown up in very poor-quality *residential* institutions and hospitals, and from case studies of clinic patients who as children were separated from their mothers during the war and received very inadequate care from other hands. It did *not* come from studies of children in day nurseries or nursery schools, although Bowlby did state that children under three 'cannot adapt to nursery schools', and that 'day nurseries are known to have high rates of infectious illness and are believed to have a bad effect on the children's emotional growth'. Only in his most recent book, *Separation*, published in 1973 [18], does he discuss at length the case against nursery school or playgroup attendance before the age of three. The case rests mainly on his theory of mother–infant bonding, supported by studies of disturbed children whose history included distress at starting nursery school before the age of three.

Bowlby's earlier writings, however, were almost

* The next ten pages are based on an unpublished manuscript by Dr Barbara Tizard of the Thomas Coram Research Unit.

entirely concerned with the ill-effects of the *total* separation of mother and child, as in hospital admissions. So far as day-to-day child-rearing was concerned, he advised parents not to go on holiday without their young children for more than a week or ten days, and even then only if the child could be left with someone she knew. No specific advice was given about shorter absences during the day, and indeed he wrote that 'it is an excellent plan to accustom babies and small children to being cared for now and then by someone else'.

For reasons that are not entirely clear, but were probably connected with a post-war movement to return women to the home, the 'maternal deprivation' theory made an instant and powerful impact. Although Bowlby's own attack had been directed at residential institutions, other authorities almost immediately interpreted him to mean that mothers should be on twenty-four-hour duty. A very influential World Health Organization publication stated in 1951 that the use of day nurseries and creches has a particularly serious and permanently deleterious effect on children [19]. Large numbers of day nurseries were closed, the number of places falling from 62,784 in 1945 to 22,564 in 1960, and nursery schools raised their age of admission to three: most of them also switched from offering a full school day to taking children for a session of two and a half hours only. These changes reversed policies which had prevailed for fifty years – from their inception, British nursery schools had taken children from the age of two, while both American and Australian nursery schools had started children on a part-time basis at eighteen months.

Had these early educators been blind to the suffering of little children? The writings of such pioneers as Margaret MacMillan, Lillian de Lissa and Arnold Gesell show that they were well aware that a young child should be very gradually introduced to school,

that two-year-olds should be in small groups, and that
their teacher needs to be affectionate and gentle. Given
these circumstances they believed that the child would
become attached to both mother and teacher, and would
be less likely to feel distress at being separated from
either than a child being reared only at home. Further,
they saw group care for at least part of the day as of
positive benefit to the child from the youngest age. This
was because the nursery could better and more safely
than a family meet the very young child's needs to be
active and to explore, and thus enable the child to use
her assertiveness to gain mastery of her environment
rather than battle with her mother.

Does a young child need an exclusive relationship with her mother?

Bowlby opposed nurseries because he argued that
children have an innate biological tendency to attach
themselves to one person, and that this attachment
differs in kind from any other attachments they form.
Separation from this person in the early years will
disrupt the bond, or prevent it from forming securely,
with subsequent personality damage to the child.
According to Bowlby, the mother's feeling for her child
will also be weaker if she does not have sole charge of her
during the first years.

Detailed studies of normal young children do not
confirm these beliefs. Rudolf Schaffer and Peggy
Emerson, in a study of Scottish infants, found that one
third were showing attachment to a particular person
by the age of six months, and three quarters by nine
months [20]. By the age of eighteen months almost all the
children were attached to at least two people, and a
third of them to five or more people. In nearly a third of
cases the main attachment was to the *father*. The
amount of time (above a certain minimum) which the
adult spent with the child did not seem to affect the

development of attachment. It was the intensity of the interaction when it occurred and the responsiveness of the adult to the child which determined the strength of the attachment. Attachments were often formed with people who did not feed or care for the child but only played with her.

The Schaffer and Emerson study suggests that most children form *multiple* attachments at an early age, and that their strongest attachment is not necessarily to the person who cares for them all day. If this is the case it would not be surprising to find that children could form attachments to both their nursery nurses and their mother, and that their love for their mother need not depend on her constant presence. Other studies have shown this to be the case, the strength of the mother–child attachment being a function of the quality and intensity of mother–child interactions, rather than of the sheer availability of the mother, or the number of care-givers.

A further consideration is that, contrary to Bowlby's belief, it may be important for a child to form *several* attachments. The mother–child relationship, as we have already seen, is not always wholly satisfactory, and in some cases may be very unsatisfactory. A child whose mother is depressed or irritable, or for some reason has mixed or hostile feelings for her, may need an alternative source of affection. Illness or other un-expected events may force a separation, leaving a child who is totally dependent on her mother in great distress. Further, a child who has learnt that comfort and affection can come from several sources is likely to be more confident than a child who fears to leave her mother's side. Sometimes grandparents, aunts and uncles can provide this source, but for children in small families, or with overburdened parents, attachments outside the family could be crucial.

Rudolf Schaffer, in a recent book, *Mothering*, provides

perhaps the clearest answer to the question posed at the start of this section:

There is nothing to indicate any biological need for an exclusive primary bond; nothing to suggest that mothering cannot be shared by several people . . .

There is no need to prolong the controversy about whether the mother must be the infant's constant companion throughout each and every twenty-four-hour day. Clearly some minimum period of togetherness is required but there is nothing absolute about how much. Beyond the minimum, it is the personal qualities the adult brings to the interaction that matters most. Provided these can be given full play there is no reason why mother and infant should not spend a portion of the day apart – the mother at work, the child at some form of day care, or in some other arrangement with which the family is comfortable.

As a final note, Schaffer adds:

Mother need not be a woman . . . some fathers may make better mothers than their wives . . . From the child's point of view, it matters little what sex mother is.[21]

What is the evidence against nurseries?

Assertions that nurseries are likely to damage psychological development are quite unjustified. There is practically no *scientific* evidence that nurseries can harm young children. By this we mean evidence which is collected systematically about a whole group of children, rather than an individual's impressions or experience of isolated cases. Thus a psychiatrist's observation that some children who have disturbed relationships with their mothers started nursery at two is *not* evidence that nursery attendance at two leads to disturbed mother–child relationships. To reach this conclusion one would have to show that a larger proportion of children who have been to nurseries since the age of two have disturbed relationships with their mothers than those who have not, *after allowing for any other differences in background between the two groups*. This would be quite difficult to investigate in Britain, because nursery schools no longer take two-year-olds and council day nurseries admit only 'priority cases', such as children of lone parents or children of physically or mentally ill parents (see Chapter 4 for fuller descriptions of these and other types of nursery). These children may have problems stemming from their family lives and circumstances, and to assess the effect of the nursery on them would involve the difficult task of finding a comparison group of children from similar family backgrounds who were not in nurseries.

There are however a number of American studies which have been able to compare groups of nursery and non-nursery children from similar backgrounds. In most cases the children started at nursery in infancy. These studies have usually been concerned with the quality of mother–child relationships and almost all of them have found that nursery children do form normal attachments with their mothers.

One popular method of investigating the strength of a child's relationship with her mother is called the 'strange situation'. The mother and child are brought into a strange room and at first left alone there. Subsequently, a strange person enters the room, the mother leaves the child alone with the stranger and then returns. Using the 'strange situation' with children brought up entirely at home and children attending nursery, aged two and a half and three and a half years, Blehar found that the younger nursery children were less interested in their mothers than the non-nursery children, while the older nursery children showed angry, resistant behaviour towards their mothers [22]. This study is often cited as evidence of the bad effects of day care, yet three subsequent studies – by Brookhart and Hock [23], Doyle [24], and Roopnarine and Lamb [25]

– using exactly the same procedure found little or no difference between the behaviour of nursery and non-nursery groups of children.

A variety of other methods have been used to investigate the child's attachment to her mother. These have included ratings of relationships from interviews with the mothers, in which Caldwell found no differences between nursery and non-nursery children [26]; and observations of mothers and children in both natural and contrived situations. In one study by Farran and Ramey, children attending nursery and aged between nine and thirty-one months were brought into a playroom in which both their mother and their nursery nurse were sitting [27]. The great majority of the children made straight for their mother, and tended to play near her and to turn to her for help in their play. Other studies, by Ricciuti and his colleagues, have shown that, while children tend to prefer their mother to their nursery nurse, they also become attached to their nurse. For example, in one study it was shown that the distress of nursery children aged eight to twelve months at being left alone, or being left with a stranger, was alleviated by the appearance of their nurse, and that they showed a similar kind of distress at being separated from nurse or mother [28]. In another study babies aged four to fifteen months were observed arriving at and leaving the nursery over a period of six months. Most of the babies greeted their nurses with pleasure, or without distress, not did they show distress when their parents left. At the end of the day most of them greeted their parents' return with pleasure [29].

Most studies of the effect of nursery attendance on young children's relationships have been concerned with the mother–child relationship. There are, however, a few studies of other aspects of the child's social behaviour. One method used has been to observe children's responses to strange children and adults. For example, Kagan and his colleagues observed children attending nursery and children being raised entirely at home, in a playroom with their mothers [30]. When a strange child and her mother were brought in, the nursery children aged twenty months less often showed alarm than the non-nursery children – fewer stopped playing or ran to their mothers. At twenty-nine months, there was no difference between the behaviour of the two groups in this situation. In another study by Ricciuti, nursery and non-nursery children of twelve to nineteen months were brought into a playroom occupied by a teacher and several older children. The children attending nursery more often moved away from their mothers and watched the older children than did the other children [28]. These studies suggest that at early ages (twelve to twenty-four months) attending nursery can help children become less fearful when meeting new people, nursery children in the presence of their mothers being more likely to look at and interact with peers than are matched children not attending nursery.

Do nurseries increase the risk of illness?

A frequently expressed objection to nurseries is that they increase the risk of infection and illness. This is clearly an important issue to investigate. Loda and his colleagues monitored the illnesses of children aged one month to five years at one nursery in North Carolina over a period of three years [31]. The findings were compared with the illness rates reported in the Cleveland Family Study for middle-class children being raised entirely at home. The overall illness rates of the two groups were remarkably similar, except for a slightly increased rate of respiratory illness (coughs, colds, sore throats etc.) in nursery children under the age of twelve months, and a slightly increased tendency for the nursery children to have raised temperatures with respiratory infections.

However, a Swedish study by Strangert found more respiratory illness and raised temperatures in nursery children up to the age of two [32]. This increased rate of respiratory illness in the under-twos was also found in children with childminders, who on average were caring for four children. It seems likely that illness rates in under-twos, certainly in under-ones, are slightly increased if they are cared for outside their homes. Both the American and Swedish studies found that this increased illness rate was about equivalent to the illness of children living at home in large families – that is, infants cared for in a large family at home, or with a number of other children at a childminder's or nursery, are all exposed to more risk of infection than a child brought up at home in a small family.

Of particular interest is the Swedish finding that nurseries which excluded ill children did not reduce their illness rate – presumably because illness is spread by children with no symptoms or only mild ones. In some of the Swedish nurseries, and also in the North Carolina nursery, only children with measles, whooping cough and chickenpox were excluded. This policy reflected the awareness of the medical authorities that excluding sick children can cause great difficulties to working mothers and sometimes lead to inadequate care of the children.

It is important to note that both the American and Swedish nurseries studied were well-staffed, had ample space and paid great attention to hygiene. An overcrowded nursery, with no immunization programme, where staff ignored hygienic precautions might well constitute a health risk.

To summarize, research on the effects of nursery care, especially on very young children, has increased substantially in the last ten years, particularly in America. The results have shown that attendance at *high-quality* nursery provision

is not disruptive of the child's emotional bond with his mother, even when day care is initiated in the first year of life. In addition, there is no indication that exposure to day care decreases the child's preference for his mother in comparison with an alternative familiar caregiver. [33]

As well as drawing this conclusion, Belsky and Steinberg – in their recent review of literature on the effects of nursery attendance – point to the limited scope of most research. Studies have rarely gone beyond the direct effects of nursery experience on the individual child and important questions concerning the impact of nursery care on parents, the family and social institutions have been ignored. For instance, does nursery attendance affect the division of child-care responsibilities in the home and influence maternal and paternal roles? How is the institution of marriage affected by nursery provision? Does nursery care affect the development, function and maintenance of social networks? What impact do nurseries have on social attitudes to the care of children, the role of women and the function of the family? Do they affect family income, the career advancement of women or absenteeism from work?

In addition to seeking answers to these broad questions, there is still a great need to study how best to look after young children outside their own homes. But certainly there is no evidence to suggest that they are harmed by this experience.

Nurseries for under-twos

We can now move away from the arid debate about whether or not nursery attendance must inevitably prove harmful to very young children. What matters in practice is not whether the child is at home all the time or spends part of her time at nursery, but the quality of care she is receiving in either place. When the child is receiving poor-quality care – whether at home or at nursery – she is likely to suffer 'bad' effects: but when the quality of care is good the child can only benefit.

What makes for good-quality care in nurseries? Some of the factors are already widely recognized. Settling-in should be gradual; the environment should be safe, healthy and generally welcoming; groups should be small; there should be continuity of staff; and the child's day should be interesting and varied, within a routine which is regular without being rigid. But perhaps what matters most is that the children should be looked after by someone who genuinely likes and is interested in them, and who can be warm and affectionate towards them – in short, someone with whom parents are happy to leave their children. These general principles apply to all under-fives in nurseries, though naturally they require to be tailored to the particular requirements of each age-group. Because of their greater helplessness and vulnerability, babies and toddlers, for instance, need more adult help and more careful attention to hygiene than older children: obviously, too, the routine, toys and activities appropriate for a one-year-old would not be suited to a three-year-old.

Despite the evidence and the previous discussion there are probably many people who still feel unhappy at the idea of very young children – and especially those under a year or eighteen months – being cared for in nurseries. For many people, this idea is likely to conjure up pictures of cold, impersonal institutions where – as in Aldous Huxley's *Brave New World* – babies spend their days in long rows of identical cots, receiving none of the individual love and attention which they would get at home.

It would be easier to allay people's fears in this respect if there were more nurseries in this country where children under two were cared for in exemplary fashion, and which could therefore serve as 'models' to be emulated. Most of the provision that is currently available for such young children is with childminders, a type of service which in its present form has many defects (we shall be discussing it in Chapter 7). The only other provision, apart from a few places in private, voluntary and workplace nurseries, is in council day nurseries (Chapter 4 gives more details of these different types of service). These council nurseries certainly offer good standards of care – most maintain high staff: child ratios and pay a lot of attention to health and hygiene – and there is no evidence that the young children who attend them are harmed in any way by going. They are however unsuitable as more general models because they are solely concerned with 'priority cases' and their main aim is to provide full-time 'substitute care'. So they do not provide a good example of how a nursery could provide a mixture of full-time and shorter periods of care, regularly for some children but occasionally for others, and be available to all families.

The lack of satisfactory models highlights the need for innovation and experiment in setting up suitable nurseries for very young children. Nevertheless we can try to imagine what such nurseries would look like, and the kind of service they could provide for local families. As we shall see in Chapter 5, it is unlikely that more than a small minority of parents would want or need full-time care for children under two, and particularly for those under twelve months. Many parents with very young children find full-time work overtaxing: at the end of the day they are too exhausted to enjoy their children, and the children themselves are often tired and irritable. There is however likely to be a much greater demand for shorter periods of care – either from parents who work, or from parents who are particularly stressed, or from parents who are neither employed nor stressed but who just want a short regular break from the demands of constant child-care. There are also many mothers who would like somewhere to drop in occasionally or regularly with their child, so that both of them can have companionship and a change of scene.

There are a number of possible ways of meeting these

needs. One approach would be small, local nurseries, run along the lines of the 'community nurseries' described in Chapter 6. Such a nursery would avoid the feeling of an impersonal institution by being based in a converted house; it would also serve a small, immediate catchment area, so that the families who used it would be likely to meet each other in the near-by streets and shops. Parents could start by 'dropping in' on an occasional basis with their babies or toddlers, so that everyone got to know everyone else slowly and gradually, working up to the time when parents could leave their children in the care of the staff. With such a procedure, a baby or young child would not be left in the nursery until she had learnt to know and trust the staff, while for their part the parents would not feel they were leaving their child with someone they knew very little about.

It would be wrong to underestimate the problems involved in setting up and running such a nursery – or an alternative type, such as an extension to the local infant school and nursery class – and there are many questions which would need to be resolved in the process. For example, a lot of thought would have to be given to the activities which would be undertaken with the children in the nursery. Would the staff simply provide, in an informal way, toys and other play activities appropriate for the children's age, or would they try and devise a more structured educational programme? What, in any case, would this programme look like? Would the nursery be restricted to children under two, or would it cater for the whole range of children up to five years? Some people might feel unhappy about 'segregating' very young children from those slightly older, but it can be difficult for little babies and toddlers if they are in the midst of several noisy and energetic three- or four-year-olds. A preferable alternative might be for the whole age-range to be together in one building, but split into age-groups for part of the day. There are also questions about staffing. Would the emphasis be on highly trained professional workers, or would it be better to recruit local people who liked young children and to give them training 'on the job'? Would it be possible – or desirable – to involve local childminders who were looking after under-twos, so that they too became based at the nursery? Finally, there is the question of cost. Because a nursery including under-twos needs a particularly high staff : child ratio, the cost would be proportionately greater than for a nursery for older children. Where would the money come from – and how easy would it be to get it?

Many of these questions, of course, also apply to provision for over-twos, and we shall be exploring them in more detail later in the book. We raise them here to show that, in this country, the development of nurseries for children under two is very much unexplored territory, which urgently needs its pioneers. None of the problems we have raised should prove insurmountable, once the commitment to tackle them has been generated. The greatest problem probably lies in the initial acceptance of the idea that nurseries for under-twos can be a worthwhile proposition, of benefit to both mother and child.

In this chapter we have looked at some of the benefits children can get from attending nurseries. We have argued that they will gain indirectly from any nursery that takes some of the stress off their mothers, and that they can gain more directly from the increased opportunities nurseries offer for play, meeting other children and adults, and developing independence, as well as from the educational experiences nurseries can provide. We have also argued that young children are not harmed by attending nursery – whether they are over or under three, or attend for all or part of the day – provided they receive adequate care for the time they are there.

There is no good reason why these benefits should not

be available to any child under the age of five; that is, there are no good arguments for restricting nurseries to 'disadvantaged' children, or children over a certain age. All young children can benefit from play, from becoming more independent, from developing relationships with other children and from educational experiences, just as all young children should be well cared for while they are in nurseries. Of course their precise needs will be different at different ages – no one imagines that the care of young babies is exactly the same as the care of three-year-olds, or that the educational needs of an eighteen-month child are the same as those of a four-year-old – and nurseries must naturally be aware of and sensitive to individual differences. Nevertheless, it is still an important general principle that:

● All nurseries should aim to meet children's needs for care, play and educational experiences – whatever their age or circumstances.

To many people, this principle will seem self-evident or simply unnecessary. It is of crucial importance, however, because the present nursery system is *not* based on this principle. At the heart of the present system is the idea that some children mainly need care, while others mainly need education – and that these groups of children require different types of nursery, staffed by different types of staff. As we shall see in Chapter 5, this division between care and education is the root cause of a great many problems and discrepancies within the present system, and is a fundamental obstacle to the kind of service we want to see.

It is also often claimed that *play* and *education* are synonymous for young children. This claim, as we argue more fully in Chapter 9, is misleading. All nurseries should pay attention to meeting each of these important functions, and not assume that the one automatically leads to the other.

In these first two chapters we have put forward our

case for nurseries, and shown the ways in which they can benefit mothers and their children. We are aware, however, that many people do not agree with what we have said, and react strongly to the idea that nurseries are as much for the benefit of parents – and mothers in particular – as they are for the benefit of their children. In the next chapter we look at some of the objections people often raise to these ideas.

3 The opposition case – some objections to nurseries

Objection 1: *'We didn't need nurseries in my day'*

For at least the last hundred years, large numbers of parents have used whatever help with child-care was available to them. From the 1870 Education Act until policy changed in 1905 parents had a right to school admission for children of three and over, although compulsory schooling did not start till five. Many parents took advantage of this policy, and by 1900 almost half (43 per cent) of three- and four-year-olds were in school – a higher proportion than are attending nursery and reception classes today [1]. These children were predominantly working-class, for the great majority of middle-class and upper-class children were being cared for by nannies and nursemaids in household nurseries. At the end of the nineteenth century, when nannies were a virtual requirement of middle-class status, they numbered anywhere between 250,000 and half a million [2].

In 1905, a Board of Education Committee asked NSPCC inspectors to seek the views of families about school attendance for children under five [3]. 479 working-class families, living in slums and rural districts, were approached, and the majority were in favour of early school attendance.

> There was no division [of views] between the better and worse class of parents . . . Many careful parents keep children at home, while others equally careful send them to school.

Among the reasons given for sending young children to school were: they were kept warm, clean and safe; they were off the streets and not likely to learn bad habits; they learnt things they couldn't at home; they were happier – and couldn't get into mischief; they were kept out of the way; they were better for the company of other children; and their mothers could work.

At the time, experiences offered to children under five in schools were often totally unsuited to their needs (see page 209). But rather than improve this by developing proper nurseries – as some were then advocating – the parents' right to places was simply withdrawn. After 1905 the number of places for three- and four-year-olds fell rapidly in the face of economic pressures and the higher priority given to older children.

After about 1910 it becomes difficult to find out anything about the attitudes of parents to nurseries, and in any case there were few available; by 1930, only 13 per cent of three- and four-year-olds were in schools. Nannies remained popular with middle-class and upper-class families until the Second World War, and child-minders continued to provide their traditional services to working-class mothers in employment. A number of reports suggest however that motherhood was at least as hard then as today.

For the average working-class woman, her day begins, continues and ends with household drudgery, the claims made on her time by husband and children are unceasing and the better the mother, the less the leisure. (*1917 – a report by the Women's Co-operative Guild* [4])

[The survey] yields a picture in which monotony, loneliness, discouragement and sordid hard work are the main features – a picture of almost unredeemed drabness. Happiness can suffer an almost unprecedented lowering of standard which results in a pathetic gratitude for what might be called negative mercies. (*1939 – from a survey on the health and conditions of 1,250 working-class, married women* [5])

To be responsible for three or four children, a house and

the welfare of a husband, twenty-four hours a day, seven days a week, all the year round is something the difficulty of which has to be experienced to be understood . . .

The most important of the non-monetary handicaps of parenthood, is undoubtedly felt by mothers . . . there is no doubt that the working-class housewife and mother is becoming no less conscious of the burden of parenthood than women in the class which employs servants. The burden is felt in the actual domestic work, in the ties which children involve and in the physical and nervous strain of the continuous care of children. Children not only make work, but make it more difficult to do . . .

Mothers have shared very little in the great decrease of working hours and the shift from heavier to lighter work. The work of running a home and caring for a family has lagged behind the general advance of living and working conditions; in present conditions, as one witness puts it, 'the price most mothers are asked to pay is too high'. (*1948 – Royal Commission on Population* [6])

There is of course some variation from one generation to the next in the circumstances and needs of mothers. Since 1900 for example, there has been a large drop in the infant mortality rate; families have become smaller; women's employment and levels of education have increased; and mothers today, though their work may be less physically demanding, probably get less help and support from friends, relatives or paid helpers like nursemaids and nannies. But whatever the variations, the demands made of mothers remain heavy and their position remains disadvantaged, *relative to the rest of society*. Because past generations have had to put up with these problems, there is no reason why future generations should be expected to do the same.

Objection 2: '*You had them – you look after them*'

This objection runs along the following lines. Having children is purely a personal affair: these days we can all choose whether or not to have children, and if people choose to have them, then they must put up with the consequences, and not expect others to bail them out. At best, this line of argument reminds mothers that it is no small undertaking to bring up children – after all you can't be much of a mother if you won't put up with some inconvenience for the sake of your family. At its worst, this argument shades into a more punitive approach, part of a long tradition that views sacrifice, suffering and pain as an inevitable part of motherhood, the price for the self-indulgence of having children or the carnality that accompanies conception: woman was born to suffer, so she'd better just grin and bear it.

This objection, it should be pointed out, is almost never applied to *fathers*. As in most issues to do with bringing up young children, double standards are readily applied to men and women. No one expects men to 'choose between family and career', or to give up their work and devote themselves to twenty-four-hour child-care for the children's first five years; paternal responsibility – unlike maternal responsibility – is *not* equated with providing constant and continuous child-care.

In any case having children is *not* a purely personal affair. Children are not the sole concern or responsibility of their parents and no society in the world today believes or acts as if they were. The welfare and development of children are matters of the greatest importance to any society – because today's child is tomorrow's citizen, care-giver and producer of energy, goods and services. Modern societies share responsibility for children with parents, showing their interest through a wide range of services and benefits for children. Moreover, if society stands to gain from its children, it has an interest in and responsibility for the welfare and happiness of parents, in particular ensuring that they are not disadvantaged through the contribution they make to child-rearing.

It is clearly mistaken to think that parents can – or

should – provide for all the needs of their children: the growth of education, health, recreation and welfare services for children recognizes that parents cannot meet these needs unaided. The essence of parental responsibility is not that parents should have to do everything for their children. Rather it means that parents should be permanently concerned – as they almost invariably are – about their children's needs, and should do their best to ensure that these needs are met, with or without the help of nurseries. This sort of responsibility does not stop at the nursery door, but naturally continues throughout the time the child is at nursery. If it is to be exercised fully, parents must have full knowledge about what happens to their child in the nursery, and must have some say over what is going on. These ideas are of fundamental importance in any discussion of nurseries, and we will return to them in full in Chapter 8.

Objection 3: ' *You can't let parents decide when to use nurseries* '

A common anxiety among nursery staff is that many parents would make decisions harmful to their children, if given the choice of when to send them to nursery and for what periods of time. Parents are often seen as ill-informed about children's needs, or even as plain callous and selfish. The pejorative phrase 'dumping the child' is readily applied to parents who ask for more than nursery staff think it right to give or who appear otherwise negligent in staff eyes – such as mothers who seem pleased to get a break from their children.

Parental judgement is not infallible: given free choice, a few parents might well press for nursery provision that was plainly unsatisfactory – either through ignorance or insensitivity, or because of a genuine conflict between the needs of parent and child. But the judgement of professionals is also fallible. As we have already suggested, many doctors, psychologists and nursery staff believe that children should spend virtually all their time, until at least their third birthday, with their mothers and that part-time nursery provision is right and best for the great majority of children aged three or four. Neither of these beliefs is supported by evidence. At a more individual level, ignorance of the circumstances of particular families, or differences in values and standards between professionals and families, can also lead professionals to misjudge situations.

However knowledgeable and sensitive professionals may be, it is still true that parents are better placed to know their own needs and those of their children, and are generally the best judges of how well their children cope with going to nursery. Research shows that, given the places, many more parents would send their children to nurseries (see page 115); it also shows that there are widespread differences of opinion between parents on the hours they want and the ages at which they would like their children to start [7]. These findings suggest that parents consider the individual needs of their children, rather than that they have a blanket desire to 'dump' them in nurseries.

We believe that parents' judgements should be respected in these matters and that professional staff should act as advisers, not as gate-keepers or legislators. Inevitably, the advice given by staff will not always be heeded, sometimes because it is wrong, sometimes because it is inadequately communicated, sometimes because, though they offer good advice well explained, other circumstances work against its acceptance. It is better for professionals to work at improving the quality of their advice and their ability to communicate it – and also to accept that their help will be rejected on occasions – than for them to deny parents the responsibility of choosing.

Objection 4: 'Wouldn't it be better to pay mothers to stay at home?'

Some people have suggested that rather than provide nurseries to enable mothers to go out to work, they should be offered a 'mother's wage' to encourage them to stay at home. The suggestion has the virtue of recognizing that full-time housework and child-care is hard, demanding and real work, and that mothers wanting to stay at home should receive some support in pursuing this choice. Its virtue, however, is far outweighed by its failings: it does not go nearly far enough, is based on a number of false assumptions, and does nothing to promote equal opportunities. Moreover, the proponents of the 'mother's wage' idea have given little thought to the details of such a scheme and its implications.

The mother's wage argument rests on three dubious assumptions. First, it assumes that mothers work wholly or mainly for money. This view has already been questioned in Chapter 1, where it was shown that most mothers, like most other men and women, do work for money but also for a variety of other reasons. It is true that some mothers, particularly those working full-time or in badly paid jobs, would stop work if more money was available, but these mothers *are very much in the minority*. The great majority of mothers actually enjoy having a job, feel the better for it and would prefer to continue at work.

The second assumption is that mothers' employment is usually detrimental to the children. This assumption has been the subject of much research (though the same cannot be said about the effects of fathers' employment – double standards again!) and the general conclusion is that maternal employment *per se* is not harmful to the children [8, 9, 10]. What is crucial is the *quality of care* received when the mother is at work, and the *mother's satisfaction* with her work; when good-quality child-care is available, and when employment is satisfactory to the mother, the effects on the child are likely to be *beneficial* – going out to work can increase a mother's self-confidence and help her be more responsive to her children.

The third assumption behind the mother's wage argument is that child-care is – and should be – wholly the *mother's* responsibility. It is at heart a move away from equal opportunities, it aims to confirm child-care as primarily the mother's role, and would limit the opportunities of both mothers and fathers to choose the combination of work and child-care which suits the family best. We would argue instead that responsibility for child-care and other family matters should be regarded as *shared* between parents: discussion should always be concerned with *parental* rather than *maternal* employment. A mother's wage, aimed to dissuade only mothers from working, is incompatible with this view.

Advocates of the mother's wage have also given inadequate consideration to the details of such a measure. Would the wage be paid at a flat rate or be related to earnings? If a flat rate was chosen, it would clearly have less impact on better-educated women in higher-paid jobs. Either way, at what rate would it be paid? If pitched at a level near the present earnings of most working mothers (who are mostly in part-time jobs) it would make little impact on mothers in full-time jobs; if pitched at their level, it would become a vastly more expensive proposition than most mother's wage advocates have been prepared to envisage. Would *men* be eligible for the benefit? If so, then the rates of benefit would have to be even higher to make it a serious option – most fathers earn much more than their wives. Finally, what would happen to those mothers who still chose to work? Would nursery places and other provision be made for them, so perhaps eroding the impact of the wage, or would their needs continue to be neglected? Alternatively, would the disincentive effect of such a wage be reinforced by other measures against working mothers – higher rates of tax or national insurance for instance, or withdrawal or reduction of child benefits?

In considering the possible impact of a mother's wage we do not have to rely purely on speculation. Such a benefit has been provided in Hungary since 1967, when it was introduced partly from concern that illness was more common among children in nurseries than among those full-time at home, but mainly to boost a flagging birth-rate. The Hungarian 'childminding allowance' (referred to below as CMA) is paid to women with children under three, provided they stay at home to care for their children, and is equivalent to a third of the average industrial wage. Jobs and seniority rights are fully protected during this period and mothers returning to work are entitled to refresher courses.

The proportion of Hungarian women drawing CMA has steadily increased since its introduction and in 1976 was 80 per cent of those eligible – leaving 20 per cent still working right through from the birth of their child. Take-up is lower among professional and other higher-qualified women, who remain at home on CMA for a shorter period on average; they feel they cannot afford too long an absence from work if they are to keep in touch with new developments in their profession (as well no doubt as getting higher pay and greater job stimulation). However only 35–40 per cent of women who do take up the allowance use it for the full three-year period, and the majority of mothers stay at home for no more than eighteen months: consequently a third of all mothers with children under three are in the labour force, a substantially higher proportion than in Britain. Moreover, because of labour shortages, a recent change permits women on leave to work for part of the year [11].

The CMA has also had certain drawbacks. There has been a growing reluctance among Hungarian employers to take on young married women for qualified or responsible jobs. Any movement to greater equality in the home has also been jeopardized, with a significant proportion of mothers claiming their husbands do less housework than before: 'the increased opportunity for the wife to fulfil the mother's function turns into an obligation to play the housewife role in full' [12]. The Hungarians also experience the problems commonly found among housebound mothers in Britain – boredom and isolation [13]. There is a growing realization that a CMA for *women* only is a major hindrance to achieving sex equality. The assumption that women can withdraw from the labour force for a substantial period of time without penalty has not proved accurate: not only is income forgone, but so too are work skills, which soon become obsolete if unused [14].

Advocates of the mother's wage often suggest that Eastern European countries such as Hungary are moving away from the widespread provision of nurseries in favour of benefits such as the CMA. In fact, the Hungarians accept that some mothers will always prefer to work; indeed it is the government's professed aim to provide young mothers with as wide a range of options as possible. Rather than contracting, nursery provision is expanding. The Hungarians provide at least twice as many nursery places as in England and Wales, despite having a population only a fifth of the size, and the number of places nearly doubled between 1967 – when CMA was introduced – and 1976 [15].

We are not opposed to giving financial support to parents who want to stay at home while their children are very young; on pages 79–80 we put forward proposals as to how this might be done. But if they are to meet the objectives of furthering equal opportunities, maximizing parental choice and increasing the involvement of fathers in child-care, such benefits must be available to *either* parent, and must be paid at such a level that they are a realistic option to all fathers and mothers. They should also be complemented by other benefits and measures – including comprehensive nursery services –

which support parents who want to work, either full-time or part-time. Only if these conditions are met can we produce a system that is fair to mothers, fathers and children.

Objection 5: 'Mothers shouldn't go out to work when so many men are unemployed'

This objection can be disposed of very briefly in one of two ways. On a purely practical level, the argument is highly dubious. Most working mothers are concentrated in a narrow range of jobs, traditionally considered as women's work. Because of their low pay, poor conditions and prospects and the qualifications required, these jobs have little appeal to men. The transfer of redundant steel workers or ship-builders to jobs as cleaners, nurses, typists or cooks is, to say the least, unlikely at present.

There is however a more fundamental reason for rejecting this argument. In a society committed to sexual equality and equal opportunities, women with children have as much right to seek work as anyone else. Unemployment such as we have today is an appalling waste. It is not made any better, except perhaps in official statistics, by driving groups of people who want to work – be they disabled, elderly or women – out of the labour market. Persistent, widespread unemployment may reduce many people to desperation, but this should be directed to the *causes* of unemployment, rather than to victimizing the weakest and most disadvantaged groups in society.

Objection 6: 'Aren't there other ways of sharing the burden of child-rearing?'

The most affluent families have always been able to buy help to protect themselves from the realities of child-care, and many of them still do. When experienced at first-hand, these realities can come as a shock:

Lady Frances Russell, daughter-in-law of the Duke of Bedford, has been having a £120 a week rest cure in a health hydro. 'I have had such a tiring time since the birth of my daughter Czarina last year. Two months ago both my nanny and the Filipino couple I had left me. As a result I had to do everything on my own. Imagine going shopping taking a child with you in a pushchair. And every time you go out in the car you have all the business of fixing the safety harness. By 6.30 in the evening I was finished ... When I get home I hope to get another couple, and in the meantime my father-in-law's valet is going to help me in the house.'[16]

For most mothers, *relatives and friends* are a more likely source of support. But this support is gradually being eroded. Increased mobility has led to the break-up of established communities, and the general decline in family size (from 6.2 children for women married in 1862 to 2.2 for women married in 1951) means there are simply fewer brothers, sisters, uncles and aunts around. In addition, married women of all ages are increasingly going out to work: the proportion aged from forty-five to fifty-four at work, for instance, has risen from 24 per cent in 1951 to 68 per cent in 1977 [17]. With increased opportunities to pursue their own lives, older women – relatives, friends or neighbours – are less able, or less willing, to offer help to young mothers, while working mothers themselves are less free to enter into reciprocal child-care arrangements with other mothers. Even when there *are* relatives around there may be personal reasons why help is neither sought nor offered: grandparents may be ill, or handicapped; or the parents might feel that looking after young children might strain them too much, or they may simply not get on well enough to make such an arrangement possible.

Despite these qualifications, relatives and friends are still an important source of care for children of working mothers, and provide a great range of informal, flexible child-care arrangements. Yet though their contribution is substantial, its quantity, availability and long-term reliability are insufficient to meet the needs of all mothers and their children.

What about *fathers*? What role do they play in child-care? Some people have suggested that in recent years fathers have taken on increasing responsibility for child-care and housework and, indeed, there have been some changes. When at home, men probably do more for their children than in the past, while the very few who take a major part in child-care have also increased. But the extent and significance of the change should not be exaggerated. A good father is expected to play with the children, take them off the mother's hands occasionally, be generally interested in their well-being, and take over in crises. Responsibility for child-rearing and the home, however, remains primarily with the mother and she still does most of the work. Recent international studies show

that husbands and children, when they help at all, tend to assist with only selected, often self-selected tasks and for a very small fraction of the total hours devoted to housekeeping. As the recent multinational time budget research in nineteen countries demonstrated, the husband spends little more time assisting the wife and mother with household tasks when she works outside the home than when she does not.[18]

The failure of fathers to take on more responsibility for home and children has become increasingly serious as more mothers have gone out to work, and continues to slow progress to sexual equality. Why is this so? Part of the problem in answering these questions is that there has been virtually no research on fathers: as far as government and researchers are concerned, men's role as fathers might just as well not exist. But the heart of the problem lies in prevalent attitudes to appropriate behaviour for men and women, which the present system of child-care so effectively perpetuates. Work plays a central part in the stereotyped view of men's proper sex role, and the demands of work are one of the major obstacles to men taking an equal share in child-care.

Men normally work the longest hours of their whole working lives when they have young children. Figure 3

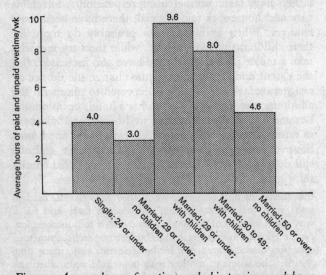

Figure 3. Average hours of overtime worked in previous week by samples of male workers in full-time work (N = 497), London area, 1970

shows hours of overtime worked, both paid and unpaid, by a sample of London men at different stages of life. Among younger married men, those with children worked three times as much overtime as those without [19]. A 1970 study by the National Board for Prices and Incomes of male manual workers in Kent, Derby and Sheffield found that men in the high-overtime group were twice as likely to have children as men in the low-overtime group [20]. Even in a recessionary period such as spring 1976, 55 per cent of male manual workers in the age-group most likely to have young children worked on average ten hours' overtime a week [21].

It is not hard to see why. Manual workers, especially, need extra pay to compensate for the high costs of bringing up children and the reduced family income when wives stop work. Overtime (usually unpaid) is also common among non-manual workers, and is often a requirement for establishing a career. Unfortunately, career-building and starting a family tend to coincide, with the family having to give way in the interest of work. A study by Gaynor Cohen of life on a private housing estate near London found that almost all the men 'felt they were at a crucial stage in the development of their careers and were optimistic about the chances of *future success, provided* they devoted their time and energy to work' [22]. This meant prolonged absence from home: 91 per cent of the men had irregular hours and considerable travelling in their jobs. As a result,

> The majority of wives in the estate did not receive (much) co-operation from their husbands. Even those who did not have to travel ... rarely saw their children during weekdays. Most needed to commute seventeen miles, leaving their houses before the children were awake and returning when they were already asleep. Fathers' lack of participation with their children was far more keenly felt by the mothers than the husbands' lack of participation within the household. Comments such as 'David has spent most of the time travelling since the babies were born; he hasn't yet learned to be a father' or 'I'm tired of being both mother and father to the children' indicated the strength of the women's feelings.

Even when they are at home, many fathers are so tired or preoccupied with their work that the amount of help they can give with the children is minimal. There are also many children who live in fatherless families. In 1976 it was estimated that there were 1,155,000 dependent children in 660,000 families headed by lone mothers, an increase of 32 per cent since 1971; a further 90,000 families with 160,000 dependent children were headed by lone fathers [23]. In addition, there are many fathers (such as servicemen and seamen) whose work often takes them away from home and whose children are effectively living in fatherless families for much of the time.

The evolution of nuclear family living means that mothers today are increasingly on their own. Cut off from friends and relatives, with husbands working long and demanding hours, they are likely to spend more and more of their days cooped up with only their children for company. Nurseries can help not only by giving mothers a break and an opportunity to rejoin the adult world, but also by bringing mothers together to meet and get to know each other at the nursery itself. One of the best ways of doing this is for nurseries to provide a whole range of services which local families might require – pregnancy testing, children's toy and book libraries, launderette facilities, bulk buying of food, adult education classes, clothing and toy exchanges, baby-sitting schemes and so on. Nurseries providing these sorts of services would be a long way from being simply child-care establishments, and would instead be an important focus of community life, actively supplementing the networks of friendship and support that have been eroded by modern living.

Objection 7: 'Nurseries alone won't solve mothers' problems'

This objection is usually put forward in a defeatist and pessimistic tone, as if the problems faced by families with young children were so great that even the best nurseries in the world would have no noticeable effect on their lives. At its most extreme it goes: 'What's the point in providing nurseries for these mothers? What they *really* need is a new flat, a steady bloke, a good job, a shoulder to cry on and someone to tell them how to bring up their kids.'

It is true that nurseries are not – and cannot be – a cure-all for the problems of mothers and young children. By themselves nurseries are likely to be as limited in effect as hospitals would be without G Ps, health visitors, proper sanitation and other public health measures. This is not to undermine the case for nurseries: rather, it emphasizes that nurseries should be only one part of a wide-ranging set of policies designed to help parents and children.

What should these policies consist of? One priority is to improve the physical environment in which children grow up: better housing; more playgrounds in parks and housing estates; good transport to increase the mobility of children and parents; buildings and larger developments planned with the needs of young children in mind. But the most important changes are required in the area of *employment*. The general objective should be to achieve a substantial shift in the present uneven relationship between employment and parenthood, with the more specific aims of securing true equality of opportunity for women in employment, and giving both parents more freedom of choice in how they combine work and child-care. Nurseries have an important part to play in achieving these aims, but they also require other measures. In the case of equal opportunities they range from changes in the educational and vocational training system to reform of employer attitudes and practices towards hiring and placing women. Greater flexibility and choice in combining work and child-care, and ensuring greater involvement of fathers with children, require another set of measures, including:

- more flexible hours (such as the extension of flexitime systems);
- leave entitlement for *each* parent at the birth of a child, with job, benefit and seniority rights fully protected during the period of the leave. As a start, both parents could have a twenty-nine week

entitlement (as mothers now do under the present maternity leave legislation) but this could extend to twelve, even eighteen months for each parent;
- the right of each working parent to a specified number of days' leave per year to undertake certain parental functions, such as caring for a sick child or settling a child at nursery or school;
- earnings-related national insurance benefits to compensate parents for loss of earnings due to take-up of these two types of leave entitlement;
- extensive vocational guidance, job placement and retraining programmes for parents re-entering the workforce after choosing to care for children full-time at home;
- greater availability of part-time work *for both men and women*, at all levels of seniority: on becoming a parent, an employee would have the right to opt for part-time work in his existing job or a comparable one.

These proposals may seem extreme. Yet they do no more than redress the present unequal balance between employment and parenthood, in which an employer is not obliged to take any account of the family needs and circumstances of employees. With high unemployment an apparently long-term prospect, they provide one means of increasing employment opportunities and tackling the anomalous situation in which hundreds of thousands want to work, while millions of employed parents are pressed for time between the demands of work and home.

The measures, especially those concerning part-time employment, also contain an element of risk. The post-war expansion of part-time employment increased both the job opportunities for women, especially women with children, *and* their concentration in the lowest-paid, less skilled and most junior occupations. Unless the part-time work option is diversified through all types and

levels of job and is adopted by more fathers for part of
their working lives, more part-time work will hinder
progress to sex equality in employment and other
fields. There are similar dangers with the introduction
of the other employment measures proposed: they make
it easier for mothers to seek work but unless taken up
widely by fathers also, they would do little for the attainment of equal opportunities.

The proposed changes in employment practice might
modify the demand for nursery services. A one-year
post-natal leave shared between both parents would,
for instance, probably reduce the demand for places for
children under twelve to fifteen months. The changes
would however be no cheap or easy alternative to
nursery provision, if implemented in full and with both
parents equally eligible; rather they are best regarded
as complementary to a proper system of nurseries.

A final point concerns the proposal for national
insurance benefits to compensate for loss of earnings.
Such insurance benefits would emphasize that early
parenthood, like retirement, is a period when families
are particularly hard-pressed and for which extra
financial allowance should be made during the relatively
prosperous years before and after having children. In
this way, the costs of child-rearing, like those of retirement, would be spread evenly over a working life-time.

Measures such as these are already being discussed
by international bodies such as the OECD and the
Council of Europe. In Sweden some of them have
already been introduced. Where there is a child under
ten in the family, either parent is entitled to leave
(twelve days a year for one child, fifteen days for two and
eighteen for three or more) for the illness of a child or a
non-working parent; for visits to child health services
such as clinics; for the birth of a child in the family; and
for visits to nurseries. Following the birth of a child,
seven months' leave can be taken, either shared between
the two parents or taken wholly by one of them. From

January 1978 this has been reduced to six months, but a
further three months of leave or part-time work will be
allowed during any time in a child's first eight years
'to give parents a possibility to stay at home when they
consider it necessary'. A special parental benefit,
equalling 90 per cent of earnings, is paid during all
these periods of leave. Introduced in 1974, the post-
natal leave was taken up by 2 per cent of eligible fathers
in its first three months; two years later, the proportion
had risen to 10 per cent, the average number of days
taken off rising from twenty-nine to forty-one. A considerably higher proportion of fathers take leave to care
for sick children [24]. These measures have been ac-
companied by a publicity campaign to encourage
fathers to take a more active part in the care of their
babies.

The most recent Swedish legislation, which came
into force on 1 January 1979, gives all parents the right
to a six-hour working day until their child reaches eight
or a full leave of absence until their baby is eighteen
months – but with no financial compensation for lost
earnings in either case. The measure has been criticized
by the Social Democrats (then in opposition) and other
groups on the grounds that it harms women's chances of
competing on the labour market – since it is mothers
rather than fathers who will mainly take advantage of
the new rights – and that it will mainly help women with
well-paid husbands. Less affluent groups, such as lone
mothers, will lack the financial resources to enjoy real
choice [25].

The Swedes however have not overlooked the contribution of nurseries. Between 1965 and 1972 there was
a four-fold increase in day nursery places, with a
further 71 per cent increase to 1975 and plans for 90,000
more places by 1981. All local authorities are required to
produce five-year nursery-expansion plans and submit
them to the Swedish Ministry of Social Affairs, which is
responsible for *all* pre-school provision in the country.

a table of places available (per 1,000 children aged under five) in each local authority (including Scotland).

Those readers who are entirely familiar with the current pre-school set-up in this country could turn directly to Chapter 5, where we look at whether these services are satisfactory.

Council Day Nurseries

Kay Mills lives in a small council flat in a largely working-class area of North London. She has two small sons – Michael, aged five, and Conrad, aged three. Her husband George used to beat her up and recently he ran off, leaving huge unpaid bills. Kay became worried and depressed and was afraid she might take it out on the kids. Her social worker managed to get a place for Conrad at the day nursery along the road, Michael started at infants school and Kay took a part-time job as a cleaner. Life has improved for all of them – Kay is less worried and the children have settled well.

The day nursery was purpose-built five years ago, and is situated on a busy main road. Conrad is in a 'family group' with eleven other children ranging from eighteen months to five years of age. He's looked after by Carol, a trained nursery nurse, and Martha, an untrained assistant; for two days a week, there's a nursery nurse student to help out. Altogether there are three such family groups and there's also a baby room for six young babies and a special group for six handicapped children. Parents pay on a sliding scale of charges, but Kay doesn't pay anything for Conrad because she earns so little.

The nursery is open from 8 to 5.30, five days a week all year round. Conrad is there from 9 to 4, just long enough for Kay to get to and from work without too much of a rush. The nursery is clean and bright with children's paintings displayed on the walls, and there is a fair-sized garden at the back. The family group rooms are small and cramped and on cold or wet days, when the children can't go out, the rooms get rather claustrophobic. There are plenty of toys around but few books – those on the shelves are tatty or torn. Books are expensive and the nursery runs on a very tight budget.

The children who come before 8.30 have breakfast. Then there is quiet play with puzzles and building bricks until the other children have arrived. The nurses may then get out paints, sand and water, but if they're short-staffed, which is often the case, it's difficult to organize these messier activities. It's particularly difficult in Conrad's room as one little girl is very hard to handle and the staff are under enough stress as it is. The children have lunch at 12 and all have to be toileted and washed beforehand. The younger ones then rest in one part of the room while the older ones play quietly. Sometimes the children have records and dancing in the afternoon and then have tea at 3.30. Kay is one of the first mothers to come, at 4.

Purpose:	To provide care for children as a substitute for what they would otherwise receive at home, where they or their parents are considered to be in special need of such help.
Provided by:	Local Authority Social Services Departments (SSD).
Who can use them:	Children defined as being in special need. Priority goes to children of lone working parents; handicapped children; children with sick or handicapped parents; and children 'whose home environment is so socially impoverished or strained that day care is considered necessary for their welfare'[5]. Families are often referred by health or welfare services.

either 9.15–11.45 or 1.00–3.30, and the school is closed during school holidays. There are twenty-six children in the class aged between three and five, and the staff consist of one trained teacher together with her assistant, who is NNEB-trained.

The nursery is well equipped, with sand, water, paint, clay, home corner, puzzles etc., available all the time, and the children are free to choose activities as they wish. Milk is on hand throughout the session and the children help themselves when they want it. Every day the teacher plans a special activity – cooking, printing, finger-painting, making masks – and the children are gently encouraged to have a go. In the term before they go up into the infants the teacher helps them to recognize and write their names. The outside play space has both a paved and a grassy area and there is no shortage of climbing apparatus, bikes, trolleys, see-saws and so on. At the end of every session the teacher reads a story to the whole class together or else they sing songs and rhymes. The children then rush out to greet their parents who are waiting outside in the lobby. Once the children have settled the parents are not invited to spend much time in the classroom.

Purpose:	To provide educational experiences for children below school age.
Provided by:	Local Education Authorities (LEA).
Who can use them:	Usually any families in school's catchment area.

Age of children:	3 to 4 years old. A very few children are 2 (1 per cent in December 1975).
Hours open:	Mostly short, two-and-a-half-hour sessions, 9.30 to 12 or 1 to 3.30. 25 per cent of children stay from 9.30 to 3.30.
Weeks open:	Normal school terms (about forty weeks a year).

Cost to parent:	Free (except lunches).

Levels of provision

Highest:	Major cities and Wales.
Lowest:	Outer London and Southern, South-Western and East Anglian counties.

Standards:	The Department of Education and Science (DES) lays down standards for premises, staffing, equipment and curriculum, in various circulars and regulations (such as Standards for School Premises Regulations, 1972; Circular 2/73). A staff:child ratio of 1:13 is considered 'acceptable', and one full-time nursery nurse (or two students) are recommended for each class[9].

Average size:	Nursery schools, which generally have two or three classes: fifty-two places per school. Nursery classes: twenty-five places per class.
Premises:	Nursery schools are separate schools with their own garden or outdoor play area. Nursery classes are attached to primary schools, but have their own play area separate from the rest of the school. Classes and schools usually purpose-built. Standards, both indoors and out, are high.
Equipment:	Usually excellent – a wide range of toys, games, books, puzzles, musical instruments, trucks, tricycles, and climbing equipment, as well as materials for imaginative play and artwork; sand, water, clay and dough for more messy activities.

Staff:child ratio:	1:11 (excluding head teachers and students). There are sufficient staff to ensure each class has a teacher and an assistant.

Staff qualifications:	Run by trained nursery teachers supported by nursery assistants. Teachers get either a three- or four-year college training or a one-year post-graduate qualification. Nursery assistants are usually NNEB-trained (see **Council Day Nurseries**).
Staff pay and conditions:	The first scale for newly qualified teachers is £3,231–£5,082. For nursery assistant rates see **Council Day Nurseries**. Teachers and nursery assistants work a thirty-five-hour week for forty weeks a year.
Number of places:	In January 1977 there were 52,260 children in 648 nursery schools and 157,601 children in 3,927 nursery classes, or 209,861 children receiving state nursery education in schools and classes combined, in 131,270 places (that is 68·3 children and 42·8 places per 1,000 children aged under five). Since there is no information on actual places available, these figures are based on the assumption that there is one *place* for every two part-time *children*. This however overlooks any wholly or partially unoccupied places; the figure for places therefore probably underestimates the number available.

Playgroups

The Smiths live in a large Edwardian terrace house. Mr Smith is a successful free-lance designer, while Mrs Smith is at home looking after their two sons – Alex, five and a quarter, and Andrew, just turned three. Andrew has recently started at the local playgroup. The playleader takes a few children just before they are three, but most, like Andrew, start soon after their third birthday, initially for two mornings a week. Mrs Smith hopes to be able to increase this soon, but with no local nursery class, demand for places is so high that she's unlikely to get more than three sessions a week.

The playgroup rents part of the local Friends' Meeting House. As well as a small kitchen, there is a sizable room, where most indoor activities take place, with a Wendy house, book corner, climbing frame and slide, sand and water trays, paints and a selection of puzzles, games, toys etc. All of these have to be stored away each Friday, to leave the room clean for weekend use by the Friends – a tedious chore but tolerated for the sake of otherwise reasonable premises (certainly better than some of the gloomy halls other playgroups in the borough have to use) and the good-sized garden that the main room opens on to.

Most mornings there are fifteen or sixteen children at the playgroup, though the numbers can go up to twenty. The day starts at 9.15, with a period of indoor play and activities, followed by 'circle time', when children and adults sit down together for a mid-morning drink, taking the register, songs, stories etc. Afterwards, weather permitting, the children usually play outside until they go home at 12, though sometimes there is music and dancing in the large hall upstairs. There are always two staff on duty plus a parent helper – invariably a mother. The rota for helping means that Mrs Smith does two or three mornings a term. The playleader and her two assistants have all completed a playgroup course, and have been at the playgroup for several years – despite rates of pay that are only just above the going local rate for cleaners and the absence of basic benefits like sickness or holiday pay.

Fixing employment conditions is one of the jobs of the playgroup committee, made up of parents and staff. Its main job is usually keeping finances in the black, relying on a mixture of fees, fund-raising and annual council grant to do this. Fees (40p a morning) and fund-raising determine how much the playgroup can pay its staff and what equipment it can afford.

Purpose:	To provide children with opportunities for play, and the chance to mix with other children; to offer support for mothers and the opportunity to learn more about children.
Provided by:	Under 1 per cent of playgroup places are provided by local SSDs; of the others, about half are run by committees of parents[10]. The remainder are provided by local organizations (such as churches, tenants' associations), child-care charities (such as Save the Children Fund) and private proprietors (some of which are registered as childminders providing part-time care; see **Registered Childminders**).
Who can use them:	Generally anyone who can afford to pay the fee and meet any other admission criteria, such as ability to help in the playgroup on a rota basis. Local authorities place and pay for some 4,850 children from their priority waiting list (see **Council Day Nurseries**).
Age of	Mostly 3 to 4 years old. Some groups take more mature 2-year-olds, usually over $2\frac{1}{2}$.
Hours open:	Mostly two to three hours in the morning – though a few also run separate afternoon sessions and a handful offer extended hours, that is morning and part of the afternoon, including lunch.
Weeks open:	Not all groups open every weekday, and even when they do, most children do not attend five sessions: 68 per cent of children attending playgroups, in the OPCS study, went to only one or two sessions a week[11]. Normally open in school terms only.
Cost to parent:	Fee charged per session attended, and varies according to length of session and other factors, including standards in playgroup and

extent of council grant to playgroup – if any.
28 per cent of playgroups replying to the 1977
Pre-School Playgroups Association (PPA)
survey got such grants, which mostly came to
less than £50 a year[10]. Fees tend to vary
according to length of session (the average, in
1976, ranging from 26p for sessions under two
hours to 49p for those over three). In 1977,
36 per cent of playgroups in the PPA survey
charged 21p–30p per session and 38 per cent
31p–40p.

Levels of provision

Highest:	Outer London boroughs, and South and South-West counties.
Lowest:	South Wales; Merseyside; Greater Manchester.

Standards and enforcement:	Standards laid down in Ministry of Health Circular 37/68; less stringent than for nurseries providing full-time care, for example staff:child ratios, where a minimum of 1:8 is recommended. Enforcement as for **Workplace Nurseries**.

Average size:	Twenty-four places per playgroup.
Premises:	7 per cent of playgroups in the 1976 PPA survey met in houses (including some registered as childminders providing part-time care). Most of the rest met in halls and other public buildings, usually shared with other organizations[12]. Only very few playgroups have their own purpose-built accommodation. Standards vary enormously and few have premises designed with children in mind. Safe outdoor play space often lacking in urban areas (in a survey of Inner London playgroups, 42 per cent lacked such space)[13].
Equipment:	Varies according to playgroup resources and space available. Many playgroups have to

regularly clear away all equipment, either
each day or on Fridays.

Staff : child ratio :	Little information available.
Staff qualifications :	Most playgroups combine paid staff (usually two) with parents helping : in the PPA survey, four-fifths of parent-run playgroups and two-fifths of other playgroups had a parent rota. Parents also help in other ways, such as committee work, fund-raising, reports. 85 per cent of playgroups in the PPA's 1977 survey had at least one trained staff member. In 71 per cent one or more staff had done a playgroup course, usually the one-year foundation course run at Adult Education Colleges for a day a week : 32 per cent had trained teachers and 15 per cent trained nursery nurses.
Staff pay and conditions :	Poor. Playleaders in the 1977 PPA survey averaged £1.91 per session and assistants £1–£1.50 (less than £1 an hour). There is usually no holiday or sick pay or other normal occupational benefits.
Number of places :	2,817 places in 126 council-run playgroups with 2,841 children on the register (that is one place and one child per 1,000 children aged under five). 381,699 registered places for an estimated 587,816 children (that is 124 places and 191 children per 1,000) in 15,581 other playgroups (plus those childminders registered for part-time care and who in practice run playgroups – see **Registered Childminders**). The estimate of children attending is on the basis of the 1977 PPA survey, which found 15·4 children on the register for every ten playgroup places; the PPA surveys, however, have a poor response rate (64 per cent and 54 per cent in 1976 and 1977, of playgroups

affiliated to the PPA), and it is always possible that responding playgroups differed in some respects from those who did not. References made above to this survey should therefore be treated with caution.

Private/Voluntary Nurseries

Robert and Clare Parker live in a large Victorian house in South London with their daughter Anna, aged three. Robert is a postgraduate student in linguistics and Clare has just obtained a grant to make a short film. Until recently they got together with friends and organized a small informal playgroup for all the children. Now they both need more time for their own work and have found a private nursery for Anna. Ideally they would have liked a place at the state nursery school, but Anna is too young and anyway the hours are too short.

The nursery is a short car ride from their home and is run in the ground floor of a sizable red-brick house, owned by the principal of the nursery. There are two rooms – one for sixteen children aged two to three and a half where Anna spends her day, and the other for the sixteen older children aged three and a half to five years. Altogether there are five staff with the thirty-two children: the principal is NNEB-trained, a Maltese nursery nurse has an equivalent qualification, a third nurse has done the playgroup course and the two others are young girls with no training at all. The staff are always appointed on a four-week trial period and if the principal doesn't like them they are asked to leave. These five staff do everything – looking after the children, cooking, cleaning etc. The nursery hours are 9 to 4 and the fees are £9 per week. If parents want longer hours they can pay £1 for each additional half hour, up until 5.30. There are a few children who come only in the mornings or afternoons, but most of the mothers are out at work, and their children come all day. The nursery is registered with the local social services department, but they rarely come to visit.

At the back of the house is a garden, much needed because the rooms themselves are rather cramped. The children play, eat and sleep all in the one room and the routine has to be tightly organized if everything is to run smoothly. The nursery is adequately equipped with an assortment of toys and play structures, but because of lack of space only a few activities are available at any one time. Anna seems a bit bored by the restricted range and Robert and Clare have asked the principal if she can move into the other room, which is slightly larger, even though she's not yet three and a half.

Purpose:	To provide care – sometimes with particular social, educational or other purposes in mind – for children whose parents can meet the fees or satisfy other admission criteria.
Provided by:	Some are provided by child-care charities (e.g. Barnardo's, National Children's Homes), colleges (for students and staff) and local community groups. Most however are provided privately.
Who can use them:	Sometimes restricted to, or favouring, local community, children with particular needs etc., but generally anyone who can afford the fees. Local authorities place and pay for some 1,630 children from their priority waiting lists (see **Council Day Nurseries**).

Age of children:	Little information available. Probably relatively few places for children under 2, though some do take children from 0 to 4.
Hours open:	Eight to ten hours a day. Most children go full-time.
Weeks open:	Usually throughout the year, except for public holidays.

Cost to parent:	Fees vary enormously, depending a lot on the quality of what is provided and how far the cost is subsidized by a local authority grant or the providing charity. Most provision however is not subsidized. In a recent report by the Local Authorities Association, six authorities reported average weekly charges of about £8 for 1975/6[14].

Levels of provision

Highest:	London, otherwise no clear pattern.
Lowest:	No clear pattern.

Standards and enforcement:	As for **Workplace Nurseries.**

Average size:	Twenty-eight places per nursery.
Premises:	From high-quality purpose-built provision to adapted short-life housing. Quality varies enormously.
Equipment:	Little information available. Likely to vary enormously. Those nurseries trying to keep costs down to a minimum may well have lower standards in general, including equipment.

Staff: child ratio:	No information available.
Staff qualifications:	Little information available. The best voluntary and private nurseries, as in all respects, will have similar standards to council day nurseries. For the rest, standards may often be lower, with use made by some of untrained school-leavers, on low rates of pay, to keep costs down.
Staff pay and conditions:	As for staff qualifications.

Number of places:	22,513 places in 799 nurseries (that is, 7.3 places per 1,000 children aged under five). No information on numbers of children actually attending.

Reception Classes

Mr and Mrs Jones live in a middle-class district of North London. Mr Jones is a lecturer at the University, and Mrs Jones plans to return to work after completing her Open University course. They have two children, Edward, six and a half, and Elizabeth, four and a quarter, who go to the local primary school. Edward is now in his third year and Elizabeth has just started in the reception class. Both started soon after they were four, as it is the local council policy to admit four-year-olds to reception classes in districts with no nursery classes.

The school itself occupies a three-storey Victorian building, flanked by two more recent annexes – the main hall and kitchens and the prefabricated building which houses two infant classes, including Elizabeth's. The class has twenty-five children, all in their first year, all under four and three quarters when they started. The teacher, with an infant teaching qualification, is assisted by a nursery nurse; there is however no arrangement for parents to help in the class, and although parents quite often chat to the staff at the beginning or end of the school day, most are in and out quickly and there is little encouragement to linger.

The classroom is a single large, bright room, decorated with children's paintings and equipped with a wide selection of activities – puzzles, Lego, a book corner, Wendy house and shop, sand tray, paints etc. At this early stage in the year, much of the day consists of free play, although, as the year progresses, rather more formal 'work' will be gradually introduced. At break-time, the children play in the infants' playground, a rather bleak piece of tarmac, with little equipment and not really enough room for the four infant classes – some 100 children in all – who use it. The class sometimes uses the playing fields or the hall for gym. Elizabeth and her classmates go to the hall twice a week to join the other infant classes for morning assembly, and this is where they have lunch, also with the older infants.

The school day starts at 8.45. Although all the children in Elizabeth's class attended for just the morning to begin with, by the first half term most stay for lunch or come back in the afternoon. Up to last week, Elizabeth's school day ended at 12, when Mrs Jones collected her, but now she has begun to go back in the afternoon and soon will be staying for lunch.

Purpose:	First class for children starting infant school (discounting nursery classes, where they exist).
Provided by:	LEA.
Who can use them:	All children starting school. The extent to which children under five are admitted depends largely on the policy of individual LEAs. Some admit very few under-fives, others concentrate on 'rising fives' (children admitted in the term before their fifth birthday), others try to take a larger number of younger four-year-olds.
Age of children:	4 to 5 years old, but most aged 5. Of the 4-year-olds, 57 per cent are 'rising 5s' and 43 per cent younger 4-year-olds.
Hours open:	92 per cent of four-year-olds attend for a full school day, the rest for mornings only.
Weeks open:	Normal school terms (about forty weeks a year).
Cost to parent:	Free.

Levels of provision
Highest:	North-East; Wales; South Lancashire.

Lowest:	Home Counties and South-East. Otherwise widely dispersed, with no clear pattern.

Standards:	DES lays down standards for buildings, staffing and curriculum in primary schools. A 1973 DES circular recommended that LEAs ensure that 'the hours of attendance, staffing, programmes, accommodation and equipment for children under five are equivalent (in reception classes) to those appropriate for nursery classes' [9].

Average size:	No information available.
Premises:	No information available. However, with many schools not built with nursery standards in mind, it seems likely that standards are often inferior to those in nursery schools/classes, especially for outdoor play space.
Equipment:	As for premises.

Staff: child ratio:	Little information available. However, in December 1975 there was on average one nursery assistant for every sixty-six children under five, compared with one for every nineteen in nursery classes [14].
Staff qualifications:	Run by a trained teacher, probably with an infant teaching qualification (see **Nursery Schools and Classes**), sometimes supported by an assistant, some of whom – though probably a minority – will be NNEB-trained (see **Council Day Nurseries**).
Staff pay and conditions:	As for **Nursery Schools and Classes**.

Number of places:	257,874 places for 268,720 children (that is 84·0 places and 87·5 children per 1,000 children aged under 5).

Registered Childminders

Mr and Mrs Johnson were both born in the West Indies but brought up in this country. They have one little girl, Dionne, twenty months, and live in a privately rented flat at the top of a Victorian house in a run-down area of London. Both work full-time: he as a bus conductor and she in a factory. Dionne spends the day with a registered minder, Mrs Brown, a twenty-five-minute walk away.

Mrs Brown is also from the West Indies. She has a two-year-old, Paul, and two older children, aged six and eight. As well as Dionne she looks after a four-year-old Indian boy, Anand, and in the afternoon she picks up her own children from school together with two other six-year-olds, who spend a couple of hours with her until their mothers come for them after work.

The minder's family lives in a small terraced house with two bedrooms and a bathroom upstairs. Downstairs is a best front room, and at the back is a small room with a kitchen leading off it; this is where the children spend the day. The room is about 11 ft square, and has a dining table with four chairs, two easy chairs and a television. Outside is a small yard.

Mrs Johnson gets Dionne to the minder at 8 o'clock and picks her up at 6. Dionne spends the day with Paul and Anand. They accompany Mrs Brown to the primary school, and to the local shops now and then. But mainly they play about in the small back room with the television on. There's a cardboard box of toys – bricks, cars, puzzles, a couple of teds, a big ball, some Lego and two or three Ladybird books. Their day is punctuated by a midmorning drink, with a biscuit; dinner at 12.30; and after dinner a rest upstairs. When the older children are back from school, it's tea and telly time for the seven children.

Mrs Brown herself has a busy day: she gets the urgent housework done and she makes meals for her family and the minded children. There's also a lot of washing and clearing up to be done for the children. Sometimes she finds time to put her feet up for half an hour – then she might do a puzzle with the children, or show them a book. It's a long day and the pay is low. She gets £9 each for Anand and Dionne and £2 each for the school-age children. Out of that she finds food and neating. There is no security of pay and no basic benefits like holiday or sickness pay. Probably Mrs Brown will go out to work herself when Paul goes to primary school.

Purpose:	To provide care – in the minder's own home – for children whose parents can meet their fees; mostly used by working mothers.
Provided by:	Individual minders.
Who can use them:	Any parent who can afford the fees and make an arrangement with a minder. Local authorities place and pay for some 1,210 children from their priority waiting lists (see **Council Day Nurseries**).

Age of children:	Little information available. Many minders – though not all – take children from 0 to 4, and some care for children over five after school and in the holidays. The OPCS survey results suggest that about half of all minded children are under 3.
Hours open:	Three quarters of the places with registered minders are for all-day care, and most of these minders will take children from 8 a.m. to 6 p.m. The remaining quarter are for part-time care, and many of these may, in practice, be small private playgroups, open for morning or afternoon sessions.
Weeks open:	Most all-day minders are available all year round, apart perhaps from a short summer holiday. Little is known about part-time minders, and how many operate in school terms only.

Cost to parent:	Fees vary, from £2 to £10 per child per week in 1976, with an average probably around £6, though higher in London [15]. By 1977–8, the average in London was about £10. The extent to which parents are expected to provide food, nappies etc. for their children also varies.

Levels of provision

Highest:	Inner London; a few Outer London boroughs and scattered non-metropolitan counties.
Lowest:	Spread wide, but mostly mining and port areas, with traditionally low female employment rates.

Standards and enforcement:	Anyone, apart from a close relative, looking after a child under five for pay, even for two hours a week, should by law be registered with the local SSD. Inspection is made before registration, when basic standards of safety, health and space are checked, though these may vary between authorities; some are reluctant to refuse registration, as it may be the only way to keep check on the minder. The SSD can also impose various requirements before registering a minder, including a maximum number of children to be taken. Frequency of subsequent inspections also varies but is usually infrequent. A substantial number of minders are not registered, and are therefore caring for children illegally. There is no information available about them.
  DHSS guidelines suggest a maximum of three children under five (including minder's own) per minder, for those providing all-day care.
Average size:	Minders providing all-day care are registered, on average, to provide 2·2 places each. Minders

	providing part-time care are registered for 6·8 places each.
Premises:	Minders' own homes, which vary enormously in size, condition, facilities. No national information, but a recent study in London found generally inadequate premises (e.g. a third had no outdoor play space)[16].
Equipment:	Likely also to vary, though no national information available. The London study however also found widespread deficiencies. Local authorities can provide assistance, with toys, safety equipment etc.; again, widespread variations in how far authorities make such provision.

Staff : child ratio :	Little information available on minders providing all-day care. In the London study, 35 per cent exceeded the recommended number of children. There is no information available on minders registered for part-time care.
Staff qualifications:	No training required or recommended. No information about training or past experience of minders, though the vast majority probably have had no formal training or experience in looking after young children. Some local authorities are introducing voluntary, part-time training schemes.
Staff pay and conditions:	Very low income, after expenses paid; a 1977 BBC programme estimated 10p an hour for caring for three children. No holiday or sick pay or other normal occupational benefits.

Number of places:	70,288 all-day care places with 31,398 *registered* minders (that is 22·9 places per 1,000 children aged under five); 17,947 part-time places, for an estimated 27,638 children (see **Playgroups** for basis of estimate) with 2,635 registered minders (that is 5·8 places and 9·0 children per 1,000 children aged under five).

No information on numbers of children actually
attending.

Workplace Nurseries

Morgan Electronics prides itself on the quality and
good name of its consumer products. To maintain this –
and the accompanying profitability – the company
needs a reliable, experienced and, above all, stable
workforce. These needs enabled the personnel department to win Board agreement to establishing a nursery
for female employees, who do nearly all the production-
line and clerical work.

The twenty-place nursery, which takes children from
the age of two, opens at 7.45. Children arrive between
then and 9 and are collected after work, from 4 till 5.15.
Once they have left their children in the morning,
mothers are not encouraged to visit till it's time to go
home. Daytime visits are felt to disrupt routine and
upset children whose mothers don't come; besides,
there's never been a great demand from mothers for
such access. The nursery is housed in a prefabricated
building on one side of the factory site, and surrounded
by a high wire fence, whose gate is kept padlocked for
the children's safety – and to prevent unchecked
journeys to and from the factory. Nearly all indoor
activities take place in the nursery's big main room, but
there is also a small room where groups of four or five
children can be taken for special activities and a staff
room-cum-office. Outside there is a grassy play area.

The day begins with breakfast for the early arrivals,
followed by periods of free play indoors and, weather
permitting, outdoors, interspersed by lunch, a post-
lunch nap for the younger children, tea, stories and the
daily routine of washing, toileting, clearing-up, laying
tables etc. There are also outings from time to time. The
staff consists of a matron, and deputy matron – both

nursery nurses – and two assistants, younger girls, one of whom has just finished nursery nurse training, the other having just left school.

Day-to-day routine is decided by the staff, but overall management policy – including admissions and the decision that children must leave the nursery if their mothers leave the firm – is the responsibility of the personnel manager. She has always taken a particular interest in the nursery, and protected it from closure during periods when higher unemployment has reduced its value in recruiting and keeping employees. The personnel department also deals with all financial matters. The cost of the nursery is partly subsidized by the company, the remaining costs being met by fees, deducted from the mothers' wages.

Purpose:	To provide care for children of employer's workforce.
Provided by:	Private and public sector employers, usually with a high reliance on female employees (hospitals, electrical engineering, textiles etc.). The employer may run the nursery directly or engage a specialist firm to set up and run the service.
Who can use them:	Almost without exception, limited to children of employees (usually women only). Preference sometimes given to certain kinds of staff. Children have to leave if mother moves job.
Age of children:	0 to 4, though only a minority accept children under 2. Some provide holiday play schemes for children over 5.
Hours open:	To fit working hours. Usually open between 7.30–8 a.m. and 5–5.30 p.m., though 13 per cent of places are in nurseries offering part-time care only.
Weeks open:	Throughout the year, apart from public and works' holidays.

Cost to parent:	Usually subsidized by firm, so below full cost. In 1976, one fairly typical factory charged £5 a week.
Levels of provision:	Sixty out of ninety-two nurseries in the North-West; East Midlands; East Anglia and Home Counties; seventy-four local authorities have no workplace nurseries.
Standards and enforcement:	Standards as for **Council Day Nurseries**. Must be registered with SSDs, who can impose extra requirements over and above those recommended in Circular 37/68. Thereafter periodic inspections. Their frequency, and the additional standards required, vary between local authorities.
Average size:	Thirty places per nursery.
Premises:	Both purpose-built and adapted. Indoor space generally good, outdoor play space often inadequate.
Equipment:	Generally adequate, but lack of outdoor space may limit larger outdoor equipment. Unlikely to be as well provided for as nursery schools/classes.
Staff: child ratio:	A survey in 1975 by the Institute of Personnel Management found that the recommended ratio for children over two – 1 : 5 – was 'not always strictly adhered to', only half actually meeting it [17].
Staff qualifications:	Run by nursery nurses and assistants under the direction of a matron. Staff usually nursery nurse or hospital nursing trained.
Staff pay and conditions:	These vary. Often in line with those in the company, hospital etc.; though sometimes related to council day nurseries. Daily hours often long; a working day of over nine hours, with no lunch break, was common in the 1975 survey.

Number of places:	2,446 all-day care and 350 part-time care places in ninety-two nurseries (that is 0·9 places per 1,000 children aged under five). No information on numbers of children actually attending.

Putting the pieces together

In England and Wales, the seven types of service just described provided some 914,676 *places* in 1977 – or 298 per 1,000 children aged under five. Of these, some 46 per cent were provided by the state sector (that is to say directly by local authorities), the remaining 54 per cent by the voluntary or private sectors, mostly in playgroups. Scottish provision is substantially lower at 209 places per 1,000 children in 1976 compared to 279/1,000 in England and Wales. The difference is largely due to low levels of private day nurseries, registered minders and under-fives in reception classes in Scotland: these classes accounted for 27 per cent of places in England and Wales, but only 12 per cent in Scotland.

Altogether some 1,221,495 children attended these types of service in England and Wales, the difference between places available and children attending being largely due to the part-time attendance of many children at nursery and infant schools and playgroups. This enables one place to be used by more than one child (e.g. one nursery school place can be used by one child attending full-time or two attending part-time; and one playgroup place can be used by one child going five mornings a week or two attending three and two mornings respectively). Figure 4 shows the proportion of children going to each type of service, and that altogether some 40 per cent of under-fives were attending one or other of these in 1977. Of children attending, 42 per cent went to state-sector services and 58 per cent

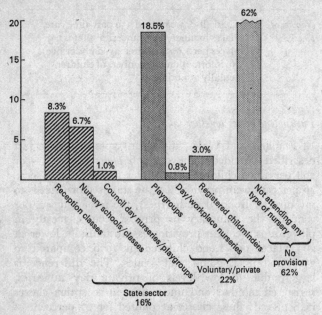

Figure 4. Percentage of children under five attending different types of nursery provision, England and Wales, 1977

to private and voluntary-sector services: 65 per cent attended part-time, 25 per cent for a full school day and 10 per cent had all-day places. As with places, the contribution of reception classes – not primarily a service for under-fives – is substantial: excluding them, only 30 per cent of under-fives attend a service specifically for the age-group.

These figures slightly underestimate the total position, as they exclude two types of service – unregistered minders and private schools (educational establishments, not to be confused with private day nurseries).

Unregistered minders. Their numbers, almost by definition, remain unknown. Estimates vary, but the evidence of surveys suggests that they may provide some 50,000 places.

Private schools. In December 1975, they provided for 29,373 children under five in England and Wales, in some 22,500 places (that is 60 per cent of these children went for a full school day, the rest part-time) : 67 per cent of the children were aged four.

Since then there have been two changes affecting these schools. *Direct-grant nursery schools,* which accounted for only 700 under-fives, have been phased out; and *independent nursery schools* have also disappeared. A handful of nurseries were previously given this special status by the DES, even though legally a private establishment can be a school only if it has at least five children *over* five. This special status was withdrawn in April 1978, and the few nurseries formerly covered by it are now the sole responsibility of SSDs, along with private day nurseries. Private schooling is therefore now limited to schools taking both under-fives and over-fives (for instance from 3 to 11 or 13).

Between them, unregistered minders and private schools probably account for about 2 per cent of the under-five population.

This summary has so far considered all under-fives as one group, but patterns of nursery attendance vary with age. Figure 5 shows the proportion of children in each of the five pre-school years going to different types of nurseries and minders; the information, from the OPCS study, refers to the situation in 1974. As the figure shows, attendance at nurseries increases with age, rising from 6 per cent for under-twos, to 19 per cent for two-year-olds and 60 per cent for three- and four-year-olds. The pattern of service use also changes: whereas childminding is the service most commonly used for children under two, its relative significance declines for older children as the contribution of other types of service increases. Playgroups are well ahead in

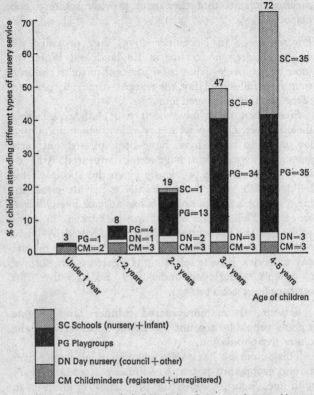

Figure 5. Types of nursery service used according to age of children, England and Wales, 1974

providing for two- and three-year-olds, but have a more or less equal share of four-year-olds with schools (reception and nursery classes and nursery schools).

If the picture that emerges from this review of services seems rather confused, it is because, like Topsy, the services 'just grew', each starting at a different period in response to different needs, and following different lines of development. The result has been chaotic, a mish-mash of anomalies, gaps, overlaps, inequalities and feuds – which we now turn to consider in more detail.

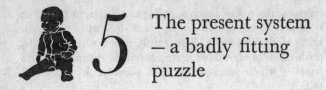

5 The present system
– a badly fitting
puzzle

In this chapter we look at the system of pre-school services *as a whole*, and ask how far it provides the kind of service we argued for at the beginning of the book. We focus on three crucial questions:

> Does the present system provide enough places for all parents who want them?
> How much choice is offered in terms of the age when children can start and the hours they can attend for each day?
> Is the present organization of services the best way to meet children's needs for care, play and education?

As we shall see, the system as a whole falls a long way short on each of these counts. Altogether, there are only enough places for just over half the parents who want them, and the vast majority of places are restricted to short sessions of two and a half hours for three- and four-year-old children. In addition, the division of services into those providing 'care' and those providing 'education' creates an unequal, two-tier system in which those children most in need of nursery education are least likely to get it. These problems are clearly not the fault of any individuals working in nurseries today, but are instead the product of deeply rooted economic and organizational problems, the effects of which can be felt at every level of the present system.

Not enough places to go round

Even when all nurseries, playgroups and other services are taken together, the total number of places available still falls far short of the number desired by parents. As we saw on pages 13–14, surveys carried out in London, Rochdale, Oxfordshire and Fife – as well as the nation-wide OPCS survey – indicate that places are wanted for about two thirds of all pre-school children in the country. Yet as we have just seen, there are altogether places for only 40 per cent of all children, and over a fifth of these are in reception classes not primarily intended for under-fives.

The situation is worse in some parts of the country than in others. Local authorities are under no statutory obligation to provide pre-school services – whereas they *are* obliged to provide primary schools and child health clinics, for example – and so the level of services in any area depends very much on the attitude of the authority concerned. Some attach considerable priority to the under-fives, and have developed high levels of state services in their area, while others do very little and rely on voluntary playgroups, private nurseries and child-minders to take care of the problem. This is shown very clearly in Table 2 below, which gives the five areas with the *highest* levels of local authority provision and the five with the *lowest*. In the Appendix we give similar figures for every authority in England, Scotland and Wales, showing the wide variations that exist for all types of services between different areas.

As well as being unevenly distributed across the country, the services are also unfairly distributed according to *social class*. The OPCS survey found that although the *desire* for places was uniformly high across all classes, the proportion of families who had got a place was much higher in professional and managerial families (40 per cent) than for the families of semi- and

Table 2. *Nursery provision in areas with highest and lowest levels of local authority provision*

Places for 1,000 children under five in:

	Local authority nursery provision	Playgroups	Private provision	Total	Reception classes
High levels of local authority nursery provision					
Manchester	212	57	21	290	84
Gwynedd	183	129	8	319	66
Mid Glamorgan	147	58	10	215	118
W. Glamorgan	124	49	7	180	134
Inner London Education Authority	125	102	64	291	55
Low levels of local authority nursery provision					
Wiltshire	1	130	29	160	70
Gloucestershire	3	159	43	205	69
West Sussex	7	172	60	239	30
Bromley	6	242	58	307	50
Kent	8	137	66	211	36

Local authority nursery provision = nursery schools and classes, council day nurseries and local authority playgroups: *playgroups* = voluntary and some private playgroups: *private provision* = factory nurseries, private and voluntary day nurseries, registered childminders: *reception classes* = number of places for children under five in these classes. For fuller details of how the figures are calculated, see the Appendix.

unskilled manual workers (24 per cent). The same unequal picture emerged when housing rather than occupation was looked at: the survey found that children whose housing was inadequate were less likely than others of the same age to use nurseries [1]. Even those children whose circumstances classify them as 'priority' admissions for council day nurseries – for example, children of single parents who have to work, or children who are considered to be severely 'socially disadvantaged' – are by no means guaranteed a place. In 1976 there were nearly 12,000 priority children on the *waiting lists* of council day nurseries, almost half the total number of places available.

The personal consequences

These figures paint their own gloomy picture of a service which is not only distributed in an unfair and haphazard manner, but which is creaking under the strain of an enormous unmet desire for places. But what does all this mean in more personal terms? The most obvious consequence is that there are countless families who do not get a place at all, and these mothers and children must forgo – or at best postpone – the benefits they might get from a nursery. Many of these families, like the mother and child below, must undergo considerable hardship and distress as a result of not getting a place. The following account, which first appeared in *Spare Rib* magazine, starts when the mother returns from a holiday to find two letters from the Nursery Officer at the Social Services Department.

Her first letter told me that my son's place in the Day Nursery was due to be reviewed. If I needed the place during the next term I should write to them with proof from my college of the subject I was studying, the length of terms and my would-be career. What nonsense – I had told them several times already, I thought, while opening the second letter. This was very short, saying that as they hadn't heard from me,

Niaz had been discharged from the nursery. 'Oh God no.' I said it quietly and sat down to think. I had told the matron that I would certainly need the place when I came back. When questioned I had emphasized that I would be going back to college the following term as I hadn't finished studying yet, and I had shown her the registration paper.

I needed to put Niaz in a nursery if I was to carry on studying. This was vital to me as I needed basic qualifications to enable me to get a job and be independent.

I went to Niaz's health visitor. She said we were no longer in her area, because we'd moved, though we were still in the same area as far as the nursery was concerned. So we went to another health visitor nearer our new house. When I explained everything to her, she said she was sorry but I must go to the Social Services – only they could help me.

I went there, rang the bell and was shown to the waiting room. I waited for a long time, exhausted by Niaz's efforts to escape and my growing impatience. At last a lady came into the room, asked my name and address, and I told her my problem. She dashed off, returning quickly with a new application. She said she was sorry but I had lost the place and would have to reapply. I took the form and staggered home.

The next day I thought I'd better make an appointment directly with the nursery officer and explain everything to her. I phoned in the morning and went that afternoon. After a long wait a small middle-aged woman called me and we went into a cubicle together. I was worried as I had left Niaz at home alone. Although he was asleep I felt uneasy. She started questioning.

'How long will you be studying for? What will you be doing after you have finished college? Which college are you going to? What's its address? Its telephone number? How long are you going to the college every day? How many days a week?'

I answered her questions patiently and politely, mentioning that I had answered them all many times before. But when she started carrying on about my would-be career I grew impatient and told her that I had left my boy alone at home and couldn't stay there any longer, that I needed the place urgently. They had discharged him on the assumption that I didn't need the place any more. Now that I am here again and need the place badly, isn't it their responsibility to put him back?

'You have left your child alone at home? Oh you shouldn't

you know, it's against the law,' she said, looking like a fox. 'You have lost his place at the Day Nursery,' she went on. 'The place is now taken by someone else and there isn't another available.'

'It is only in the afternoons,' I said. 'Surely it is not impossible.'

'There are many people on the waiting list, a great many people, and all have been waiting a long time,' she finished. 'Sorry, you must wait, we can't do anything.'

I walked home confused, questioning myself and getting nowhere, with a picture in my mind of her fox face, repeating the cunning words 'you shouldn't have left him alone you know, it's against the law'. I ran the rest of the way, rushing into the room to find him awake, crying his eyes out.

I stayed at home a few days thinking over and again what I could do. I couldn't go back to college while he had no nursery. He was too young to take to college with me and the weather was too cold anyway to do the journey with such a small child. And there were no facilities at college either. I thought I must try to see whomever I could, go wherever I had to and probably someone, somewhere should be able to tell me what to do.

One morning I phoned a local social worker whom I used to know and asked if we could see her, explaining why. I was given an appointment for a few days later. She listened carefully as a good social worker always does and let me do all the talking. Then I asked what she could do. She said it was difficult but she would contact Social Services and let me know the result.

When I took Niaz to the children's clinic I saw his new health visitor. I remembered how the other one had found the nursery place herself, how helpful and understanding she had been. I found this one cool and indifferent. I told her politely that I thought she could show me an alternative and tell me what to do; she said that was not her job and she didn't know much about it.

For nearly two months my life had been paralysed and I had missed a term. I was unable to concentrate and do any reading at home either. The next term would start in January and I really wanted to go. It was not just not going to college that made me feel so frustrated, but sitting at home feeling idle and undecided and not knowing what to do next. Besides, it made me feel bitter, angry and cruel, and Niaz was the one who was being hurt most. Now I was hitting him nearly all the time and it seemed everything he did was wrong.

At night when everywhere was silence, between tiredness and depression I would visualize single mothers with more children than me and dread the difficulties they have to face. Now I could see why a perfectly normal human being would turn into a cruel beast.[2]

When the demand for places exceeds the supply, those who control the supply have to introduce a *selective system*. As this mother's account shows, this takes its most extreme form in the council day nursery system, but it also occurs in nursery schools and classes (particularly for the allocation of full-time places) and even in playgroups (to decide how many sessions a child can attend). Wherever it occurs, a selective system is almost guaranteed to bring out the worst in people, whichever side they are on, and it is almost inevitable that selfishness, tension and ill-feeling will arise. Mothers will put their child's name down at birth for a place in a nursery school; they may exaggerate their distress or make false claims about their circumstances in order to get a day nursery place; they will compare notes as to why one person has been allocated a place or extra sessions when they have not, and may accuse the staff of unfairness and favouritism.

For the staff themselves the situation can also be trying and unpleasant. When the pressure on places is great, it has to be decided who is most deserving and needy – is it the single mother who has to work to support herself and her child, or is it the Bengali woman cooped up in a small flat with three young children, none of whom speak English? Not only is it impossible to be fair in such circumstances, but the whole process is disagreeable for all concerned. Nor do the effects of a selective system stop when the selection has been made. If a mother has been given a place because her circumstances are particularly unfortunate, it is more than likely that the staff will see her as an 'inadequate mother' and treat her and her child accordingly; for her part she may resent having had to reveal her private circumstances in order to get a place, while at the same time she may feel she cannot tell the staff of any improvements in her life in case her place gets taken away.

State resources and 'low-cost' provision

The present shortage of nursery places is a direct reflection of the chronic lack of resources which has characterized pre-school services over the years, and in particular reflects the low priority and lack of commitment shown by the state towards mothers and young children. Nurseries – like any other service, such as schools, hospitals or child health clinics – cost a good deal of money to set up and run, and, as with any other service, large-scale improvements are not likely to be made without considerable financial and political commitment from the state. Yet the state's contribution to pre-school services in this country has always been – and still is – pitifully small. In 1977 council day nurseries and playgroups, nursery schools and classes provided between them only about 162,000 places, and these for a total pre-school population of three million children. In contrast – and as a direct result of this neglect from the state – there has been a vast boom in the number of children cared for by *voluntary* and *private* agencies, such as private nurseries, playgroups and childminders. In 1977 these forms of child-care provided over 495,000 places, three times the number of places in state pre-school services.

The two government departments responsible for pre-school services – the DHSS and the DES – are well aware of the situation. A joint circular issued in January 1978 noted that 'the Departments recognize that the resources available for the under-fives are still far short of what is needed to make adequate provision for the group' [3]. Their solution – in a time of economic restraint and public expenditure cuts – has been to advocate the increasing use of 'low-cost' services – that is, playgroups and childminders. This policy was spelt out in 1976 by Dr David Owen, then Minister of State for Health, in a foreword to an interdepartmental conference on 'Low Cost Day Provision for the Under-Fives':

The theme is 'low cost'; we did not meet to discuss the desirable, we want to grapple with the attainable ... We could improve the provision for the 0–5s substantially by spreading the low-cost best practice which already exists, proven and documented on the ground. I suggest this spreading of best practice should now be our central objective. [4]

It says a lot for the status given to nurseries that a government minister can seriously advocate 'low-cost' services – after all, we do not hear much talk of 'low-cost universities' or 'low-cost motorways'. But it is easy to see why 'low-cost' services are so attractive. A service based mainly on playgroups and childminders is far cheaper to run than one based on nursery schools and day nurseries, as the outlay is confined to small grants to playgroups, toy allowances and other limited help for childminders, and paying council workers to spread the development of these forms of service.

To focus entirely on the cost to the state is to see only a small part of the picture. Good child-care services are not cheap to run, and any service which claims to be 'low-cost' is either being subsidized by its parents and staff or is of poor quality – or both. This can readily be demonstrated by a direct comparison of the main forms of state and low-cost services (see Chapter 4). Compared with state services, low-cost services:

- are more expensive for parents
- use poorer premises, often with no outdoor play area
- have less money for toys and equipment
- use predominantly untrained staff
- offer staff low pay and poor conditions of work.

These discrepancies no doubt go a long way towards explaining why so many parents who use low-cost services would prefer their children to go to state-run nurseries. The OPCS survey found that almost a third of mothers who were using playgroups would have preferred their child to attend a nursery school or class, compared with only 3 per cent for whom the opposite was true. Childminders are even less popular than playgroups: the OPCS survey found that 'for the great majority of the children who were with childminders, other forms of provision would have been preferred'; and the TCRU survey found that only two out of 229 mothers interviewed would use a minder if other forms of child-care were available [5].

We are not suggesting there is no place for either playgroups or childminders – or for volunteer workers more generally – in an ideal nursery system. Nor are we saying that all nurseries must be lavishly equipped in expensive premises, or staffed solely by highly trained professional workers. What *is* important, however, is that all forms of child-care should reach certain acceptable standards regarding premises, outdoor play space, and equipment; that the great majority of staff should have some sort of training, receive decent pay and get adequate conditions of work; and that there should be a thorough system of inspection and regulation to ensure that these standards are met. There is no reason why playgroups and childminders should not develop to meet these requirements, but, as we shall see, such developments will almost certainly require a substantial input of resources if they are to be implemented. A good nursery service cannot be provided on the cheap, and policies which advocate low-cost solutions must be treated with the suspicion they deserve.

Restrictions on places

We argued in Chapter 1 that if nurseries are to be of
maximum benefit to parents, they must offer parents a
genuine choice regarding the age at which their children
can start and the hours they can attend for each day.
At first sight it seems that the present system does offer
this kind of choice, for, as we saw in Chapter 4, it is
made up of a wide range of different types of service,

*Table 3. Restrictions on places provided in different
types of nurseries*

Form of child-care	Restrictions on age	Restrictions on hours	Other restrictions
Playgroups	Mostly 3 and 4 years although some take over 2½s	Short 2½-hour sessions	Most require mothers to help on rota
Reception classes	Older 4-year-olds only	Mostly full school day	—
Nursery schools and classes	3 and 4 years only	Mostly short 2½-hour sessions	—
Private nurseries	Few take under 2 years	—	Cost may be prohibitive
Workplace nurseries	Few take under 2 years	—	Employees only
Council day nurseries	Some don't take babies	—	Priority children only
Childminders	Some don't take under 2 years	—	Depends on minder

offering a variety of hours and starting ages. A closer inspection, however, reveals that this variety is very much an illusion. As Table 3 shows, there are quite severe limitations on the kinds of places which are available, with the overwhelming majority of places consisting of short sessions of two and a half hours for three- and four-year-old children.

The overall effect of these restrictions is as follows:

- If your child is under three, you will not get a nursery place – either full-time or part-time – unless you are a 'priority' case, or have a nursery at your work, or can afford a private nursery. Otherwise you will have to use a childminder.
- If you need full day care (seven plus hours) for your child, much the same applies, whatever the age of your child.
- If your child is over three and you need a full school day (six hours), you may be able to get a full-time place at a nursery school or class (though your chances will be small): if your child is approaching five she will probably be able to start infant school.
- If your child is over three and you need only a short session (two and a half hours), you are almost certain to get a place, though not necessarily in your first choice of service.

Not only are there severe restrictions on the type of places available, but these places are usually offered on a 'take it or leave it' basis: parents must fit in with what is offered or go elsewhere. Of course there are many good-natured nursery staff who are prepared to bend the rules in special circumstances – such as allowing a child to start nursery school at two and three quarters because she seems 'ready', or letting a 'mornings only' child stay till after lunch on Friday because her mother works late that day – but there are also many nurseries which make it extremely difficult for parents to have any choice over the hours their children attend.

'I've had some upsets in there [day nursery] because I wanted Rachel to stay longer. It was like a Catch 22 situation. I had to get involved with the health visitor who said I should get a social worker. I didn't want a social worker. I got one and asked him if he could add weight to my request. I had a very confusing and annoying time with the social worker, which is still going on. He's done nothing practical for me. He goes around trying to be an amateur psychiatrist, which annoys me ... The nursery have agreed to let Rachel stay on now, but the fact that I had to get a social worker and that he did nothing to help me really upset me. I felt infantalized by the way they all treated me. They couldn't believe *me*: they had to have someone representing me, like in court. It all got me very confused and upset.'

What do parents want?

The overwhelming emphasis on short two-and-a-half-hour sessions for three- and four-year-old children is of course a direct reflection of the belief that children should not be separated from their mothers until they are three years old, and then only for a few hours each day. As we saw in Chapter 2, this belief is not based on strong or convincing scientific evidence, but has nevertheless been accepted by both government departments responsible for pre-school services – the DHSS and the DES – as well as by the Pre-School Playgroups Association (PPA). Many parents, however, do *not* share this belief. Table 4 shows the demand for different kinds of places in the TCRU survey of three different areas of London.

The survey clearly shows that many mothers would like their children to start at nursery long before the recommended age of three years. Altogether, 46 per cent of mothers with children under three wanted some sort of nursery place; this desire increased with the age of the child from 17 per cent for babies to 73 per cent for two-

Table 4. Percentage of children whose mothers want nursery places for them, in three areas of Inner London, by ages of child

Hours wanted per day	Age of child					All ages
	0-1	1-2	2-3	3-4	4-5	
Place not wanted now	83	56	27	10	9	36
Place wanted for –						
1-4 hours	1	10	31	43	31	25
5-6 hours	0	8	8	24	36	15
7+ hours	16	26	34	23	24	24
Total wanting place	17	44	73	90	91	64

year-olds. The survey also shows that less than half the mothers wanting a nursery place wanted 'part-time' hours, that is four hours a day or less. Even within this group, there is a spread of hours wanted, from the two to two and a half hours of an average playgroup or nursery school session to the three or four hours that might well include a child staying through for lunch. A similar number of mothers wanted all-day care (seven hours or more), while just under a quarter opted for around a full school day (five to six hours a day).

How typical are these mothers? The large nationwide survey by the OPCS suggests that on the question of *age* they are probably typical of mothers throughout the country. The OPCS survey found that places were wanted for 46 per cent of all children under three – 20 per cent for children under one, 41 per cent for children between one and two, and 72 per cent for children aged two to three. These figures are almost identical to those of the TCRU survey. On the question of hours, we can be less certain, as the OPCS survey did not ask mothers the precise hours which they wanted. However, it is likely that the demand for full-day care amongst the

London mothers is untypically high; this sample contained a higher than average proportion of single and
immigrant mothers – both groups with high rates of full-
time employment.

Even with these qualifications, it is still clear that the
present system fails on several counts to provide what
parents want. For a start there are very few places for
children under three – despite the fact that parents
want places for almost half of all under-threes – and the
few places that are available are practically all full-time.
For the mother who wants a short regular break from her
baby or toddler there is virtually nothing, and often the
most she can hope for is a place at a 'Mothers and
Toddlers Club' or a 'One O'Clock Club'. These clubs
usually meet for an hour or two once or twice a week and
provide somewhere for mothers to get together while
their children play: often there is a paid leader who
supervises and plans activities. Many mothers find them
extremely valuable, but their usefulness is limited
because mothers must stay with their children all the
time: they are in no way a substitute for a proper nursery.

It is also clear that many mothers do not find short
two-and-a-half-hour sessions particularly useful, and
would prefer longer hours – though not necessarily all-
day care – if they had the choice. It is not hard to see
why: a session may nominally last two and a half hours,
but after a mother has settled her child in, talked to the
staff and other mothers, and walked home, she is unlikely to have more than an hour and a half before she
has to set off again to collect her child. That hardly
gives her time to wash up and tidy the house, or go to
the launderette, let alone have any time to herself. As
one mother told us:

'I wouldn't put her in part-time nursery – from my point of
view it's no use at all. You've got to haul them all the way up
the road in the mornings and then you've got to go back again
two hours later. Doesn't give you time to do anything worthwhile.'

Short sessions are even less use for working mothers. There are very few jobs which can be fitted in between 9.30 a.m. and 12 noon, or between 1 and 3.30 p.m., and even 'part-time' jobs usually take up at least three or four hours a day. If mothers using the short sessions at playgroups or nursery classes want to work, they must inevitably use some other arrangement as well:

'From my point of view I'd like him to go longer than that [9.30 to 12 o'clock] as that doesn't really give you any chance to work in the mornings. I'll have to come to some sort of arrangement to have him picked up at 12 and given lunch because that would give me half a day if I could pick him up at 2.'

Indeed the present system of services is particularly badly suited to the needs of working mothers. Some women are fortunate enough to find arrangements which suit both them and their children: they may have a nursery at work, or know of a good and reliable minder, or be able to afford a private nursery or nanny, or have a friend or relative who will happily collect their child from playgroup and look after her until the mother gets back from work. But other women are not so fortunate. Many mothers, unable to make suitable child-care arrangements, stay at home and try to reconcile themselves to not working. Other mothers have no alternative but to go ahead with an arrangement they find less than satisfactory: this may consist of a minder who provides sub-standard care, or a relative who may resent having to look after their child day after day. Some mothers have to rely on complex arrangements which involve several forms of care: for example, a relative may collect the child from a morning playgroup, give her lunch, then take her on to an afternoon nursery class, from which she is collected by her father. Such arrangements may well be satisfactory in some cases, but usually they are not: the child is passed from pillar to post, while each extra 'link' in the chain means an added chance of its breaking.

Some women are forced to take jobs at unpleasant or anti-social times of the day – such as early morning or evening cleaning, or evening shifts at factories – so that their husbands can look after their children while they are at work. This kind of arrangement may well be very common, but it has severe drawbacks. The work is likely to be monotonous and badly paid, and such arrangements drastically reduce the time when the mother and father can be together, with or without their children. In addition, it often means that the person looking after the child is tired from work or is actually trying to sleep while the child is awake – hardly ideal for anyone. Finally, many women try to combine child-care and work either by working at home or, more rarely, by taking the child with them to work. Again, such arrangements may well be satisfactory in some cases – one pictures the novelist working at her desk while her child plays contentedly in the garden – but all too often they are not. Much home-work consists of boring and badly paid work (such as cutting out material or addressing envelopes), and further emphasizes the isolation and loneliness of mothers with young children. In addition, as anyone who has tried it will know, it is extremely difficult to combine any sort of work with child-care, and in practice either the work or the children will suffer – if not both.

In Chapter 3 we argued for a number of changes in employment and national insurance benefits, which would make it easier for both parents to combine work and child-care. It is hard to predict the effect such measures would have on the demand for nurseries, particularly if all parents had access to good-quality nurseries which offered flexible hours for children of all ages up to five. Overall, it is possible that the demand for all-day care for children under twelve months would fall – although for older children it might still be well above the level currently available in state, voluntary and private nurseries – while there would be an increase in the demand for part-time places, ranging between two and six hours a day, as more mothers sought employment and, hopefully, more men opted for periods of part-time work.

While we cannot be certain what the precise demand for nurseries will be in the future, there can be little doubt that many parents, just as they do at present, will want their children to start before they are three years old and will want places lasting longer than the customary two and a half hours a day.

Care and education – who's responsible?

We have already seen how the doctrine of maternal deprivation severely restricts the kind of places which are available, and acts as a major barrier to the development of services for children under three and for children of working mothers. But there is also an *organizational* barrier standing in the way of these developments, namely the division of services into those primarily concerned with *care* and those primarily concerned with *education*. This division is deeply rooted in the history of pre-school services – it dates back at least to 1918 – and has far-reaching effects on virtually every aspect of these services.

Care services are primarily the concern of local authority social services departments, who on a national level come under the DHSS. They are responsible for ensuring that all playgroups, private nurseries and child-minders in their area provide adequate standards of care, which in practice means checking that regulations on staff–child ratios, space, hygiene and safety are met. They also provide council day nurseries for children who 'cannot be adequately cared for at home'; as we have seen this is a highly selective service where places go to 'priority' children only.

Education services are primarily the concern of local education departments, who on a national level come under the DES. They are responsible for providing nursery education – in schools and classes – in their area. Unlike council day nurseries, nursery education is intended to be non-selective and available for the general benefit of all children, rather than just for an 'inadequate' minority.

One consequence of this situation is the anomalous position of playgroups. As we have already seen in Chapter 4, they are the most widely used type of service and are generally open to any local family able to meet their usually modest fees and other admission requirements, such as parents helping on the rota. They also include a disproportionately high number of middle-class children: in the OPCS survey they were used by 22 per cent of middle-class children, but only 17 per cent of working-class children. Yet they have become the responsibility of social services departments, whose whole orientation is towards providing selective services for the most disadvantaged and disabled. This contradiction can lead to strange happenings: a local social services department, which restricts day nursery admission to children with 'priority' needs, may at the same time be paying regular grants to all playgroups in its area, including those in the most privileged and affluent areas.

The difficulty of 'placing' playgroups in a divided system also shows itself if we consider the purpose of playgroups for children – to provide opportunities for *play* and *social contact* for them. This does not really fit into either care or education, though in practice the activities offered in better playgroups and nursery schools may be very similar and many playgroup workers and teachers share the same ideas and approaches to working with pre-school children. Yet most teachers would deny that playgroups provide 'education' – or at least 'proper' education – while playgroups themselves would rightly deny that their function was purely care. We raise this point not to introduce a debate about the relative merits of playgroups or nursery schools, but to show the problems of fitting more recent developments and ideas into the archaic split between care and education, whose continuation owes more to inertia and vested interests than to any rational argument relevant to contemporary needs.

One of the other main consequences of this organizational division is that no single department has responsibility for services *as a whole*. In practice, both the government departments mark out what they consider to be their proper area of concern, and neither of them is prepared to take any responsibility outside this area. Their attitude to working mothers is a particularly good example of this ostrich-like behaviour. A recent statement by the D E S declared that:

> The primary aim of nursery education is to provide young children with educational experiences and all children can benefit from it to some degree. This aim is clearly distinct from the aims underlying the provision of care facilities, whether in local authority day nurseries, creches at work places, or with childminders or foster-parents ... *while the provision of nursery education goes some way towards meeting the care needs of, for example, the children of working mothers, it is unlikely to be sufficient in itself.*[6] [Our italics]

The DHSS and its predecessor, the Ministry of Health, have been even more explicit than the DES about their lack of concern for working mothers:

> ... as far as day nurseries are concerned, they have been provided by local health authorities since 1945 primarily to meet the needs of certain children for day care on health and welfare grounds. *Their service is not intended to meet a demand from working women generally for subsidized day-care facilities.* [7] [Our italics]

This vacuum in overall responsibility means that certain groups of mothers and certain groups of children are the responsibility of no one, and are left high and dry. If you are a child over three with a non-working mother or a child under five with a family in very great social need, you may be catered for by your local education or social services department. Otherwise you are the responsibility of neither department. So, if a group of local women are campaigning for more nursery places for working mothers, they are liable to find themselves passed from one department to another – each may show some degree of sympathy to their cause, but ultimately they will both take the line that it is 'none of their business' to provide them with services. Precisely the same effect occurs at the national level, where the current division of responsibility acts as a major obstacle to any change in the system.

What is particularly frustrating is that in the late sixties a golden opportunity presented itself for sorting out the situation once and for all – yet it was not taken up. A committee was set up under the leadership of Frederic Seebohm to report on the planned reorganization of social services departments, and one section of the report dealt with services for children. The committee was severely critical of the existing division of responsibility at the pre-school level, and noted that this fragmentation had had a disastrous effect on the development of services. Nevertheless it still went on to recommend that pre-school services should remain divided – exactly as before!

A divided and divisive service

Another disturbing consequence of the split between care and education is that it effectively limits the number of children for whom nursery education is available. In many cases this means that the children who might benefit from it most are least likely to get it. This of course is not a deliberate policy on the part of individual nursery schools, many of whom go to great lengths to try to give places to those they think are most in need, but rather is due to the disregard which the education service pays to children's 'care' needs. Because nursery

education is offered only in term-time and in predominantly short sessions, it is available only to those children
whose mothers are able and willing to accommodate to
such hours. Such a situation inevitably favours the
middle classes – compared to their working-class counterparts, middle-class mothers are less likely to work
full-time, and if their working hours do not fit in with
nursery school hours they are more likely to organize
child-sharing rotas with other mothers or pay people to
cover the gaps. In contrast, the children who are least
likely to get nursery education are those whose mothers
work long hours, a category which includes a high
proportion of immigrant or single-parent families.
These children will most likely be with childminders or,
if they fall into a 'priority' category, at council day
nurseries: either way they will not get the benefit of
nursery education.

The other side of this coin is that council day nurseries
become almost entirely populated with 'priority'
children, resulting in a virtual segregation of the most
'disadvantaged' children in one type of nursery. As a
result, children who, by any criteria, would most
benefit from nursery education are instead placed in an
environment where their educational needs are often
explicitly ignored: as one matron said to us, 'we mustn't
teach them anything here – that's for the schools to do'.
This matron may be more extreme than most, but she
does reflect the general lack of educational orientation
in council day nurseries. Most nursery nurses are not
trained for an 'educational' role, and often do not know
how to devise educational activities for the children.
They are in any case hampered by lack of resources:
their allowance for books, toys and other equipment is
much smaller than that given to teachers in nursery
schools, in spite of the fact that children spend a much
longer day in the day nursery than they do in nursery
schools or classes. In addition, the pressure of continually

working with the most disadvantaged children – and their families – can have a severe effect on staff morale, and drastically lower their perceptions and expectations of the children.

Feelings of low morale among day nursery staff are inevitably aggravated by numerous discrepancies between their pay and working conditions and those of nursery teachers. As Chapter 4 shows, day nursery staff work a longer week than nursery teachers, get less pay, and have shorter holidays. Moreover the teaching profession places little – if any – value on the qualifications and experience of day nursery staff. If a qualified nursery nurse with ten years' experience in a day nursery wants to train as a nursery teacher she finds her experience and qualifications count for nothing and that she must start entirely from scratch. The overall message is clear: working in a day nursery is a second-rate job compared with working in a nursery school or class. The fact that council day nurseries are chronically short-staffed and have a very high rate of staff turnover shows that many nursery nurses are aware of their low status and are dissatisfied with their jobs.

In this chapter, we have seen how the present system of pre-school services fails to meet any of the three requirements which we believe should underlie a good nursery service. There are nowhere near enough places for all parents who want them, and those places which are available are severely limited in what they offer, particularly to working mothers and for children under three. In addition the division between care and education services has a crippling effect on almost every level of the present system.

It is clear that if our three requirements are to be met, we do not need simply 'more of the same'. Instead a radical re-thinking is required of the whole orientation and organization of pre-school services in this country. Changes are needed at many levels, ranging from a long-term government commitment to mothers and their children, to changes at grass-roots level in the kind of service which is offered to them.

There are signs that such changes are beginning to happen. In the next chapter we look at how people working within the services themselves are starting to come to grips with some of the problems we have outlined.

6 New approaches to old problems

Tackling the problems

In this chapter we look at projects which are trying to tackle some of the problems discussed in Chapter 5. While no single project can hope to deal with the overall lack of places, other issues are being confronted. Various schemes are grappling with the problems of short and inflexible hours, the split between care and education services, and to a lesser extent the lack of provision for under-threes. New projects are springing up from different sources – local authorities, voluntary bodies and charities, neighbourhood groups of parents. We look at what each project has to offer in terms of both its immediate value to children and parents, and its potential as a model for the future.

The information given here is mostly based on visits carried out between spring 1976 and summer 1978.* Many of the schemes are experimental and *there may well have been changes since our visits*. Nevertheless they bring to light important issues and serve as valuable examples of the kinds of solutions being tried.

Extended-hour playgroups

Most playgroup sessions last about two and a half hours – too short to be of value for many mothers,

* More information on many of the schemes discussed in this chapter is given in two recent publications from the Equal Opportunities Commission [1,2].

particularly those who go out to work. In an attempt to provide a more useful service some playgroups are now extending their hours beyond this time. They provide lunch for the children and then continue into the afternoon.

The *Save the Children Fund* have ten extended-hour playgroups, all but two being in London. The one we visited is unusually well housed and equipped for a playgroup. It is based in purpose-built premises set in a large pleasant garden, well equipped with swings, climbing frames and a large sand-pit. Indoors, the staff arrange the quieter activities – like cutting-out and model-making – that need more concentration. The playleader writes of the day:

> The programme is flexible in that the children's hours are staggered to fit into family schedules. Some children come to the playgroup from 9.30 to 12.30. Younger children come from 1 to 2.30. Others fit in between these hours. No child stays longer than four hours per day. Between ten and thirteen children stay for lunch each day and there are thirty children on the roll altogether. Children who stay to lunch bring their own food (now weaned away from sandwiches to cold meat, eggs, etc.) and this is supplemented by raw vegetables, fruit, soup, etc. as appropriate. It is a highly social lunch and everyone, including adult visitors, seems to enjoy the occasion.

The playgroup is staffed by one leader and two part-time assistants, and a special helper comes in at lunch-time to help with the serving of food.

A number of extended-hour playgroups have been supported by *local authorities*. We visited one set up by the London Borough of Islington, an authority which runs or gives financial assistance to fifteen of these playgroups. The one we saw is in an old and decaying part of the borough, with many immigrants and working mothers. The building was originally used as a day nursery, and the playgroup was started when the nursery moved to new premises. It is bleak on the outside but inside bright paint makes the bare bricks more cheerful. The playgroup has the use of two rooms: a large playroom where the children spend most of their time, and a smaller room used for group activities where they rest after lunch. There is also a kitchen, where meals are cooked and where the children eat. The playroom opens on to a stark concrete yard which has no fixed play equipment such as swings or a climbing frame. Otherwise the playgroup is quite well equipped.

The playgroup is open from 8.30 to 4.30 (although other Islington playgroups are open only from 9 to 3.30). It closes for three weeks in the summer, and for a shorter time at Christmas and Easter. There are twenty children who stay for a full day and another nine who come for the morning or afternoon only. The youngest child is two years old. There are three trained playleaders, one untrained assistant, a cook and a cleaner, both mothers of children using the playgroup. There is no rota of parent helpers as most of them are working, but some parents make a contribution to the group, helping with sewing or looking after plants. Others drop in from time to time to help with the children, but not on a regular basis.

We also visited an extended playgroup in a church hall. The hall is lofty and rather dark, with no decorations or children's pictures on the wall. One end is piled high with chairs and tables, for the use of church members in the evenings and weekends. The only outdoor play space is a car park at the front of the building; this opens on to the street, but can be roped off to keep the children in.

Up to twenty-two children attend from 9 until 2, four days a week, forty-two weeks a year. Nearly all the children are over three, though the playleader will take the occasional two-year-old. These children are cared for by two trained playleaders, who also cook, wash up, clean, do the books – in fact do everything. This puts a great burden on them, especially around lunchtime, when one is in the kitchen cooking, leaving the other to supervise twenty or more children. No parents help in the morning but one comes in to help with lunch. Despite some disillusionment with parents, the staff keep going, offering extended hours because they see this as a real need in the area.

We were impressed by the stamina and determination shown by the playleaders in the face of great odds – lack of staff, equipment and support. Not surprisingly, however, the standard of child-care was poor. Some of the children spent a lot of time racing noisily about the hall on tricycles, distracting others who were trying to settle down to the play activities set out on tables. There was not much equipment – five jigsaw puzzles, only one of which was complete, a limited supply of Lego and about fifteen old, tatty books in the book corner. The adults were not very involved in the children's play.

These three examples show that extending playgroup hours needs thought and extra funding to be successful. When it is done well it provides a welcome addition to pre-school facilities in an area, particularly for mothers who work part-time. It can also be useful to non-working mothers who feel that a short session does not give them enough of a break.

What are the problems that face a playgroup wishing to give children a longer day? The first is likely to be premises. Many groups are held in church halls and have the use of only one large room, and perhaps a kitchen; there may not be good outdoor play space. Equipment often has to be cleared away and stored at the end of each session and brought out again afresh at the beginning of the next. These disadvantages – bad enough in a short-session playgroup – present far more difficulties when hours are to be extended. Cooking facilities are needed, as well as storage space for food, crockery, pots and pans. Space is also needed for children to rest after lunch, as well as a separate room for children who do not want to sleep, and storage space for sleeping mats and blankets.

Staffing is also likely to present problems. At first sight it might seem that an extended playgroup could be run by the same number of adults as an ordinary one, but working longer hours. This however does not take account of the extra work involved in preparing, cooking and serving a meal, washing up and clearing away. Extra staff are needed to cover the lunch period, and to make sure that all staff can have a break. There must also be cover for staff absences and holidays – especially if the playgroup is to be kept open more or less throughout the year. This means extra funding: either by increasing the fee to parents, or by local authority grant, or both.

At least one social service department has taken note of these additional requirements and decided that groups wishing to provide longer hours can no longer be registered as playgroups, but must re-register as community day nurseries and meet more stringent conditions. In the case of the London Borough of Hackney these include outside play space, a rest area, proper catering facilities and one member of staff for each five children attending. If a playgroup's application is approved, Hackney Social Services Department will give grant aid to help the group meet the necessary requirements. In Islington the Social Services Department will provide the greater part of the playgroup's funds on condition that staff are paid on a standard scale and fees to parents are not raised above a certain level. Even so, the playleaders still get very much less than nursery nurses or nursery teachers.

Are playleaders adequately trained to provide extended-hour care? Playleaders are usually local mothers with no previous training who take a short training course one day a week for a year. While this training may be adequate for short-session playgroups, it may not be sufficient to cope with the additional responsibility of caring for children all day. In addition, playleaders for extended-hour playgroups are unlikely to have much help from parents. The PPA emphasizes the importance for all playgroups of having a rota of parent helpers, but it is often difficult to have a regular rota in extended-hour playgroups, as so many parents are working elsewhere. In some of these playgroups a few non-working mothers may be able to help on a rota, but this could easily create tension, with the rota mothers becoming resentful of those who cannot give time. Of course there are other ways for parents to be involved – helping with laundry, being on the management committee, sewing, mending toys – but the fact remains that the rota is a key element in defining playgroups. Inevitably these extended-hour playgroups have moved away from this definition, and this raises the question of whether they are in fact still playgroups.

The PPA itself does not welcome the trend. According to Delphine Knight, PPA national advisor: 'It would be a pity to see first-rate playgroups close because of falling numbers but I think I would prefer that to seeing them turn into second-rate day nurseries' [3].

While nobody wishes to see an increase in second-rate day nurseries, there is probably some potential for developing good-quality extended-hour playgroups, although this will be possible only in playgroups where premises and staffing are suitable and where adequate funding is made available. These are unlikely to provide for children under two, as conditions are usually not appropriate. They are probably best suited to three- and four-year-old children who require longer part-time places (say four or five hours) rather than full-day care. As such they could well become a welcome service for mothers working part-time.

Extended-hour nursery schools and classes

One effect of the division between 'care' and 'education' is that education services pay little regard to the hours of care a child may need. Most sessions at nursery schools and classes last only two and a half hours, and, as with playgroups, these hours are of limited use to many mothers. Even a full-time place at school (9.30 – 3.30) may present problems for a mother working full-time. Several nursery schools and classes are now offering longer hours, so that some children who attend for a full school day can stay later in the afternoon and in some cases arrive earlier in the morning. Most of these schools also operate play schemes in the school holidays.

Two nursery classes in Islington – Montem and Penton Infants – have recently extended their hours till 6 p.m., and five more schools in the borough are planning to do so. About ten children in each school stay on after normal school hours. They are all thought to be in particular need of a place, and are often referred by a social worker or health visitor. Places are not available simply at the parent's request, although some places are given to children of working mothers.

At Montem, the children move after school into a different room (formerly unused owing to falling numbers at the school), and an effort is made to create a 'homelike' atmosphere, as unlike school as possible. There are adult-sized armchairs, a settee and a television, and a selection of toys not found in the classroom. Some of the children may go out with an adult to buy food and later help to prepare the tea. Others watch television or cuddle up on the sofa for a story. The children are cared for by two local women: they are employed during the day as helpers in the infants school and so are familiar figures, chosen more for their personal qualities than for any paper qualifications.

The cost of the scheme is mainly met by the social services department, who pay for staff salaries, food and toys. Overheads such as caretaking, heating and lighting are covered by the education authority. Parents pay only for meals.

Blagdon Road Nursery School in Reading is open from 8.30 to 6.30, for forty-nine weeks of the year. In practice, no child spends the whole ten hours in the nursery, and not all children at the school use the extended hours. Those who do are selected on grounds of 'social disadvantage' or because they have working mothers. These children spend the school day in an ordinary classroom, but outside school hours they are in a separate building. The staff use the extra time to give the children more individual attention, for example with speech and language development. Additional teachers and other staff are employed to cover the longer hours and holiday periods, and they all work shifts. Families pay only for meals.

Extending the hours of nursery schools and classes is clearly a good way to use existing resources – particularly as the falling birth-rate means that more empty classrooms are becoming available in schools. These schemes are unlikely to suffer the same problems as extended-hour playgroups: schools are usually better housed and equipped than playgroups, and the direct involvement of the local authority means that adequate standards of care will be maintained. They are a useful measure which can make nursery education available to many children who would not otherwise get it, and have an important role to play in the development of future services.

If extended-hour schools are to be developed more widely, however, a number of issues need to be resolved. The first concerns the *selection of children*. At present these schemes do not aim to give a wider choice of hours to *all* parents using the school, but instead restrict places to children in 'special need': this means that a child with working parents may not get a place unless her family circumstances are sufficiently 'deserving'. This selective policy is particularly likely to be enforced if social services departments are putting up some or all of the money – understandably enough, when they may have several hundred 'priority' children on their waiting lists. There is the danger that, as with council day nurseries, these schemes will become a low-status service, in which 'priority' children are grouped together at the end of the day. It would be a far healthier and more valuable service if it could be made available to *all* children in the school who needed longer hours.

There is also the danger that these schemes will perpetuate very stereotyped notions of 'care' and 'education'. At Montem the after-school period is explicitly seen as a 'caring' experience, very different from the rest of the school day; the children are taken out of the classroom to a 'homelike' room where they are looked after by warm motherly figures, eat tea and watch TV. In contrast the after-hours staff at Blagdon Road are teachers (and their assistants) who use the time to give the children extra educational help. These different approaches no doubt reflect the fact that at Montem the scheme is funded by the social services department, whereas at Blagdon Road it is supported by the education authority. Both approaches, however, are likely to reinforce the idea that education and care are very separate activities, carried out by different sorts of staff in different environments. This is clearly not so: as we argue in Chapter 9, helping an adult buy food and make tea can be a valuable educational experience for a young child, as can watching TV and discussing the programme with an adult. Likewise playing educational games and getting individual attention from a well-liked teacher can be a warm and caring experience. If nursery schools and classes are going to offer extended hours on a regular basis they should not be based on stereotyped notions of care and education, but instead be part of a well-thought-out daily programme designed to meet the needs of *all* children for care and education, however long they are in the building.

Nursery schools and classes could also consider another kind of 'extension' – to include children under three. This idea has not really been tried out in this country –

mainly because of the official view that children under three should not be at nurseries – although it has in other parts of the world. The Kramer School in Little Rock, Arkansas, for example, offers a comprehensive nursery service for children up to the age of six, and elementary schooling from six to twelve. The advantage of this set-up is that the children do not have to move from one school to another when they reach compulsory school age; in addition the presence of an under-threes unit in an infants school could be an educational experience for *all* the children! On the other hand the idea of children being in 'school' from a very early age could be un-appealing to many people, and great care would be needed to ensure that the under-threes unit was small, intimate and suited to the needs of very young children.

'*Link-up*' schemes

Another effect of the care/education split is that local authority day nurseries do not have an educational orientation – there are very few trained teachers on the staff and the equipment and activities are often limited. Several London boroughs – including Haringey, Ealing, Hammersmith and Islington – have introduced 'link-up' schemes in which day nursery children attend a near-by nursery school or class for part of the day.

We visited seven of these schemes altogether. In one typical scheme, the children arrived at the day nursery from 8 o'clock onwards and the early arrivals had break-fast. At about 9 o'clock the six oldest children were gathered together by two of the nursery nurses, outdoor clothes were put on again, and they all set off for the local nursery class, five minutes walk down the road. The nurses saw the children into the classroom and then returned to the day nursery. The six children were then faced with a different set of staff and a group of twenty-four different children. None of the children seemed noticeably disturbed by the experience, although we were told that when the scheme first started the children ran wild when they got to the school. The day nursery children tended to stick together in spite of the teacher's attempt to integrate them with the rest of the class, although one child had obviously developed a close friendship with two other children in the class. Although there was more equipment at school and it was in much better condition than that in the day nursery, the range of activities was similar in both places – sand, water, dough, creative artwork, puzzles, physical apparatus and so on. On the day we visited, the teacher had organized some finger-painting and three of the day nursery children joined in; later she sat down with two of the children and helped them trace their names into a workbook. At 11.15 the two nurses returned to collect the six children so as to get them back and washed in time for lunch at 12: this means they missed the group story session at the school.

What do these children gain from this brief daily excursion to school? The walk and change of scene may be of value, and the children love going out, but the same could be achieved by regular outings to shops, parks, bus stations, etc. without a trip to school. But what about the educational benefit? How different was the children's school experience from the day nursery? Apart from finger-painting and tracing their names the children were doing very similar activities in both places and they did not mix in with the rest of the children in the class. The advantages appear to be limited. The drawbacks however are numerous. It is obviously wasteful for a child to occupy two places in different nurseries, and as a general policy this would be an inefficient use of resources. In addition, its application is restricted, as such schemes can happen only where a day nursery and nursery school or class are situated close by and where the matron and headteacher are prepared to co-operate. More seriously, such schemes reinforce the notion that care and education are necessarily separate processes carried out by different staff in different types of nurseries. A far better solution would be for nursery nurses to be trained to adopt a more educational approach, and for day nurseries to get equipment comparable to that found in the schools.

Teachers in day nurseries

A different way of tackling the same problem is for trained nursery teachers to be employed to work in day nurseries. In some cases the teacher is employed by the social services department; in others by the education authority. In the schemes we visited the day nurseries were organized into 'family groups': that is, each room contained nine or ten children between eighteen months and five years, who were looked after by two nursery nurses. The teacher was not attached to any particular group but was responsible for planning educational activities for *all* the children. For example she would choose a topic to be worked on during the week, such as shape or colour, and then suggest activities that the nurses could provide on this topic, offering them help and guidance. Sometimes she would organize activities herself, or work more intensively with a small group of the older children.

This sort of scheme avoids some of the difficulties of the 'link-up' schemes: children are not moved from one nursery to another, and do not take up two places at once. It can make the work more interesting for all the nursery staff, and at best can form a kind of in-service training for nursery nurses: as one matron said 'they have developed a greater awareness of the individual child's development and of his educational requirements'. Problems and resentments could arise, however, if the teacher works shorter hours and has longer holidays than other staff, although in most of the nurseries we visited, some sort of averaging-out or shift system had been adopted. The major drawback again is the separation of 'educational' staff from 'caring' staff, and the continued emphasis on education as a separate activity. In one of the nurseries, for example, records on the child's language and intellectual development are kept by the teacher, and records on her social and emotional development kept by the nursery nurses. As with the link-up schemes, this idea serves only to reinforce the split between care and education, and goes no way towards tackling any of the basic problems.

Combining day nurseries and nursery schools

A different way of bringing care and education together is to set up day nurseries and nursery schools on the same site. The Dorothy Gardner Centre in London and the Gamesley Pre-school Centre in Derbyshire are both examples of this type of 'combined' centre. Both were purpose-built and are run jointly by the social services and education departments, and although all the staff and children are present in the same building, there are effectively two separate services running in parallel, each administered separately. At the Dorothy Gardner Centre there are even two management committees, one for the day nursery and one for the nursery school. There are two sets of children – those attending the day nursery mostly come for a full day all year round and the age range is up to five years; those attending the nursery school come either mornings, afternoons or a full school day, the school is closed during normal school holidays, and the children are aged three to five years. There are two separate waiting lists and different admissions policies – day nursery children are admitted 'according to need', whereas nursery school children can attend 'on demand'. Sometimes there may be empty places in the nursery school even though there are children on the waiting list for the day nursery. At Dorothy Gardner the service is free for all children, thus avoiding potential anomalies of different systems of payment, but at Gamesley a complex system of charges operates. During term-time and normal school hours the three- to five-year-olds pay only for meals. If they come earlier or stay later than school hours they pay by the hour, and during school holidays they pay means-tested day nursery rates. The under-threes pay means-tested rates all the time.

In both centres there are two sets of staff – day care staff paid by the social services department and nursery school staff paid by the education department. At Dorothy Gardner there are three different heads in the one centre: a matron to run the day nursery, a head-teacher for the nursery school and a principal who co-ordinates the overall work of the centre. The nursery nurses work longer hours, get shorter holidays and are paid less than the teaching staff. Finally there are two sets of equipment, often duplicated – although the nursery school allocation for buying equipment is considerably larger than that of the day nursery.

In what ways can the children benefit from this sort of combined centre? How do the day nursery children receive both care and education? When they are mature enough, at two and a half to three years, the day nursery children move across to the nursery school area for part of the day. Sometimes a nursery nurse goes with them to make the transition easier. The children can benefit from the educational experiences of school, the wider range of activities and equipment and the different approach of the trained teachers. They also have the chance to mix with children who are not from such 'deprived' backgrounds. Meanwhile the younger children who are left in the day nursery receive extra attention from the nursery nurses. The older children return to the day nursery for tea in the afternoon and stay there until it is time to go home. During the school holidays (twelve weeks in all) this system breaks down – the school closes, the equipment is locked away and the staff disappear.

In some ways these combined centres resemble the

link-up schemes, with children moving from one service to another for part of the day. The centres have the advantage that the move can be made gradually and that the building, teaching staff and children are usually familiar to the child before going across to the school. The disadvantages are similar to those of link-ups – caring services and educational services remain separate except for a bridge which passes children from one to the other. In practice all the old traditions and divides of nursery school and day nursery are simply being maintained in a new setting – indeed, by putting them side by side the anomalies in admissions, cost, equipment, staff pay and conditions are made even more glaring. Although the quality of the service is excellent in these centres, they do little to challenge the fundamental split between care and education.

Co-ordination or integration?

The four types of scheme we have just described – extended-hour schools, link-up schemes, teachers in day nurseries and combined centres – are all attempts to *co-ordinate* different aspects of care and education services. This policy of co-ordination is currently being encouraged by the DES and the DHSS. In March 1976 the two departments issued a joint circular to local authorities spelling out the general desire for co-ordination, and followed this up in January 1978 with another circular recommending specific ways of doing this [4, 5]. Among their recommendations were the four schemes we have just described, as well as schemes co-ordinating playgroups, childminders and health services.

These co-ordination schemes should no doubt be welcomed as attempts to do *something* about the present situation and, as we have seen, some have more to offer than others. None of them, however, can be said to have solved the basic problems arising from the split between care and education: indeed, bringing together different aspects of the two services in some cases serves only to show up the anomalies and discrepancies between them. At best these schemes have helped to alleviate some of the more unfortunate effects of the split: at worst they serve only to perpetuate and reinforce it.

These experiences show that attempts to co-ordinate care and education are merely papering over the gigantic crack between the two different services. The problems caused by the division are too deeply rooted to be cured by patch-up jobs at local level; they require instead a fundamental change in the basic organization and policies of pre-school services. The basic question is not how to co-ordinate services, but rather how to *integrate* them to provide the best possible service for parents and their children.

What measures would be needed to accomplish this aim?

- *Responsibility for all children under five should be given to one department at national and local level.* Of the two, education departments are probably best suited for the job. If nurseries are to be available for all parents who want them, it is more appropriate they are provided by education departments, with their well-established tradition of providing *universal* services, than by social services, whose function has always been to provide for 'needy' groups. In addition, even excluding reception classes, education authorities currently provide for about seven times as many pre-school children as do social services (210,000 in nursery classes and nursery schools, compared to about 32,000 in day nurseries and council playgroups).

- *Local authorities should be required to ensure sufficient nursery places for all parents who wanted them.* The authority would not necessarily have to supply all the places itself: there could be a role for voluntary nurseries, playgroups and childminders (see Chap-

ters 7 and 10). It would however mean an end to
selective services such as council day nurseries.

– *Parents should be able to choose the age when their
children started, and the hours attended for each day.*
Education departments would thus have to provide
for children under three, as well as for children
after normal school hours and in school holidays.
They should also be required to take on similar
responsibilities for older, school-age children.

– *Staff training, pay, and conditions of work should be
rationalized.* The existing anomalies between the
teaching and nursery nurse professions would be
removed by creating a single, integrated profession,
with a common-core training, and unified conditions of work. Playgroup staff and childminders
might also be integrated into such a scheme.

– *All nurseries should aim to meet the needs of all children
for both care and education.* This would partly follow
from integrating the approaches of nursery
teachers and nursery nurses, but would also involve
new methods of working. A fundamental re-thinking would be needed of what constitutes care and
education for young children (see Chapter 9).

– *Anomalies in what parents are charged would be removed.*
The simplest, fairest and most rational way to do
this is to model pre-school services on other school
and child health services, and make them *free*. The
cost would thus be met (through rates and general
taxation) by the population as a whole, so acknowledging that young children are the responsibility
of *everyone* and that the society of tomorrow will
depend on them. A free service also spreads the
cost to the parent over a working life-time, rather
than loading it all on a time in their lives when
they are particularly likely to be hard pressed
financially.

If these six steps were put into operation a new form of nursery would have to evolve, one that was freely available to all families in a given area, which offered them choice as to when their children started and for how long they stayed, and which aimed to meet all children's needs for care and education. Such a comprehensive, integrated and flexible 'nursery centre' would obviously be quite different from the nurseries we have looked at so far. However, a few nurseries in this country are already developing along these lines, and these nurseries can give us a very good idea of what an ideal nursery centre of the future might be like. We look first at the Thomas Coram Children's Centre, and then at the idea of a community nursery.

Thomas Coram Children's Centre

The Coram Children's Centre opened in January 1974 in the Bloomsbury area of London, taking over from a council day nursery which had previously used the building. The aims of the Centre are:

(1) To provide a comprehensive range of services for pre-school children and their families, living in a defined catchment area around the Centre.

(2) To integrate and co-ordinate the efforts of all those concerned with the upbringing of young children: doctors, teachers, parents, nursery nurses, health visitors, social workers, etc.

(3) To meet the different needs of individual children and their families by offering as much flexibility as possible in terms of both the range of services provided and the availability of each service.

How successful has the Centre been in achieving these ambitious aims?

Availability: Although the original aim was to provide enough places for all children living in the immediate neighbourhood, the catchment area is slightly too large for this, and there has to be a waiting list. Some selection takes place according to social need and problems, but on the whole the children in the Centre come from a wide range of backgrounds, and they reflect the social mix of the local community. The Centre is *not* operating a service purely for 'disadvantaged' children.

Although the original aim was to take children of all ages up to five, the Centre has been unable to provide for very young children. Nevertheless it has been able to take increasing numbers of two-year-olds; at the end of October 1976 there were six children under two, twenty-five between two and three, twenty-three between three and four, and twenty-seven over four [6]. The Centre is free; parents pay only for lunches.

Flexibility: The Centre is open from 8.30 to 5.30 for fifty weeks a year, and each child attends for the hours that suit her and her family. Not only can parents choose the initial hours of attendance, but these can be altered later, usually at the parents' request. The following examples, drawn from children attending in October 1978, give some idea of what this flexible approach can mean in practice:

Jasmine, aged three and a quarter years, entered the Centre in September 1977. She began by attending between 10 and 4, five days a week. In April 1978, her hours were extended to 8.30 to 4 so that her mother could attend more English classes.

Jim, aged three years, was admitted in May 1978 and attended three mornings a week, 10 to 12. In September, his hours were extended to 10 to 3 for five days a week at his mother's request, because he had settled and enjoyed going, and to give his mother more time to devote to his baby sister, born earlier in the year.

Alan, aged four and a half years, was admitted in September 1978 for five mornings a week. He settled well and enjoyed going, and his hours have been extended; they are now 9 to 3. He and his younger brother (nine months) are looked after by their grandmother during the rest of the day.

Luke, aged four years, joined the Centre in November 1976, and attended five days a week, from 9.30 to 12.30, to begin with. His mother took a course for one day a week, and he was able to stay until four on that day.

Chris and Pat, twins, aged two and three quarter years, began attending the Centre in January 1978, from 9 to 11.30. Lively girls, living in cramped accommodation, their hours have been gradually extended, at first until 12.30 and now until 2.30, at the Centre staff's suggestion.

Mary, aged four years, who usually attends from 9 to 12.30, stayed in the afternoons for two weeks while her mother had another baby, having tea at the Centre on a few occasions when her father could not collect her earlier.

Given such readiness to provide hours of attendance suited to the needs and circumstances of individual children and parents, labelling places as 'full-time' or 'part-time' becomes irrelevant and an inaccurate way of describing the true variety that exists.

Integration of care and education: There is one head responsible for running the Centre, who is qualified both as a teacher and as a nursery nurse. She leads a team composed of teachers, nursery nurses, assistants and students, and steps have been taken to reduce the differences between their working conditions. All full-time staff work the same number of hours per week (thirty-seven and a half), whatever their training, and nursery nurses and assistants get six weeks' holiday a year instead of the usual four. All staff work shifts, and holidays are staggered throughout the year. Some discrepancies still remain, however: teachers get twelve

weeks holiday a year and are paid on the Burnham
scale, whereas nursery nurses and assistants are paid on
the lower Joint National Council scale.

The Centre is organized into four family group
rooms, each with fifteen to twenty children aged from
just under two up to five years. A trained teacher is in
charge of each room and nursery nurses, assistants and
students work alongside her. To some extent the traditional roles of the staff have been broken down – all
staff participate in physical care such as wiping noses,
toileting, dressing; all help with domestic chores –
setting tables and so on; and all are involved in the more
'educational' activities like story-reading, quiet play
sessions for older children and planning the day's
activities. Teaching and caring are done by teachers and
nurses alike. The staff in each room meet fortnightly to
discuss various aspects of their work – how to help
individual children, planning activities, daily routine,
educational work etc. There are also monthly meetings
for all the staff in the Centre. The aim of all these meetings is to give the staff the opportunity to assess their
work and to make changes when necessary: in a Centre
such as this, where new ground is continually being
broken, it is particularly important to keep evaluating
all sides of the work.

Other services: Two paediatricians and a health visitor
provide a weekly child health clinic at the Centre, and a
speech therapist comes twice a week to work with the
children, parents and staff. The Centre employs a
social worker, who has her own room there and is
available to help parents at any time. It also offers a
wide range of other facilities to families: toy and book
libraries, a children's bookshop, a mother and baby
group, a conversation group for parents who speak
little English and a launderette.

The Coram Centre has been largely successful in

meeting its aims. It provides a flexible service which is available for most parents in the neighbourhood, as well as a wide range of other facilities for families with young children. As far as possible the distinction between 'care' and 'education' has been eliminated: the problems and difficulties which remain stem mainly from differences in training, pay and hours which cannot be tackled adequately at local level. Coram's success in integrating services within one centre owes much to the fact that it is administered by a charitable body, the Coram Foundation. Although the Centre receives a sizable grant from Camden Social Services Department, the borough does not impose rigid conditions, thus allowing it to develop in a flexible and responsive way.

Community nurseries

Community nurseries offer a different kind of model for a nursery centre. They are situated in the voluntary sector, outside the traditional framework of day nurseries and nursery schools, and therefore do not have to fit into any of the established moulds. About a dozen community nurseries have sprung up since the early seventies, virtually all in London, and all started by groups of parents or other local people. They serve a small neighbourhood and receive grants from the local authority.

In some respects community nurseries resemble playgroups, and a few have developed from extended-hour playgroups, but they usually offer longer hours and have places for children under three. Unlike playgroups they have premises exclusively for their own use; most are based in converted short-life houses (empty houses which are due to be demolished), though others are in prefabricated units, and in one case in a converted church. Most community nurseries are small, with places for no more than twenty-five children at a time. Decisions about running the nursery are taken jointly by parents and staff together – a radical departure from normal practice, and one we will look at more closely in Chapter 8.

The Children's Community Centre in the London Borough of Camden is the oldest and probably the best-known community nursery. Started in 1972 by a group of local women, many of whom were involved in the Women's Liberation Movement, it is based in a converted house, and provides fifteen places for children aged two to four years. It is open from 8.30 to 6, forty-eight weeks a year. There are two full-time staff, and most parents work regularly in the centre on a rota basis. All decisions are made at a weekly meeting of workers and parents [7].

To what extent do community nurseries offer a flexible and integrated service? For a start, they do not divide the children into two categories of 'priority' and 'normal'; instead, all children living locally are eligible for a place. In addition, hours of attendance are not rigidly laid down, but vary according to what the family wants, what the child can cope with, what space is available. In practice most parents choose full-day places because they have jobs outside the home and because there are few other nurseries providing full-time places, but in principle most community nurseries are flexible and responsive to parents' wishes. Most are unable to take toddlers and babies – lack of suitable facilities and limited funds mean that the majority of community nurseries do not meet the conditions laid down by social services departments for children under two. With better funding on a secure and regular basis, and with permanent high-quality premises, community nurseries could provide for the whole age-range up to five.

Community nurseries have also managed to get right away from any preconceived notions of 'care' and 'education'; staff are not employed on this basis and do not see their roles in this way. Some nurseries do employ teachers and nursery nurses, but they are chosen as much for their personal qualities, beliefs and experiences as for any paper qualifications or formal training. All staff work as educators, just as all are care-givers, and they try to meet the children's needs as they arise: washing hands, answering questions, cuddling, discussing families and friends, reading stories, pointing out shapes, colours, sizes and so on. In most community nurseries there are no staff hierarchies and everyone is paid at the same rate.

The idea of community nurseries has not yet been widely developed in this country, but in the State of Victoria, Australia, there are about a hundred such nurseries already open or in the process of starting up. These nurseries – or neighbourhood centres as they are called – are normally run in ordinary domestic housing and they receive funding from the Federal Government's Office of Child Care, provided they meet certain conditions. Parent involvement in management is one such condition, a topic we discuss fully in Chapter 8. In addition, centres must be open to any child living in the neighbourhood and cannot be provided for selected groups. Funding is also conditional on the provision of some all-day places and it is further laid down that fees must be related to parents' incomes. Neighbourhood centres meeting these conditions receive a grant to buy and convert a suitable property, and money to equip and run the nursery based on a standard payment per place, children under the age of three receiving a higher amount.

These neighbourhood centres are able to provide the kind of integrated and flexible service we proposed earlier on – full-time and part-time places are available to all children living locally and many have places for children under three. Some centres also provide a range of other activities depending on local circumstances, for example holiday and out-of-school care for school-age children, food co-operatives, equipment pools and toy libraries, swap shops, drop-in facilities and so on.

Nursery centres for the future?

In their different ways, the Thomas Coram Children's Centre and community nurseries like the Children's Community Centre and the neighbourhood centres in Australia show that the idea of a flexible and integrated nursery centre can be realized. Both the community nurseries and the Coram Centre have had the initial advantage of being *outside* the state nursery system, and so have had more freedom to experiment and dispense with preconceived notions of how nurseries should be provided. However, there is no reason why local authorities could not provide nursery centres run along similar lines to the Coram Centre, and also give financial backing to community nurseries and other voluntary initiatives – as the London Borough of Camden has done with both the Thomas Coram Centre and the Children's Community Centre.

Despite some similarities between the two types of centre, there are also important differences. The most obvious one is *financial*. The Coram Centre is generously funded and is very much seen as a demonstration project, exemplifying the best of current practice. Staff:child ratios are high, the premises good, the equipment is superb, and the Centre can afford a large number of extra facilities. In contrast, most community nurseries are run on shoe-string budgets, and have to make economies all along the line; for most, funding is their greatest single problem, and this inevitably detracts from what they can provide. This suggests short-sightedness on the part of local authorities: community nurseries have great potential as a model for future nurseries, and should be given the funds they need to realize their potential.

The other main difference between the two types of centre stems partly from their respective *sizes* and *premises*. The Coram Centre has eighteen full-time child-care staff and places for seventy-six children, while the Children's Community Centre has two full-time staff and places for fifteen children. The Coram Centre is based in a large two-storey building originally designed as a Child Welfare Centre, with a large play area and garden, while the Children's Community Centre is housed in an old terraced house with a small back garden. These differences inevitably affect the atmosphere of each centre and shape the relationships between staff and children, and are further reinforced by the different approach of the staff. At most community nurseries the staff explicitly aim to provide a 'homelike' atmosphere and emphasize the similarities between parents and staff, while the Coram Centre emphasizes the 'skilled intervention' of professionally trained staff in helping children's development. Clearly, both approaches have their merits (in Chapter 9 we look at some of the educational advantages for children of being in a 'homelike' environment), and it would be wrong to say one was the 'correct' approach while the other was not. It could well be argued however that small, informal centres are particularly suited for very young children (those under three), and if nurseries are to be developed more widely for them, the community nursery idea could be extremely valuable.

Many people believe, however, that if young children are to be cared for outside the home the right place is *not* in a nursery, however small and informal, but with a *childminder*. We now turn to consider what childminders have to offer.

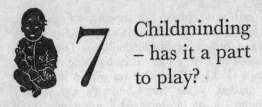

7 Childminding – has it a part to play?

Childminding has become, almost overnight, one of the hottest issues in the pre-school world. For years it has been neglected and often despised, but the recent cold economic climate has led government and other organizations to start promoting it as a model for the future: minding, it is claimed, is an ideal low-cost solution to the day-care needs of working mothers. Many of these organizations – such as the Central Policy Review Staff ('Think Tank') [1] – have claimed that minding in fact offers *better* care than nurseries, particularly for children under three.

Minding is an issue on which people take up strong and opposing positions. For instance, Sonia and Brian Jackson of the National Educational and Research Development Trust take the view that, while much minding is poor, improvement can be made cheaply (by short informal training courses, and the provision of toy libraries and playgroups), and that since minding is a community response to need ('a back-street system that people have themselves built out of adversity') it should be recognized and built on as an important resource in 'breaking cycles of deprivation'[2]. In contrast the view that minding can be a good, cheap service, run by motherly women who do not need or wish for the conditions of employment that most of us assume (regular pay, insurance, holidays and pension schemes), has been forcefully opposed by the TUC. In their view minders are workers like any others, and should be paid and employed like any others; they argue that only by turning minders into local authority employees can a good-quality service for children and their parents be ensured[3].

Which of these views is correct? What sort of service do minders in fact provide? These questions are not easy to answer, mainly because *so little is known about minding*. It is essentially a *private* service, provided by private individuals in their own homes, and as such presents a fairly impenetrable front to researchers and mothers alike. It is not even known how many minders are operating without being registered (which is in any case illegal), and estimates vary from thousands to hundreds of thousands. Most opinions on minding are based on personal experience at local level or on hopes and assumptions, and horror stories abound. Brian Jackson has described 'Dickensian' scenes in which large numbers of children are herded into small dark rooms, and others tell of children tied to chairs or strapped to carry-cots while the minder goes out shopping or even to work[4]. Such stories, as Willem van der Eyken puts it, 'have given rise to popular legend, in which the childminder has become the personification of neglect, of greed, and of ignorance'[5].

We have no wish to endorse this popular legend, and do not believe that minding should be condemned out of hand because of the few cases of neglect and cruelty which undoubtedly exist. Nevertheless we are convinced that minding does not on the whole provide a service which in any way compares with what a good nursery could offer, even for children under three. This is not because minders are cruel and neglectful, but rather because the very nature of minding means that the conditions under which minders work, and the attitudes they have to their work, provide major obstacles to achieving good child-care, although there are of course notable exceptions. Much of what we say is based on detailed research carried out by two of us (Berry Mayall and Pat Petrie); where this has been published we refer to it as the TCRU minding study[6].

Minders and the law

Minders are required by law to register with the local authority, who will specify the maximum number of children that they can look after (usually three, including any of the minder's own children). The law stipulates that minders must be 'fit' to do the job and 'adequate' in 'qualifications or experience'[7]. Since nothing is specified as to what these words mean, and since most of the emphasis in the law and in circulars sent out by the DHSS on interpreting the law is on *safety and health* requirements, it is virtually impossible to refuse registration to someone if she can meet these requirements. Almost anyone who applies to be registered as a minder will be accepted; indeed, the authorities sometimes register women thought to fall below adequate child-care standards in order to keep an eye on them and to stop them from minding illegally.

Once registered, a minder can offer care ranging from the admirable to the appalling, and there is little the authority can do in law to deal with the appalling. To de-register a minder who is giving a poor service is virtually impossible (unless she contravenes the health and safety part of the law), since it involves making a case in court that she is 'unfit' to care for children; neither can she be required, as an alternative to de-registration, to improve her standard of child-care.

The law makes few demands on minders. Instead, the responsible ministry, the DHSS, makes recommendations on staffing, accommodation, equipment etc. for minders, as if for council day nurseries. The standards recommended for minders are however consistently lower than those for day nurseries. On staffing, for instance, it is recommended that day nursery staff should be trained or in training, but that 'some opportunity for training' should be offered to people working in private nurseries; and for minders 'it might be appropriate to organize ... short courses'. In practice, too, standards at day nurseries are more consistent, and are maintained by the local authority at a higher level than those at minders. Most day nursery staff are in practice trained or in training, while minders are not. Most day nurseries do have good equipment (toys and furniture) for the children; this is not so at very many minders. The fact that standards at day nurseries are in general higher than those at minders is a measure of the low priority put on minding by the local authority. Many local authorities still do no more than register minders, and in these cases little control is exercised over the kind of care the children receive. And even in boroughs where considerable efforts are made to visit and encourage minders to offer good care, most of the money spent is on the salaries of minding workers rather than on training and equipping the minders themselves. Very few authorities will bring the minder's house up to standard for her, and keep her supplied with toys for the children. Minding workers often operate on pitifully small allowances for toys and equipment; we have heard from such workers, for instance, that they were unable to register as a minder because the allowance did not run to a fireguard or a baby buggy.

Minding as a job

A minder's only income from her work comes from what she charges parents. The amount varies wildly: in 1976 the DHSS estimated that the current rate in England varied between £2 and £10 per child per week[8], and at the time of writing (summer, 1978) the rate in London is between £7 and £12. Out of this income the minder must feed the child, heat the premises, perhaps wash and dry clothes; she must pay for any equipment and for wear and tear of her furniture, her wallpaper and her belongings generally. She may also, if she wishes, provide toys and outings for the children. Toys, paper and paint get used up quickly, ice-cream and fares are non-returnable items. However you calculate the minders' *net* income, it is clear they are doing the job for pocket money and not for a living wage.

Perhaps the main incentive for minders to operate outside the legal market (in other words, not to register) is that they can take in as many children as will give them a reasonable income. Many registered minders also take more children than they are registered for, often with the knowledge and tacit consent of the local authority. In the TCRU minding study fourteen of the thirty-nine minders interviewed were looking after more than three children, including their own under-fives, and six of these were looking after six or more children. Many minders make a bit extra by taking school-age children before and after school and in the holidays; at these times they may have at least half a dozen children to look after.

The minder has none of the real benefits that most full-time workers take for granted, such as holiday pay, sick pay, national insurance or pension. The payment she gets is insecure – parents can remove a child when they like. She has no help, and is in sole charge of the children from the time the first one arrives until the time the last one leaves. The minder's day is often nine, ten or eleven hours long.

Most minders do not see their work as constituting a 'proper job' – rather it is a way of getting some extra money that fits in well with their domestic situation and commitments. Many have young children of their own and want to be at home to look after them anyway. Other women take up minding after their own family has left home; this is the 'granny-figure' who may have started minding when asked to care for a grandchild. There are others who want to earn some money but are not well enough to go out to work. We have met minders who had a long-term disability, like a heart condition or a bad back, and some who were advised by their doctor to mind children as an antidote to depression. There are also those whose husbands do not want them to go out to work, but who will tolerate this home-based occupation.

It is particularly striking how few women take up minding because they are *interested in working with children*. In the TCRU minding study only five of the thirty-nine minders gave this as their reason for minding. In contrast, a Schools Council study of 578 nursery teachers found that almost 90 per cent gave 'vocational' reasons (such as 'wanting to work with children', 'interesting work') as their main reason for entering the profession[9].

A few minders make a long-term job of minding: some have been doing it for fifteen or more years. Many, however, mind only for as long as they want to be at home, and that often means for the early years of their children's lives. After that, the need or desire to earn a proper wage and participate in the wider world sends them out to work. Since many women do not register as minders until their own youngest is on her feet and able to hold her own, their working time as a minder may be only two or three years. In the TCRU study, a third had been in the job for less than three years, and just over a half for less than five years, while a larger study by the Community Relations Commission (CRC) found that 40 per cent had been in the job for less than two years, and 65 per cent for less than five years[10]. This is one reason why many children spend only a short time with a minder before moving on. In the CRC study forty-eight mothers of minded children were asked about the numbers of placements their child had had, and why the child had been moved each time. Eight of the children had been to two minders each, and eleven to three or more. At nine of the minders, according to the mothers, the reason for ending the placement was that the minder had stopped minding.

What kind of care do minders provide?

From the children's point of view, minders' homes may present all the restrictions and disadvantages which they experience in their own homes (see Chapter 2). Most minders are not well enough housed to provide a large play space where children can run about, climb and explore or engage in messy or creative play, as they would at a nursery. The minder may have no outside space at all, or she may live above ground level in a block of flats with little or no access to communal play space. Some houses open directly onto busy streets. Most minding takes place in big cities, especially among poor and immigrant families; for many children, being minded will mean *going from one poor housing situation to another for their day care.*

The minder is also unlikely to provide *toys and play equipment* that in any way match up to what nurseries and playgroups provide. Toys are a cost to her out of the money paid by the parents, and to provide a supply of appropriate toys for a varying age-range of children would be a considerable drain on that money. Many minders rely on what they have in the house, 'left over' from their own children's younger days, and this stock of toys, broken and incomplete, may be all the minded child has to play with. A common sight at minders is children extracting odd bits of different toys from a large cardboard box – a piece of a puzzle, a few bits of Lego or sticklebricks, a car that has lost a wheel – and sitting fiddling with them.

As we have seen, most minders do not regard themselves as professional child-care workers; for them, *the job of minding is a side-line* to their main occupation, which is their domestic responsibilities and commitment to their own family. The amount of attention they give the minded child may be slight compared with what a mother may give, or with what a nursery nurse or teacher or playgroup leader may see as her role. A minder may consider that it is mainly to the mother that she is offering a service, by keeping the child warm, fed and clean while the mother works. And because a minder works in her own home she may find the demands of the domestic side of her life more difficult to separate off than she would if she left home and its demands behind her each day. When her own pre-school child claims her attention, when her older child returns home from school, bursting to relate all the day's events, and when her husband comes home, ready for his meal, the mother and wife cannot ignore their demands.

However well motivated the minder, she is in any case *hampered by her routine housework*: cooking, washing-up, cleaning and clearing-up, laundry, putting the house to rights for the return of her own family. If she is minding a baby, she will have to prepare his feeds, possibly at a different time from the other meals, change his nappies and perhaps wash them. So a baby, who needs pretty well full-time attention in his waking hours, will have to compete with these chores, as well as with older children, for attention. And the older children, too, need plenty of attention – above all conversation, affection and patience. Minders will tell you that they only get a chance to sit and play with the children for perhaps an hour in the afternoon.

For many people one of the attractions of minding is that it offers a natural environment to the child – not just that she spends her day in a home, but that she can make forays with the minder into the ordinary life of the community, to the shops, on the bus, to the playground, to other people's houses, and so on. Our interviews with minders in London suggest that, on the contrary, the minder's day has just *too many commitments* – so that she has to rush in and out dragging the minded children with her. In any case, expeditions with children of mixed ages can be a major task. If you live at the top of several flights of stairs, or at the mercy of a lift, you face complicated manoeuvres with prams, buggies and children, and many minders do not have adequate transport for the children they are minding. Many have to go out on two, four or even more trips a day, just to take children back and forth to primary or nursery school. Under these circumstances, the trip is probably not much fun for the accompanying child. The other side of this coin is that trips just for the fun and interest of the children may well be few. Of the thirty-nine minders interviewed in the TCRU study, a third said they had not been out with the children at all during the previous week.

The routine demands of the day may also mean that rest time for the children has to be when it fits in with those demands, not when the children want a rest. If the minder herself is to get a break she will probably try to get all the children to rest at the same time, whether they want to or not.

Do minders give motherly care?

The main argument usually proposed in favour of minding is that the child will become attached to the minder and will receive 'motherly care' from her. This, it is argued, will compensate for whatever defects minding may have, such as poor play space and lack of toys. Our experience of visiting minders and mothers suggests that the relationships they develop with the children are quite different. The TCRU minding study points to a striking contrast here:

There is usually a great deal of interaction between mother and child during the course of an hour-long interview. At the outset, the child often sits close to the mother for several minutes, then gets down to play, returns to her, climbs on her knee, asks for food or to watch the television, or wants her to play. He shows her toys or cries for attention. In fact, the child's behaviour towards his mother impedes the flow of the interview. The mother responds to the child with caresses, talk, diversionary tactics or punishment. Sometimes she will break off the interview to meet his requirements and apologizes for the interruption. Throughout there are frequent interactions between the mother and the child, which suggest the strength of the underlying relationship. Many of these are initiated by the child himself, responding in a situation where his mother is giving her attention to a stranger. The mother, meanwhile, initiates less interaction in order, no doubt, to expedite the course of the interview. We found by contrast that the minders had virtually no difficulty in concentrating on the interview because the children were surprisingly undemanding of their attention. And not only did the minder not initiate interaction with the child, but almost invariably the child attempted little or no interaction with the minder.

We have frequently seen a child who is lively, affectionate and naughty with his parents sit quiet, sad and strangely good at the minder's. Such a child makes few demands on the minder and indeed minders often comment that children are easy, no trouble, never naughty.

Why is there such a difference between the relationships a child forms with his mother and with a minder? We think it is because the minder has not established a relationship with the child in which she encourages and responds to his actions and signals, stimulates him to talk and play and enjoys his company. This process happens naturally enough when the child is your own, but when it is someone else's child it needs working at and *many minders are not aware of the need to work at forming a relationship with a child not their own.* Indeed, many of them consider that looking after other people's children is just like looking after your own – you don't need to learn how to do it. When we have asked minders whether they think there are things they need to know in order to help them in their job, the most common response by far is that once you've been a mother yourself you know how to handle children, you have nothing to learn. But the minder is not looking after a child continuously from birth, as she did with her own, so she and the child have to build a relationship with each other when he first comes to her. Although this may be easier if the child is very young, in practice children move in and out of placements at minders: in any one year a minder may have through her hands half a dozen or more children of varying ages.

Some possible consequences for the child are indicated by a language test carried out on twenty-eight minded children in the TCRU minding study. All the children were aged two to three years. The test showed that most of the children in the sample (85 per cent) were functioning below average, and a quarter of them were functioning at a level which gave serious cause for concern (in technical terms, 1.5 or more standard deviations below average). What was particularly disturbing was that nothing was being done about the situation: none of the seven most backward children was getting any specialist help, and two of them had not attended child welfare clinic for at least a year.

How does minding suit parents?

Advocates of minding often picture it as a flexible system whereby the community meets its own needs for day-care places. Minders, so the argument runs, will spring up where they are needed, parents will seek them out, and needs will be satisfied. But there is of course no guarantee that enough minders will spring up, or that they will provide exactly what the parent wants. In practice a mother often has difficulty even finding a minder, let alone one with whom she is satisfied. Armed with a list of registered minders – often out of date – she may go from door to door only to be told 'no vacancies', or 'no babies', or even 'no coloureds'.

If a mother does find a minder for her child what kind of service will she be offered? First, the good side of the picture. Most minders provide whatever hours the parent asks for, including journey time to and from work, as well as the hours spent at work. Some will accept the idea that the child will come and go at different times on different days, to fit in with a parent's shift-work. We have met a few who were happy to keep children overnight or even for the weekend. And if the relationship established is a happy one for all concerned, it is sometimes possible for the minder to go on helping once the child is at primary school – by taking her before and after school, and in the holidays. Some bring out books of photographs of 'their' children, going back over the years, children with whom they have kept up contact, and for whom their home has become a second home.

But there is no guarantee that things will go as well as this, nor that they will go well at all. As we saw in Chapter 5, the OPCS survey found that parents are less happy with minding than with any other form of care. The TCRU minding study found that nearly half (thirteen) of the twenty-eight mothers interviewed wanted to remove their child from the minder, and another five thought that the child should go, either now or later, to a playgroup or nursery school as well as to the minder. Few parents would choose a minder if a suitable nursery place was available. Evidence on this is forthcoming too at an international level. A study of day care for under-threes in six countries has found that most parents, offered a choice of nursery or minder care, opt for the nursery [11].

Many of the difficulties between parents and minders result from the direct money transaction. From the parents' point of view, minding is a service they have probably chosen as second-best (many parents we have met have at least inquired about day nurseries first), yet the minder must be paid. There is very little hope of a subsidy here, as there would be if the child were at a council day nursery. Paying the minder can take up to a quarter of a mother's pay – more if she has two under-fives. Some parents are angry when they see few toys at the minder's; they expect a good service because they are paying for it, even though they may recognize that for the minder what they pay is little enough. Minders from time to time have to put up their rates: they are often reluctant to do this, and diffident about asking, but they are pushed into it by the rising cost of food and fuel. Parents may resent this additional charge, which has not been met by a rise in their own wages.

The local authority does not offer a guarantee that all their registered minders will offer good, basic standards of care: good food, fresh air and exercise, and opportunities to talk and play with adults and children. Whether you knock on a good minder's door is largely a matter of chance, and parents can form little idea about the minder before they agree to leave their child. They may not necessarily learn much more as time goes on. Mothers often say how little they know about how their child spends the day, and they worry that she isn't talked to, played with or taken out. Frequently, too, parents and minder are in conflict about such things as when and whether to give a child a rest, or when and how to start toilet training.

Some of these difficulties could probably be resolved if parents and minders could get to know each other well and could establish a habit of discussing the child's needs. But it is usually difficult for parents to spend much time at the minder's – it is after all her home. In most nurseries and playgroups parents spend some time settling the child in when she first starts going; at the same time they get to know the staff, and can assure themselves that the standard of care is adequate and that the child is happy there. The child may spend half an hour the first day, an hour the next, and so on, first with her parent and later on her own. This rarely happens at a minder. Most parents cannot afford to pay for the child's place while this settling-in proceeds; and they usually have to be at work anyway. Furthermore, some minders and parents do not consider that gradual settling-in is important. It is easy to see therefore why parents and minders often mistrust each other, since they have had little opportunity to get to know each other and establish a good relationship.

The other main dissatisfaction parents have with minding is that the placement is so insecure: the minder can stop taking the child whenever she pleases. Parents are well aware how distressing it is for their child to be abruptly moved. For the mother, the ending of the arrangement means she must start again, and look for another minder at the same time as trying to hold down her job. This often means frantic attempts to find something suitable in the space of a weekend. Mothers may refrain from asking how the child spent her day, whether she ate her dinner, or how long she slept, because they fear the minder will construe such questions as criticism of her methods and standards, and may ask for the child to be removed.

Finally, because minding is private and because the local authority has little control over it, parents have no assurance of a minimum standard of care, no assurance of support from the local authority in cases of difficulty, and no source of redress in case of serious complaint.

Government (double-)thinking on minders

It is clear that, compared to what a nursery can offer, childminding provides a poor service to parents and their children. Yet, as we have already seen, minding is currently being encouraged by central government, particularly for children under three. Does this mean that government departments are actually unaware of the defects of minding? Or is it rather that they are deliberately encouraging a form of care they know to be inadequate?

The joint circular published by the DHSS and DES in January 1978 suggests that they are well aware of the inadequacies of minding [12]:

While education should be an integral part of the care provided for children outside their home, it is particularly important for children in the care of childminders ... *because children who are merely minded are more likely than other children to be denied the social and intellectual stimulation that is important to their development,* the Departments attach great importance to fostering links between childminders and nursery schools, classes and teachers, with child health clinics and with voluntary groups working in this field – pre-school playgroups and toy libraries for example. Such links can help to break down the isolation experienced by many minders as well as broaden the experience of the children in their care. [Our italics]

These official recommendations raise a number of serious and disturbing questions. The recommended cure for inadequate minding is supposedly in nursery education and playgroups – which are almost entirely for children *over* three. Does this mean that it is acceptable for children *under* three – for whom minding is specially recommended – to be 'denied the social and intellectual stimulation that is important to their development'? This stimulation is surely necessary for children of *all* ages – recall that the children found to be backward in language in the TCRU minding study were all under three. Even for children over three, to offer a part-time nursery place is to offer the child a good deal less than she would get if she spent all day with caring and stimulating adults. Is it a good idea in any case to set up a service in which a three-year-old goes from home to minder to nursery school to minder to home? Even supposing minders felt like co-operating – a big assumption given their busy day – isn't that too many journeys, too many people for her to cope with? *But if minders, as the circular suggests, are not good enough, why should we be relying on them as child-care workers anyway?*

The joint circular also recommends that authorities should look at ways in which minding can be *improved*, and indeed there are several schemes under way at present which aim to do this. These fall into two categories: those that rely on the voluntary participation of minders, and those in which the authority takes minders more directly under its wing. We look at each type of scheme in turn.

Voluntary schemes

Various approaches have been adopted in recent years. A first step has often been for local authorities to take minders off the bottom of social workers' 'case-lists', where they usually lie neglected for lack of time, and to appoint *workers with special responsibility for minding*. Their job is to keep more efficient records of minders' names and addresses, specifying how many children each one is registered for, the ages of the children she may take, and the names and addresses of the children she is currently minding. This task looks easy enough but in practice it may be extremely difficult. Though the local authority is empowered to collect the information, the minder's co-operation is vital; since she may have through her hands a dozen or more children in a year, she will have to be efficient too. Unless she has a phone, she will have to write, or wait for a visit from the local authority worker, to bring the information up to date.

Local authority workers may also act as *home visitors* to minders, helping them sort out problems and offering informal teaching in child-care. Toys may be offered as gifts or on loan; equipment, such as double baby-buggies, prams and high chairs may be provided. Minders may be put in touch with one another for encouragement and support, and to help each other out in emergencies. Again, much depends on the minder's willingness to co-operate. Workers in this sort of scheme usually acknowledge that they are reaching only some of the minders on their patch – about a third is a figure often mentioned. Minders may not see the worker as having any sort of part to play in their working life; they may resent 'the welfare' coming into their home;

or they may simply say they are too busy to deal with yet another person, another commitment, in their already busy day. Much depends, too, on the expertise of the worker: teaching child-care to experienced mothers is after all a delicate business.

Some authorities arrange *groups* for minders to attend: these groups are often seen as therapeutic, and as promoting self-help. Minders discuss their problems with regard to the children, the parents, and the local authority. Difficulties of the job may seem more tolerable when shared. They may as a group decide on a common rate to charge for each child, thus eliminating under-cutting by other minders and door-step arguments with parents. Some groups have devised contract forms to be signed by parent and minder when the child first starts at the minder's: these usually set out the financial agreement and include vital information, like the name of the child's GP and an address or telephone number where the parent can be contacted during the day.

Other areas have opened *drop-in centres*, where the minder can spend time when she chooses, and which the children can use as a playgroup. She may leave the children in safe hands there while she has a break or does some essential chore, such as heavy shopping or visiting the dentist; she may welcome the opportunity to meet other minders and mothers, or perhaps take part as a helper or playleader in the children's activities. There may be a toy library where the minders and children can choose toys for the week, and at the same time widen their knowledge of what toys are currently available.

Many groups or drop-in centres are used by the authority as informal settings for *teaching*. A local authority worker may lead discussions on child health and development, the situation of immigrant children, or on the importance of talking and playing with children. While the minders get together in one room the children play together in another. A more ambitious idea is to organize *short courses* for minders – usually a series of six to twelve discussions or lectures led by local authority workers, doctors, health visitors, teachers and others working with young children.

The success of these schemes obviously varies according to the staff and minders involved – although toys and toy libraries are almost universally welcomed. Some minders again say they are too busy or too old to learn new approaches, or that as mothers themselves they have nothing to learn about child-care. Some feel that their status has been raised – they feel more confident about the value of what they are doing, they feel less isolated, happier about dealing with parents and with the local authority. Some have benefited from the support and help of other local minders, especially in emergencies. Some have even become so enthused with the possibilities of working with children that they give up minding altogether and train as playleaders!

The most important point about all these schemes however is that participation is entirely voluntary; it is impossible to avoid the suspicion that a good deal of effort may be put into preaching to the converted. It may well be that those minders whose practice most needs improvement are never reached at all. Even for those who do participate, there is no guarantee that they will put into practice the ideas that have been suggested to them.

Finally, we must again emphasize that most minders do not stay in the job for very long (see page 169). This means that any attempts to improve minders once they have registered and begun minding may begin to take effect just as they move on to another job.

Minders and 'priority children'

A few local authorities are attempting to take the bull more firmly by the horns and are paying minders directly to look after 'priority' children. This is particularly attractive for local authorities with long waiting lists, as it means that more 'priority' children can be cared for without setting up new day nurseries.

There are various versions of these schemes. Some local authorities sponsor particular children – they pay the minder directly to look after the child, and may offer a retainer of half or all this amount for periods when no sponsored child attends, in order to hold open the place. The minders may be specially selected: in Humberside, for instance, recruitment to the scheme involves interviews and taking up references [13]. Other boroughs will pay any minder for any child she takes who falls within a 'priority' category. In a few boroughs, the authority asks that the minder attend a training course in return for this payment. In Edinburgh a course takes place at a day nursery; it includes teaching sessions and practical work at the nursery. There is a further course at a local college of education on one day a week for thirty weeks [14].

The most thorough-going scheme of this kind is the Groveway Project in Lambeth [15]. It was set up as a research project with 75 per cent of the cost paid by Urban Aid and 25 per cent by the local authority. Minders are paid a salary to care for priority children and their work has now become an accepted part of the day-care services in the borough. Applications are invited from those interested in becoming salaried minders, and after initial selection applicants are given six weeks' training based in the local (Groveway) day nursery. They are paid while training, but must reach an acceptable standard before taking children into their own homes. They are paid on the same scale as trainee nursery nurses, plus expenses (50p per child per day). The minders meet regularly at the nursery, and 'their' children spend this time with one of the nursery groups. There is also a regular fortnightly meeting with the training tutor, and the children attend a playgroup during this time. Minders are visited by day nursery staff about once a month. Parents pay for this service, as for day nurseries in Lambeth, on a means-tested basis. It is reckoned that the cost per place to the local authority is no less than that of a day nursery place.

A full report of the project has been written by Phyllis Willmot and Linda Challis, who suggest that each council day nursery in the borough could provide half as many places again by adopting this system. They are convinced that high standards of care are achieved by the minders, and that the day nursery itself has benefited from the project. Through their visits to minders, the day nursery staff now have much more contact with the local community and are more aware of the characteristics and problems of the area.

What do these schemes have to offer? In many cases the minders are hand-picked, and it is not surprising that those reporting on the schemes think that the care offered is of high quality. The schemes also offer a welcome flexibility in hours that day nurseries do not usually provide, and are probably of great benefit to many of the children and parents. However, the pay offered, even at Groveway, is not high and the amount offered for expenses is not enough to cover the cost of looking after a child: the minders are in fact subsidizing the local authority out of their own or their husband's pocket. Lambeth staff have suggested that more account should be taken of wear and tear, food, toys, outings and treats by offering a more generous rate per child, or by arranging for the minders to claim back expenses. Some doubt must also remain about the quality of care given to the children, since, as far as we know, there has been no systematic attempt to evaluate it. The present schemes are small enough to be highly selective in choosing staff, and for the minding to be carefully observed and improved; probably these minders are exceptional. If the schemes were widened it would almost certainly be necessary to offer a salary that would draw good people out of other jobs – and even then there must be some doubt whether sufficient suitable applicants could be recruited.

Do these schemes offer a better service to parents than ordinary registered minding? Do they have more say in the care of their children? Is it easier for them to get to know the minder, and establish a good relationship with her? One major step forward is that bargaining about money is removed, and so conflicts and misunderstandings may be reduced. In addition, the minders are more carefully selected and may be more sympathetic to parents. But the child – and her parents – are still stigmatized as members of a 'priority' group, and, as in council day nurseries, this will inevitably affect the relationship between minder and mother, as well as influencing how the minder relates to the child. This, of course, is hardly a criticism of the schemes themselves, but rather of the underlying problems of operating a selective system.

Has minding a future?

The future of minding depends very much on what happens *outside* minding. It is likely that if a comprehensive nursery service was made available, minding could well become superfluous and would simply wither away. However, if minding *is* to continue as a recognized form of child-care it cannot be allowed to remain as an inadequately regulated and sub-standard private enterprise. Instead, it must be brought under the wing of the local authority and fully integrated with other child-care services. Several of the ideas currently being tried out at Groveway should be taken up and extended further:

- Minders should be paid on the same scale as other child-care workers and offered comparable conditions of work, such as holidays, sick leave and national insurance. This idea has already been implemented to some extent in France, West Germany, Denmark and Sweden.

- Minding should be recognized as a demanding and responsible job, and people should be carefully selected and trained for it. As in the Groveway scheme, this training could be based in a nursery and minders could learn on the job as well as having more formal instruction, very much as nursery nurses do today.
- Once trained, minders should be attached to a nursery centre, working partly there and partly at home. They would be seen as part of the nursery staff and parents would have access to all the nursery facilities.
- Parents would ideally choose whether their child spent all her time at the nursery, or whether she spent some time in the minder's home. Many would prefer the former, but some parents might see advantages in the domestic setting. A child who found it difficult to adapt to group care might be happier with a smaller group of children and one adult. A minder who lived very locally or who was already a friend might be seen as an ideal answer for a parent who wanted occasional care or care for an hour or two a day for a baby. A parent who occasionally needed to leave a child over night or late in the evening might be more readily helped by a minder than by a nursery.

If these changes were fully implemented minding would be a much more attractive proposition for parents, children and the minders themselves – indeed it would hardly be fair to go on calling it 'minding'. These changes would not however be cheap, and it is likely that an improved minding scheme would cost as much per place as a local authority day nursery. Whether minding would still be as attractive in these circumstances to its present advocates in government and elsewhere very much remains to be seen.

8 But what about the parents?

Parents and staff: communication and control

In this chapter and the next we look at two issues which are of fundamental importance for *all* nurseries: the role of parents and the question of what the children are learning. We start by looking at the relationship between staff and parents, focusing in particular on the issues of communication and control. First we look at the extent to which parents and staff communicate their knowledge of the child, discuss their approaches to child-care, and share ideas. Later we consider the more contentious issue of control and decision-making in nurseries, looking in particular at the role parents might have in this process.

Two worlds

The child who goes to nursery spends her time in two different worlds and is cared for by two different sets of adults, her parents and the nursery staff. Both play an important part in the child's life and both contribute to her happiness and development. But living in two worlds, while offering variation and enrichment, can also be troublesome and confusing. The child may suffer if different approaches to child-care are practised in the two settings or if parents and staff do not discuss what they are each doing. This is particularly obvious in such areas as feeding and toilet training: a child might be praised for trying to feed herself at nursery, but scolded by her parents for the sticky mess she makes at home; or she may be obliged to sit on the potty at fixed times in the nursery, but given free access at home. Such differences in approach could be distressing for the child and may also slow down her development.

These problems could be avoided if parents and staff saw themselves as partners in the process of caring for young children, working together towards a common approach, communicating freely with one another and sharing their experience and knowledge of the children. This would lead to better understanding of the children by parents and staff alike, and in these circumstances the children's happiness and development would be enhanced, rather than diminished. Discussion could range over all aspects of child-care, not just the physical areas of feeding, toileting and sleeping, but also including children's play and learning.

Communication in a day nursery

What actually happens in nurseries at present? How much contact *is* there between nursery staff and parents? How much discussion of the child's daily experience at nursery and at home? How much consultation about aims and methods? These were some of the questions explored in a research project on Parent Involvement in Nursery Education directed by Barbara Tizard of the Thomas Coram Research Unit. The project took place in seven nursery schools and classes and one local authority day nursery, all of which were selected because of the staff's interest in working with parents. Since one of us (Gill Pinkerton) worked closely with the day nursery on this project, we shall describe this aspect of the work in some detail. Although this is an account of one particular day nursery, it is likely that the issues involved apply to other nurseries as well.

The research worker began by looking at the existing relationships between staff and parents. She did so by taking note of all conversations that took place between them during a typical week, and noted approximately how long they lasted. Relationships seemed to be friendly and agreeable, and as many as 80 per cent of the parents had some contact with staff every day. (Usually the mother brought and collected the child, but in a few cases it was the father, or an elder brother or sister.) The vast majority of conversations, however, were simply greetings or chats about the weather, clothing or parents' jobs. Conversations about the child's health and welfare were much less frequent, and when they did occur, simple information only was conveyed – such as whether the child had eaten breakfast, slept after lunch or bumped her head. There was little conversation about what activities the children had taken part in at nursery or at home and virtually no discussion about either the child's progress or how parent and staff approached such matters as feeding, toileting, play and so on. Furthermore almost all the conversations were very brief, usually lasting about a minute or less. Thus beneath the friendly chat there was very little communication of any real significance [1].

A very similar picture was found in the nursery schools and classes in the project. Barbara Tizard wrote:

In these schools parent–teacher conversations were serving a largely social function. Home and school were seen as separate experiences by both teachers and parents, and little mutual exchange of information occurred.[2]

How far this is generally true of other nurseries we cannot say, but the similarity between the day nursery and the seven schools is striking and suggests that this type of friendly, but limited, relationship may be fairly widespread.

Having completed these initial observations in the day nursery the research worker interviewed most of the parents and staff. The interview revealed that although both parties thought it was in the children's best interest to discuss the care of the children together and to co-operate with one another, both felt there was not enough communication going on in practice. Almost three quarters of the parents said they would like to know more about what their child did at the nursery. Yet if both saw the need for more meaningful communication, why was it not occurring?

Part of the problem seemed to be the lack of an appropriate time for discussion. There were no evening meetings or individual appointments to talk to staff and the only opportunities were when children were brought or collected. These times were far from ideal: parents were frequently in a hurry, since two thirds were going out to work, and staff were often too busy to stop and talk for long. In addition many of the parents refrained from asking too many questions because they were worried about being seen to interfere. The staff, for their part, did not go out of their way to converse with the parents as they were simply not aware of the parents' keen interest in discussing their children's experiences and progress. These factors all contributed to limiting communication.

The next step was to discuss the findings of the observations and interviews with the staff. During this discussion one nursery nurse very honestly said she thought she was failing to communicate with the parents about things which really affected the children. She admitted she had been unaware of the parents' genuine concern and willingness to talk. Her courage and ability to criticize herself enabled other staff to express similar feelings and it then became possible to discuss how communication might be improved. Without this realization on the part of the staff, and their openness in expressing their own limitations, it would have been very difficult, if not impossible, to introduce any changes at all.

The staff and research worker decided that a good

way to inform parents about life at the nursery would be to make a video-film of a typical day and to invite parents to come and watch it, either in the afternoon or in the evening. Every parent received a written personal invitation and a creche was held for the evening session so that no one was prevented from coming because of baby-sitting problems. The response was overwhelming – every child was represented by one or both parents. Only three parents did not come – one mother had to look after her sick baby (her husband bravely came alone, having visited the nursery on only one other occasion) and two fathers were working shifts. The staff later confessed their surprise at the excellent attendance – they had not expected some of the parents to come, believing that they were not very concerned about their children. The presence of almost every mother and father at the meeting helped to dispel the staff's preconceptions about these 'uninterested' parents.

As well as seeing the video-film, parents were given written information about activities provided at the nursery, a sheet of rhymes and songs, a list of suitable books for young children and a booklet describing various aspects of the day nursery. Comments and questions were invited after the film was shown and a wide range of topics were raised for discussion. One parent, seeing her child cutting out shapes on the film, said that Michael always wanted scissors at home, but she did not let him use them because they were too dangerous. She did not know there were special children's scissors and has since bought some for him to use at home. Another mother was surprised to see her child using a knife and fork at the nursery as she still gave her a spoon at home. And when Sarah's mother saw the children painting the nursery windows on the film she realized why, to her dismay, Sarah had tried to do the same at home. But it was not only the parents who learnt about the children. One of the nursery nurses finally understood why Yasmin, a four-year-old Indian girl, was so clumsy using cutlery. She had been unaware that Yasmin and her family ate with their hands at home and the child had simply never used cutlery before starting at the nursery.

These comments, amongst many others, revealed just how little parents and nursery staff knew about the child's everyday life at nursery and at home. What appeared to be very obvious information was often not communicated – each party assumed that the other must already know. It was clearly a mistake to make this kind of assumption, as can be seen from this letter written by one of the parents after the meeting:

On behalf of my husband and myself I wish to thank you all for a very pleasant and informative evening. Although Christopher has been at the nursery for over two years now we found there were a lot of things going on which we were not aware of, such as the frequent visits by the doctor, also the outings to the parks and shops.

Seeing the film also served to reassure some of the parents that their child was happy and well cared for at the nursery. One mother expressed her feelings like this:

I don't know if the other mothers are like me but I had guilt feelings because I put Clare in nursery, you know, and I felt 'oh, have I done right or have I done wrong?', but seeing her there and seeing how she was enjoying herself and really loving it, that really put my mind at ease again ... I feel great since I watched the film, you know, that made me understand that I was being stupid. I was just trying to tie her to my apron strings.

During the meeting, parents and staff expressed the desire for more contact of this kind and since then meetings have been held regularly. The main value of this work with the day nursery has been to demonstrate the need for more meaningful communication between parents and staff, showing how a channel for such communication can be opened up and used.

Communicating the aims of nursery education

The exchange of simple information seems to be relatively straightforward, once the need has been recognized. What appears to be more difficult is the communication of aims and methods. The importance of explaining aims to parents is often stressed in nursery schools and classes, where, in contrast to day nurseries, the teachers have definite educational aims. Indeed one of the indicators of good practice put forward by the National Union of Teachers is:

Nursery teachers develop and maintain good links with the child's home and are aware of the value of educating parents in the range and purpose of educational activities which their child experiences at nursery school.[3]

But how easy is it to do this? Nursery education is based on the free play approach (see Chapter 9) and consequently it is often difficult for parents to see *what* the children are learning, other than to play and mix with other children. This was certainly the case in five of the nursery schools and classes involved in the Parent Involvement project, where even after the teachers had made determined efforts to inform parents about nursery education, communication had apparently failed to be effective. Barbara Tizard summed up the position:

Though during the year most parents had become well informed about *what* their children did in the nursery class or school, few understood *why* the activities were provided, and how they were supposed to help the child.[4]

In the course of interviews, parents and teachers were asked why the nursery provided specific materials – sand, water, paint, books, puzzles, Wendy house (home corner) – but their answers were often very different. All the teachers, besides mentioning the children's enjoyment of the materials, stressed their potential for learning. This was not true for many of the parents, particularly the immigrant families.

Many Asian mothers were baffled by the purpose of all the equipment except for books, although sometimes they produced ingenious explanations for them: 'Sand – all English people like the seaside; as it is so far away they bring some to school, to remind them of the beach'; 'Water – so as to get them interested in washing up.'

The teachers valued sand and water as important for developing mathematical and scientific concepts, for example, volume and the properties of materials. What the mothers saw, however, were children making sand pies or filling bottles with water, having a good time no doubt, but with what relevance to maths and science? Clearly the teachers had not adequately spelled out what the child is supposed to be learning in these activities. Indeed to do so effectively probably requires particular communication skills – and teachers would probably have to be specially trained for the purpose.

Who makes decisions? The role of professionals

While few people would doubt the importance of effective communication between nursery staff and parents, a more contentious issue is that of control and decision-making in nurseries. How much say should parents have over what happens in the nursery? Should all important decisions be made by the professional staff or should parents and staff be jointly responsible? Do parents have a right to some control over their children's care and education? There is a wide range of opinion to be found throughout the pre-school world.

At present parents have little say in what goes on at state nursery schools or day nurseries (playgroups, as we shall see later, are somewhat different). Most of the decisions affecting the day-to-day running of the nursery – such as choosing equipment or planning activities –

are made by the professional staff. The DES and DHSS lay down certain standards for premises, staff ratios etc., and make recommendations about what should be going on, and there are teams of inspectors and advisers who ensure that standards are universally maintained. The parents thus take on the role of clients, passively in receipt of a service over which they have no direct influence. All decisions are made by professionally trained people who, it is believed, are qualified to do so by their special knowledge, skills and expertise.

The advantage of this system is that it ensures accountability to the *public at large*: if a state nursery is opened in any part of the country the public can be assured that certain minimum standards are met, and if they are not the local authority can be held responsible. The disadvantage, however, is that individual nurseries are not directly accountable to those *particular parents* who use them. While acceptable standards are ensured, there is no responsiveness to the varying needs and desires of different groups of parents. Parents are excluded from making decisions about their own children, and are obliged to hand over responsibility to professionally trained people. Their confidence as parents is thus undermined and they come to believe that what happens to their children can be determined only by qualified experts – they, as parents, have no rights at all.

The tendency for professionals to take over control of ordinary people's lives is not, of course, peculiar to nurseries: it happens in other fields such as medicine, architecture and town planning. One of many arguments against it is that the professionals may not always be right. There are some post-war housing estates, for example, which are now being demolished at great expense because architects designed them badly in the first place, and we have already seen that many child-care professionals believe – incorrectly – that children under three are harmed by attending nurseries. A further argument is that some decisions do not depend on specialized knowledge but must rely heavily on people's *values and attitudes*. The decision to appoint a male nursery teacher, for example, will depend – all other things being equal – on whether members of the appointments board *want* to employ a man. Specialized knowledge and expertise will have little bearing on this type of decision.

To argue for more control by parents does not mean that we do not value professional skills and expertise. Working with young children is a difficult and responsible job, for which people should be properly selected, trained and paid. This, however, does not mean they should be given total control over what happens in the nursery. Instead the aim should be to counterbalance the staff's skills and expertise with the parents' own views and knowledge, so that a more equal partnership between the two can develop.

Parent involvement in managing schools

Specific recommendations for involving parents in the management of schools have been recently put forward by the DES-sponsored Taylor Report, *A New Partnership for Our Schools* [5]. Although the management of nursery schools was excluded from the report, being outside the terms of the inquiry, the Taylor recommendations are very relevant to the present discussion. The main recommendation was that every school should have a managing body responsible for running the school, composed of four different parties who would be equally represented: the local education authority, the staff, the parents (and, where appropriate, pupils) and members of the local community. Taylor argued for more direct control of individual schools by people with a legitimate concern and interest:

Whatever the Government, the local Council and the education experts between them decide about schools in general, every school is a special place, the school around somebody's corner. No two schools have exactly the same needs or problems, and that is why the first recommendation of my Committee is that every school, big or small, should have its own governors to look after its interests.

The Taylor report was welcomed by John Hall, Secretary to the National Confederation of Parent Teachers Associations, which represents over a million parents:

> This Report represents a wonderful opportunity for parents. Let's hope they take advantage of it to the full. For the first time parents will be an effective voice in the government of schools.[6]

In marked contrast the teachers' unions responded with hostility, viewing the report as a definite threat to the professional status of teachers. Fred Jarvis, General Secretary of the NUT, condemned the report as a 'busybodies' Charter' which would impair the education of children. The report, he said, suggested handing over the running of schools to 'management by unaccountable committees'. Terry Casey, General Secretary of the National Association of Schoolmasters/Union of Women Teachers, said that 'the union was not "anti-parent" but could not allow non-professionals to pass judgement on teachers' [7].

The Taylor report provides one model for more democratic management structures in state nursery schools and day nurseries – though as these fall outside the scope of the Committee, the precise relevance of the model to them remains untested. It can also be questioned how far the model could or should be applied separately to individual parts of a school – would it be possible or desirable, for instance, to set up a management sub-committee for each nursery class, making recommendations to the school's main committee and having particular functions delegated to it?

Despite these queries, the Taylor report has placed the whole question of more democratic school manage-

ment firmly on the political agenda – the onus is now
very definitely on the politicians, who must decide if
new legislation is to be introduced. Other countries
have however already introduced legislation which
lays down a more democratic management structure.
In Norway, for example, all state kindergartens are
required to have a management committee composed of
two parents, two staff and two members appointed by
the local authority (similar to the Taylor recommendations, but without representation from the local community). The duties of the committee include the
appointment of staff, recommending children to be
admitted, suggesting activities for the children and so
on. The parent representatives on the management
committee are elected by a Parents Advisory Committee
made up of *all* the parents and guardians.

> The parents advisory committee shall look after the interests
> of parents and children so as to ensure the provision of adequate
> facilities for the development and activities of children.[8]

Embodied in this sort of structure is an implicit
respect for parents' views and interests, and a recognition
of the need for close contact between home and kindergarten. Decisions are made by professionals and parents
together.

In America there have been recent moves to give
parents more control in schools, the aim being to create
an active partnership between parents and professionals.
Legislation over the past fifteen years has specified the
involvement of parents in schools for young children.
As in Norway, this includes selecting teaching staff,
the curriculum and other educational issues. In a
recent article in the *Times Educational Supplement*, Donald
Peters points out the advantages of the American system
to *both* parents and professionals:

> Teachers gained a greater understanding of children and
> their home context and could therefore make greater efforts to
> match their teaching to a child's capabilities. Parents learned

more about and were more sympathetic towards the difficulties faced by teachers. Both found they could gain from the support provided by the other as they worked together for the well-being of the child.[9]

The American experience suggests that teachers, as well as parents, have much to gain from this partnership. What appears initially to be a fundamental threat to teachers may in fact turn out to be a tremendous source of support.

Parents and playgroups

Although parents have no voice in state nurseries in this country, the picture is different when we look at *playgroups*; for the essence of a playgroup is parent involvement. In many playgroups this may simply mean helping out on a parents' rota, but in others it can extend to participating in management by way of a parents' committee. The fact that parents can have a role in management and decision-making reflects the basic philosophy of the playgroup movement, which aims at increasing parents' responsibility in matters concerning child-care and helping parents to gain confidence in themselves as parents.

This emphasis on the *parent's* development as well as the child's is one aspect of playgroups which differentiates them from nursery schools and classes. In the latter the focus is more exclusively on the child's educational experience. Given this difference in orientation it is perhaps not surprising that parents are offered different roles in the two types of service: active in playgroups, passive in nursery education. But there are probably other factors at work as well. In many playgroups parents are necessary for the survival of the playgroup – the parents' committee applies for funds, employs staff, manages the books, pays the bills and so on – work which most playgroup staff cannot reasonably take on in addition to the daily job of running the playgroup. This is not the case in schools, where funds are guaranteed by the state and where the headteacher carries out much of the other administrative work as a recognized part of her job. Parents are simply not *needed* in the same way. Furthermore, as we mentioned earlier, in the state sector there is a well-developed system for maintaining standards – teachers must register with the DES, advisers and inspectors visit the schools regularly and so on. The system can operate efficiently without direct management by parents. This is not true for playgroups. Although the PPA attempts to carry out the function of ensuring acceptable standards through its own network of advisers and by running its own courses for playgroup leaders, it has neither the resources nor the machinery of the DES and LEAs to do so effectively. This therefore allows more *direct* control by the playgroup parents' committee.

Another reason why parents adopt a more active role in playgroups than in nursery education is that there is less distinction between 'parents' and 'staff'. Many staff first become involved in playgroups as parents, before going on to do playgroup courses, often while their child is still at playgroup. Although some of the staff may have completed the playgroup leaders' course, this training does not have the same status as a teaching qualification, and therefore does not have the same effect in distancing the 'qualified expert' from the ordinary parent.

The difference in attitudes between playgroup staff, teachers and nursery nurses was clearly brought out in a Scottish study by Joyce Watt. Various types of staff were asked to give their opinions about the role of parents in management. Watt reports her findings as follows:

Teachers and nursery nurses were almost universally against it. 'No, definitely no', 'parents don't want it', 'you can become so democratic no decisions are made', 'professionals are here to make decisions', 'parents should have no power of decisions

on policy; only the right in relation to their own children to
question and ask'.

Playgroup staff accepted the principle, acknowledging it as
basic to the playgroup philosophy. 'It's fundamental, it's
what playgroups are about', 'it's all-important – we must
learn to question the experts'.[10]

But what actually happens in playgroups? By no
means all playgroups are managed by parents; only 55
per cent of those replying to the PPA's 1976 survey had a
parents' committee, the rest being managed by charitable
organizations (such as the Save the Children Fund), the
Church, tenants' associations and in some cases by one
or two committed individuals [11]. Even where playgroups do have a parents' committee, some of the staff
may be ambivalent about management by parents.
This was clearly the case for some playgroup staff in
Joyce Watt's study.

Others adhered to the principle but interpreted it narrowly:
'it's important when it comes to raising and using money, but
not for the day-to-day running of the group', 'it's important
to ask their opinion, whether you take it or not', 'we've only
two parents on the committee. We really provide a service;
this was stipulated when the playgroup started ... that it had
to be firmly under the church's control' (community playgroup supervisors). Some supervisors acknowledged the
frustration of the principle in practice: 'we used to have free
play completely, but the mothers didn't like it; they insisted
on the discipline of "sitting down to do things"', 'in principle
management by parents is right but I get so frustrated with it;
I even have to ask for scissors'.

What does a parents' committee actually do in practice?
To what extent is it primarily an administrative and
fund-raising body? How much time is given to discussing what the children are getting from the playgroup experience? Does the committee serve as a
channel for parents and staff to talk about the progress
and problems of individual children? In our experience
a good deal of the meeting time tends to be absorbed

discussing financial and administrative issues, and while this may be crucial for the continuing stability of the playgroup it can mean that other issues concerning the children are given insufficient attention. In some playgroups the staff may discuss such topics informally with parents, but in others the staff themselves become the real arbiters of how the playgroup should run, as teachers are in nursery schools and classes.

If there is a trend towards the staff having greater influence than parents – and at this stage we are only suggesting that this *may* be happening – it is likely to be because paid workers are increasing in playgroups (91 per cent in the 1977 PPA survey employed at least one person) [12] and because staff tend to stay put, while parents pass through quickly. This rapid turnover of parents – many having children at playgroup for only four or five terms – has become more marked as education authorities open nursery classes and admit more and more four-year-olds to reception classes. In this situation parents are likely to be involved in management for only a short time, giving them less opportunity to build up knowledge and skill, and their commitment is bound to be less. In these circumstances staff will understandably assume more control.

Although playgroups no doubt offer parents a more active role than most nursery schools and classes, this does not necessarily mean they have much more influence over what their children are doing. Indeed the playgroup literature pays little attention to this issue of control. Parent involvement in playgroups is often seen primarily in terms of giving mothers support and helping them to become better parents. In the *Penguin Book of Playgroups*, Lucas and McKennell describe the mothers' experience of the playgroup as follows:

They see their child being dealt with by experienced people and discover how different sorts of behaviour problems are handled. They will notice the sort of activities being offered and what toys are used. *Without knowing it, they will be learning how to be better mothers.* [13] [Our italics]

The playgroup movement has achieved much in its short history; in particular it has demonstrated the potential for parental involvement in nurseries. What is at question is just how far this potential has been tapped and what changes may be occurring in playgroups over time. Our *impression* is that although many parents are often involved in rotas and management committees their role is often quite limited, particularly in the crucial areas of the aims of playgroups and how the children spend their time there. If the pioneering work of playgroups is to be built on to achieve greater influence, there needs to be careful assessment of what parent involvement means in practice: the playgroup movement – infant of the 1960s – is now strong and large enough to stand more rigorous examination of its health and development.

Community nurseries: parents in control

In Chapter 6 we discussed the merits of *community nurseries* as small and informal nursery centres. Here we want to focus on the role of parents, looking in particular at the oldest community nursery, the Children's Community Centre (CCC), in the London Borough of Camden.

Although there are some similarities with playgroups in that the CCC – like other community nurseries – was started by parents, serves a local area and exists within the voluntary sector, there are still clear differences in approach. At the CCC emphasis is placed on giving parents some degree of *control* over their children's experiences, not in order to make them into better parents, *but as a fundamental right to which all parents are entitled.* Some of the parents and workers at the CCC place this philosophy within a broader political context, viewing child-care as just one area amongst many (housing, health, environment) where people should aim to make their own decisions about matters affecting their everyday life, rather than letting professionals take over.

All decisions concerning the CCC are made at a weekly meeting of parents and paid workers, and although the workers have a voice at the meetings, the parents, by virtue of numbers, are effectively in control. Indeed, as one of the functions of the meetings is to decide on the appointment of staff, the workers are in fact employed by the parents. Other topics at the meeting include sharing out administrative work (maintaining the building, buying food, ordering equipment); discussing basic attitudes to children (for example, how far children should be allowed to express their aggression); deciding on a theme of activities for the following week (for example plants, animals, the body, the senses, time); deciding which new children should come; discussing individual children; and so on. The meetings have two main purposes: one is to make all decisions affecting the running of the centre, and the other is to provide an opportunity for communication between parents and staff about the children's experiences and behaviour.

Our aim is to discuss one or two children each week – but only if their parent(s) are there. This is always useful to parents and workers as it makes the crucial link between the home and the centre; does the child behave differently in each place? Is she treated differently? Does the parent act in the same way in both places? How do people on the rota react to the child? In this way important issues are raised about attitudes to child-care, and discussions can take place not, as it were, between a lone parent and a group of professionals, but among a group of people who know and care for each other's children and who can share their problems and learn from each other.[14]

The experience of the Children's Community Centre raises a number of important issues about parent control.

What if a policy decision must be made and agreement cannot be reached between parents and staff? Supposing, for example, that the majority of parents wanted their children to be taught to read but the staff disagreed, on the grounds that pre-school children are not ready for such formal activities. What solutions would be open in a situation like this of fundamental conflict? In a nursery like the CCC where parents have ultimate control the workers could do one of the following: either they could argue the case against teaching reading and convince the parents of their point of view, or they could re-think their position and submit to the parents' wishes. If neither of these was a workable solution, they would ultimately be obliged to resign. In practice disagreements may never become as polarized as this, and in any case, opinions amongst the parents may be wide-ranging, with parents disagreeing amongst themselves on various issues. Even when conflict does arise it need not be a negative experience. It is far healthier and may be more productive to confront and discuss any differences of opinion, even though it may be upsetting at the time, instead of allowing resentment to build up. In this way an active parent body which is prepared to challenge the reigning philosophy can encourage a positive discussion of current pre-school practice, and could introduce exciting new ideas. As we shall see in the next chapter, there are various possible aims and methods besides the prevailing free play approach.

Some opponents of parental involvement in decision-making would argue that many parents do not have the necessary skills and knowledge to make wise decisions about their children's care and education. This objection misses two very fundamental points: first, that parents are continually making decisions about their children's care and education, and secondly, that parents probably know their own children better than anyone else does. Teachers can often learn a good deal about children from parents, as long as they are prepared to listen and accept what parents have to say. Indeed, teachers could perhaps do more to encourage the parents to talk about their children, helping less articulate parents to express their views.

When it comes to the theory of education, however, and to a more abstract discussion of aims and methods, some parents may have considerable difficulty. As we saw earlier from the Parent Involvement Research Project, teachers found it very difficult to explain their aims and methods and many parents find it hard to grasp the basic ideas, let alone contribute to active discussion. This could be remedied if teachers were given help to put across their ideas to parents as part of their training and if material (such as leaflets, video-films etc.) were produced specially for this purpose. This would require a fundamental change of attitude on the part of the professionals, moving towards *sharing* their knowledge and skills rather than retaining their expertise exclusively for themselves.

If parents *were* to play a more active part in decision-making, both in the state nurseries and in community nurseries and playgroups, who would these parents be? Would we inevitably be giving educated middle-class families the advantage? The Children's Community Centre had to face this issue and one of the parents voiced this problem in her contribution to the Centre's pamphlet:

The Sunday meetings also expose another area of class difference. Most of the middle-class parents are fairly articulate. They are at home with abstract argument, full of jargon and references to authors one may or may not have heard of. It is not surprising that many parents lose heart and seldom come to meetings.[14]

Of course working-class people are not necessarily unconfident and inarticulate, as the strength of the trade-union movement clearly demonstrates, but many working-class families may not feel able to participate in decisions about education. These families may in any case be under considerable daily pressure and have less time and energy to contribute than more favoured middle-class families. While this is not an argument against the basic idea of parent control it should be borne in mind as a potential problem to be tackled. One possible solution might be for the local authority to employ someone to act as a 'parents' advocate', particularly in working-class areas, encouraging parents to express and argue their views and giving them help and support in doing so.

Yet another issue is that of accountability. In play-groups, standards of premises, equipment, outdoor play space and so on vary enormously, and to a large extent their quality depends on the effectiveness and energies of the management committee. Does this mean that when parents play an active role we are giving a better service to the children of more involved parents? How can high standards be ensured if a nursery is accountable only to the parents who use the service? A balance must be struck between ensuring that certain minimum standards are met while at the same time giving parents direct influence over how the service runs. Part of the problem at present is that playgroups and community nurseries tend to receive minimal financial support from their local authorities and are under constant pressure just to survive. Community nurseries are under particular stress as they offer longer hours and take younger children, and their running costs are therefore considerably higher. If they are to provide high-quality care, then voluntary initiatives where parents play an active role must be guaranteed adequate long-term funding, in return for which the nurseries would meet certain minimum standards. This need not restrict each nursery's autonomy and initiative.

Perhaps the most fundamental issue of all is whether parents actually *want* to be involved. The Children's Community Centre experience suggests that many parents *do* want to take an active part in making decisions, and greatly value the opportunity to do so. Two of the parents wrote about their feelings in the CCC pamphlet:

... being involved in the aims of the Centre in the collective decision-making, I feel I have never had to feel guilty or insecure about 'leaving' my child in a place where 'they' take care of him in a way I know nothing about, by people who are supposed to be 'experts'.

I finally came to the conclusion that this centre was what most people want, to be able to have some say in what goes on with your child during the time you are away from them. The weekly meeting gives everyone a chance to discuss their feelings about what has happened or what's going to happen.

There were however many parents at the Centre with neither the inclination nor the time to participate in this way. These parents were not sufficiently involved to contribute to the pamphlet, so we cannot hear their views directly. But this is a problem faced by all community nurseries – how to involve more parents in the affairs of the nursery? How can the idea be put across that the nursery is more than just a place to leave children, but is a place for parents as well? Perhaps it just has to be accepted that while some parents want this type of involvement, others may not. And until it is commonplace for parents to be offered control it is impossible to know just how many would welcome it.

It is the parents – not the staff – who have ultimate responsibility for their children's upbringing. If they are to exercise this responsibility properly they must know what happens to the child while she is at the nursery, and they must be able to exert some control over what is happening to her there. All nurseries should therefore organize times for parents and staff to share their knowledge and experience of each child, and to decide together what that child most needs to develop healthily and happily. In addition, all nurseries should have a democratic management structure whereby parents have the opportunity, if they want to use it, to take part in decision-making; those decisions should cover the selection of staff, times of opening, admissions policies, and what the children should be learning.

But what *might* the children be learning in nurseries? We turn now to look at some of the options which are open.

9 Early education – there's more to it than play

As we saw in the last chapter, many parents feel confused about what and how their children are actually learning at nurseries. They can see that the children enjoy going, that there are lots of other children to play with, and plenty of interesting toys and equipment for them to use. But the main activity in most nurseries is quite clearly 'play', and it is not at all obvious that any 'learning' is going on. So what *is* nursery education all about?

Learning through play

It is easier to understand the modern approach to nursery education by comparing it with the practices of a hundred years ago. In the combined nursery and infant schools of late Victorian Britain the classrooms usually consisted of tiered galleries in which up to a hundred young children sat, arms folded, in rigid rows, while the teacher stood at the front and taught the whole class at once. The curriculum consisted mainly of the '3Rs' (reading, writing and arithmetic), which were taught almost entirely by rote-learning methods, interspersed by short breaks when the children were marched around the yard. A graphic account of these grim conditions was given by a Board of Education Inspector in 1905:

Let us now follow the baby of three years through part of one day of school life. He is placed on a hard wooden seat (sometimes it is only the step of a gallery) with a desk in front of him and a window behind him, which is too high up to be instrumental in providing such amusement as watching the passers-by. He often cannot reach the floor with his feet, and in many cases he has no back to lean against. He is told to fold his arms and sit quiet. He is surrounded by a large number of other babies all under similar alarming and incomprehensible conditions, and the effort to fold his arms is by no means conducive to comfort or well being ... He usually spends the first day or two in tears, rising at times to sobs of so disturbing a character that he has to be sent into the playground, in charge of an older scholar, to make a noise where it will not interrupt the work of the other children. If he cries quietly he becomes aware of the following proceedings. A black board has been produced, and hieroglyphics are drawn upon it by the teacher. At a given signal every child in the class begins calling out mysterious sounds: 'Letter A, letter A' in a sing-song voice, or 'Letter A says Ah, letter A says Ah' as the case may be ... I have actually heard a baby class repeat one sound a hundred and twenty times continuously ... [1]

Not surprisingly, many humane educators of young children revolted against this harsh system of education, and the ideas of such people as Friedrich Froebel gradually became the dominant beliefs in the nursery world. Froebel – who started the first kindergarten in Germany in 1837 – believed that children have a tremendous natural ability to learn through following their own interests. Nurseries, he argued, should not try to teach children things they are not interested in or ready for, but should be places where children are as free as possible to play, explore, discover and, above all, be happy. More recent support for these ideas has come from the theories of Swiss psychologist Jean Piaget, who argued that children learn mainly through their contact with the physical world around them. He claimed that concepts such as volume and weight cannot be directly taught by an adult: instead the child gradually acquires them through manipulating objects of different shapes and sizes, or through pouring sand or water from one container to another. Such activities should not be dismissed as mere 'play' – rather, they are an integral part of the child's learning.

These ideas have become almost totally accepted in the pre-school field *and it is now firmly believed that children of this age do most, if not all, of their learning through freely chosen and self-directed play.* Much of the play equipment in nursery schools is specially chosen to promote particular kinds of learning: there are climbing frames and tricycles for developing muscular co-ordination and balancing skills; puzzles and construction toys (such as Lego) for developing more precise manipulative skills; sand and water trays, each with a varied assortment of containers and funnels, to help children learn about shape, size, volume and weight; and dressing-up clothes and Wendy house to develop the children's imagination through fantasy play. Nursery schools also encourage creativity and self-expression through activities such as painting and drawing, making models and playing musical instruments.

This emphasis on play does not mean that teachers are largely unnecessary in nursery schools. Their role is to decide how the various activities should be arranged about the room and which play equipment to put out each day: they may also organize a 'main activity' (such as cooking or making a collage) for each session, and they will usually end the session with a short period of stories or music. In recent years teachers have been encouraged to intervene more in the children's play, talking to them in order to develop their 'language', and introducing basic concepts such as colour, shape and number into the conversation. But despite this increased emphasis on the role of the teacher, the fundamental idea underlying all nursery education is still that children learn best through freely chosen and self-directed play.

Is play the only way to learn?

There is undoubtedly much to admire in the principles underlying nursery education today, and particularly in the realization that young children learn best when they are happy, interested and absorbed in what they are doing. The emphasis on play in a carefully planned, child-centred environment, the considerable freedom allowed children in their choice of activities, and the general lack of pressures or educational demands all contribute to making nursery schools happy and enjoyable places, where no child is condemned as a 'failure'. At the same time, however, there is a real danger of nursery educators becoming complacent and dogmatic in thinking that the present approach is the only way to achieve these ends. In recent years a number of people – both inside and outside nursery schools – have begun to question the exclusive emphasis given to play in nursery education, and psychologists such as Barbara Tizard, Corinne Hutt and Peter Smith have begun to ask whether play is indeed the only – or best – way for children to learn. In reviewing the evidence which is currently available, Peter Smith concludes:

There are no good psychological reasons for emphasizing free play more than other activities, as far as learning in young children is concerned. It seems likely that what children learn or gain through play can just as well be learnt in other ways, as long as adequate motivation is present. We should still value free play as being enjoyable and a way of gaining experience. But we should not put it on a pedestal above other ways for children to learn about and cope with the world around them. [2]

If this conclusion is correct, we could well be in for an exciting era of experiment and innovation in nursery education, as nursery staff develop and put into practice new ways of helping young children to learn. Already a number of fresh ideas are being tried out in British nurseries, and in the rest of the chapter we look at some of these new developments.

The Schools' Council Language Project

The idea that nursery teachers should intervene more in children's play in order to develop their language has received much impetus from a large and popular Schools' Council project on 'Communication Skills in Early Childhood'. The project – which ran from 1973 to 1976 – was directed by Joan Tough from the University of Leeds, and arose from a study she carried out earlier on the use of language by children from different social backgrounds. In this study, one group of children had parents who followed professional occupations and had received higher education, while the other group came from homes where the parents had received the minimum period of education and followed unskilled or semi-skilled manual occupations. The children were observed at three years of age while playing with other children, and their spontaneous talk was recorded and analysed. It was found that children in both social groups used language equally for certain purposes – such as 'self-maintaining' (maintaining their rights and property during play), 'directing' their own or others' activity, and 'reporting' on present experiences. However there were other types of language which were mainly used by the middle-class children – such as 'logical reasoning', 'predicting', 'projecting' and 'imagining'. Examples of these types of language are given below:

Self-maintaining	'I'm the captain of this boat and I don't want you to sail it'
Directing	'You take your lorry over there and put a load on it and then push it hard down this hill'
Reporting	'It's nice at my aunty's but I wouldn't like to stay there for ever'

Logical reasoning	'You're the daddy and you'll have to go to work 'cos daddies do'
Predicting	'I'm going to put some more bricks on that tower and then I'll put this flag on and it'll all come crashing down'
Projecting	'It's hot in the desert and I think you'll get sand blowing all over you'
Imagining	'And the witch gets on the broom stick and then the cat jumps on and they fly away'

Joan Tough concluded from this study that the more extended and analytical uses of language (logical reasoning, projecting, predicting and imagining) were probably used much less frequently in working-class homes, and that the working-class children simply lacked the experience of hearing language used in this way. Yet these uses of language mark the possession of important *verbal thinking skills*, which are likely to be essential for much subsequent school learning. At the same time Joan Tough did not believe that children would acquire these uses of language simply through their play; rather, they would have to be fostered through the systematic intervention of skilled teachers. This idea became the focus of the Schools' Council Project[3, 4, 5].

The organization of the project was complex and extremely thorough. It was based on small working groups of about fifteen to twenty nursery and infant teachers, who met every few weeks over a period of two years. At the meetings the teachers played and discussed video-tapes prepared by the Project Team in Leeds, and after each one tried out the suggested techniques in their own schools. At the next meeting they reported back and discussed their findings with the other teachers. One or two of the group members took on responsibility for co-ordinating with the team at Leeds, and there were frequent meetings and conferences to discuss the progress of the project.

During the first year of the project discussions focused on ways of observing children in the classroom and recognizing the different ways in which children use language: the teachers were thus developing skills and techniques for *appraising* children's use of language. The appraisal was based primarily on the main categories of language use identified in Joan Tough's earlier research. In the second year of the project the teachers discussed and tried out techniques for *fostering* these uses of language in the classroom. The main method employed was to engage individual children in *dialogue* – that is to talk to them with particular objectives in mind. A number of strategies were developed for use in these dialogues, some of which are illustrated in the sequence below. Here the teacher approaches Tom as he finishes making a boat, and uses the opportunity to help him report on how he made it.

1. T:	Tell me how you made your boat, will you?	*Orienting strategy*
2. Tom:	I cut it like that.	
3. T:	You cut it? I wonder what it was that you cut?	*Enabling: checking*
4. Tom:	A piece of wood.	
5. T:	Oh, I see – how did you cut the wood?	*Enabling: follow-through*
6. Tom:	I got a saw and I got a piece of wood out of that box and I cut it.	
7. T:	Oh, did you hold the wood in your hand to cut it?	*Enabling: checking*
8. Tom:	No, not in my hand.	
9 T:	How then did you cut it?	*Enabling: reminder of follow-through*
10. Tom:	I fastened it in that thing – with the handle.	

11. T:	Do you mean the vice on the bench?	*Enabling : checking*
12. Tom:	Yes, the vice. And then I cut a bit off one side – and then a bit off the other side. Look, you can see it.	
13. T:	Yes, I can see it very well. And I can see you did a lot more than cut it. What is this here?	*Sustaining* *Enabling : focusing*
14. Tom:	It's a sail and I made it.	
15. T:	How did you do that?	*Enabling : follow-through*
16. Tom:	Well – I got some stuff from the box over there. And I cut it.	
17. T:	Not with the saw this time?	*Enabling : checking*
18. Tom:	(laughs) You can't cut this stuff with a saw, you have to have scissors.	
19. T:	So you cut the sail with scissors from the white material – what then?	*Enabling : follow-through*
20. Tom:	Well, it had to go on a stick to hold it up and that's a lolly stick.	
21. T:	I can see it makes a good mast for the sail.	*Sustaining*
22. Tom:	Mast – yes, a mast.	
23. T:	Did you have to buy a lolly and eat it so you could have the stick?	*Enabling : checking*
24. Tom:	No, I don't know who did – not me, somebody did.	
25. T:	Yes, I think somebody must. What are you going to do with your boat now?	*Enabling : follow-through*
26. Tom:	Miss C says I can put it on the making table – that's so they can all see it.	
27. T:	I think it's a very good boat. I think Miss C will be pleased to see it.	*Concluding strategy*

As this example shows, the project teachers were encouraged to use children's spontaneous interests and play activities to help the children talk and think about what they were doing. Unfortunately, little systematic attempt was made to evaluate the project, so it is not known how many teachers managed to incorporate the new methods into their practice, and how many continued much as before. Nor do we know how effective the methods themselves are in developing children's thinking and language. It may well be that conversations like the one above are extremely useful in helping children be more thoughtful and aware of what they are doing. On the other hand, some people might be unhappy that all the questions in this conversation are coming from the teacher, with the child playing a relatively passive role.

Some people may also have doubts about the assumptions underlying the project, particularly those concerned with the language of 'disadvantaged' children (a term often used interchangeably with 'working-class'). Is it really true that these children are deficient in a wide range of verbal thinking skills? Or is it rather that they possess the skills but do not readily use them in the strange and artificial environment of school? Perhaps it is more important to try and reduce the artificial nature of schools and nurseries – as we describe later in this chapter – than to develop new and unnatural ways of talking to the children. After all, no parent – irrespective of social class – would use anything like a conscious 'dialogue strategy' when talking to their children, and perhaps many children would find it odd when their teachers start talking in this way.

The project has undoubtedly been a great success with teachers. The first stage attracted over 1,500 nursery and infant teachers to ninety-two working groups, and about 1,350 of these stayed on for the second year. These figures not only reflect the great interest and enthusiasm which the project initially aroused, but also demon-

strate its success in retaining teachers' interest throughout the two years – the drop-out rate, compared with
most forms of adult education, is remarkably low.
Clearly there are many nursery teachers who feel that
traditional practice can be improved on, and who are
eager to take up new ways of working with children.
Indeed, the main achievements of the project have
perhaps been in giving teachers methods for looking at
and assessing individual children, and in showing them
there are ways of working with young children which
go beyond free play, but still retain the child's interest
and enjoyment.

Two other projects are also looking at ways in which
nursery teachers can intervene more in children's play.
One of these – a Schools' Council project directed by
Geoffrey Matthews from Chelsea College – is concerned
with introducing *mathematical* ideas into nursery schools.
Although operating on a smaller scale than Joan
Tough's project, it is based on similar ideas, and encourages teachers to intervene more systematically
in children's play in order to promote particular
mathematical concepts. In another project, Peter
Smith of Sheffield University has been looking at the
effects of 'fantasy play tutoring' on nursery school
children. This is an idea from Israel and America, in
which a 'play tutor' intervenes in the children's pretend
games, feeding in ideas and helping to sustain the game.
Several American studies have shown that this kind of
intervention not only increases the level of children's
play, but also leads to gains in language and thinking
skills. Peter Smith has found similar gains among
English children: however, his research suggests that
these gains are mainly due to the close contact between
tutor and child, rather than to the play tutoring *per se*.

Swimming for under-fives

While much can be done through intervening in children's play, there are still many things that children cannot learn in this way, and for which different teaching methods are required. This applies particularly to skills such as reading, writing, playing a musical instrument or swimming. This last activity was discussed in a report prepared jointly by the Redgrave Educational Trust and the Advisory Centre for Education [6]. The report argues that one of the prime reasons for teaching young children to swim is safety: every year more than a hundred children under five are drowned in Great Britain alone, and drowning kills more children in this age-range than in the range from five to fourteen. Children do not have to be good swimmers to improve their chances of surviving a fall into water: being able to float, or tread water, or feeling sufficiently confident not to panic, can all help if an accident occurs. There are, of course, other advantages to teaching young children to swim: it can improve their general health and physical co-ordination, as well as giving them tremendous confidence and satisfaction. There is also the joy of simply splashing around in the water, which is particularly appealing to children of this age.

The report describes an experimental project in Cambridgeshire in which three- and four-year-old children attending nursery school were taught to swim by a specially trained nursery teacher. The project ran for about two terms, and the children were taken for lessons three times a week. By the end of the project seventeen of the twenty-two children who had taken part were described by their teacher as 'water safe' – an American term meaning they could swim or paddle their way to safety if they fell into deep water. None of the children were 'water safe' when the project started. A few of the children became very good swimmers, and were able to swim and dive in at the deep end. The writer of the report, Lindsey March, gives her own impressions of their progress:

I first saw the children on the last day of the summer term. The largest number of lessons any of them had had was thirty. Three of the most experienced children were taken to the diving board in the deep end of the main pool. They paddled along the board in their flippers, and bounced, and plop! in they went like so many ducklings into a pond, and dog-paddled to the side.

For the head of the school the most noticeable effect was the good health of those taking part – they were away from school much less frequently than the other children. The great majority of parents also commented favourably on the experiment.

'An increased confidence and self assurance that really did seem to stem from her swimming experience...'

'A very positive love of water grew and a delight in being in it...'

'Made a tremendous impression on our child...'

'Really out-weighed all the other things happening at the nursery school at the time...'

'Last year's holiday was a delight to all of us and many on-lookers because she was able to swim at such a young age...'

The Cambridgeshire project was obviously a great success – but how easily can the idea be taken up by other nurseries? Some nursery schools and day nurseries already take small groups of children to the special training pool at their local baths. Although the children may not be learning to swim systematically, as in the Cambridgeshire project, they are nevertheless gaining confidence in the water. In one day nursery we know, visits to the local pool were introduced at the initiative of parents – a good example of parents exercising some say in what their children do at nursery. Parents accompany the staff and children for swimming sessions whenever possible, as it's important to have plenty of adults at hand.

A problem for many nurseries is getting access to a pool which is warm and shallow enough for very young children. Most pools in this country are at least 2ft 6ins. or 3ft deep at the shallow end – too deep for the majority of under-fives to stand up safely or comfortably. There is also the water temperature: small children get cold more quickly than adults, and in any case all learners need water which is warmer than average as they are not kept warm by swimming. Specially designed and heated learner pools are obviously one answer, but a more ambitious solution is for nurseries to acquire their own pools. The ideal in this respect is the Vanessa Nursery School in West London, which was designed around a swimming pool at the instigation of Vanessa Redgrave – she had apparently been very impressed at the effect which learning to swim had had on her own child. Few schools can hope to emulate the Vanessa, but it is still possible to set up a smaller pool in an existing school without vast expense. Nursery classes in infants schools are particularly well placed for this kind of venture, as the cost – and use – of the pool could be shared with the rest of the infants school.

What methods are used to teach swimming to the under-fives? Can nursery teachers be easily trained for the purpose or can specialist swimming teachers be trained to work with younger children? In this country the idea of teaching such young children is relatively new, and there are very few courses for teachers who want to be specially trained. The methods used in the Cambridgeshire project were originally developed in California, but the child-centred principles on which they are based would be very appealing to most British nursery teachers. The project teacher put great emphasis on the children's enjoyment and curiosity, and she was concerned throughout that being in the water should be fun. Before any lessons started she got the children to blow bubbles in basins of warm water at the school, and when they felt confident at doing this, she encouraged them to put their faces under the water. When the children could do this for a count of ten they were ready for their first lesson. In the pool itself the teacher devised games to make each lesson more interesting and she encouraged the children to make up their own games as well. At each stage she concentrated on developing the children's confidence and enjoyment before proceeding to the next stage. As with the Schools' Council Language Project, this project shows that young children can be helped to develop skills by methods which go beyond the traditional free play approach, but which still retain the child's interest and enjoyment.

Play and 'real life'

One of the dangers that arises when nurseries become exclusively devoted to play is that they become cut off from the wider realities of life, and thus create unnecessary restrictions on the kinds of things children might be learning about. In a typical session of nursery education the children will spend almost all their time playing with toys and puzzles, or painting and making models, and their interests inevitably become centred on these activities. The nursery staff are also in danger of becoming 'play-centred': they spend all day surrounded by toys and play, putting out and putting away play equipment and talking to the children about their play. It is rare to see staff involved in the activities they provide for the children – such as painting or digging in the sand – and rarer still to see them carrying out 'adult' work, such as cooking or sewing, mending a bicycle, mixing cement or going to the shops. Conversation between staff and children thus tends to focus on play, toys and nursery activities, as these are the only experiences they have in common. In addition the children tend to get an unnatural and one-sided view of the staff, who can often appear to be people without lives of their own. Even when children express an interest in the staff as people, the teachers often put up their 'professional' barriers and reveal very little about themselves.

The idea of separate institutions exclusively devoted to children's play and cut off from the mainstream of adult life is very much a product of modern industrial societies. In pre-industrial societies children were much more integrated with the adult world of work and social activity, and acquired valuable learning experiences through directly participating in these activities. Such societies can still be found today, as we can see from the following description of a contemporary East African village:

A child of three to four years of age is helping his mother to sort out the dry from the wet coffee beans which have been laid out in the sun. In carrying out this task he is demonstrating and perfecting those skills of visual discrimination, concept formation and fine manual control which his western counterparts acquire through play with picture dominoes, manipulative toys and the like ... two of his siblings, just a few years older, are washing the family eating vessels. They are not 'playing' at housekeeping, they are actively engaged in it, and by so doing are incidentally acquiring the conceptual knowledge about the properties of water which the western school system aims to impart through play with 'water trays'.[7]

It would be a mistake to idealize African childhood, just as it would be wrong to hanker after a return to pre-industrial Britain. Almost all pre-industrial societies are characterized by high levels of infant mortality and childhood disease, and the work which children do – or did – in such societies is often harsh, boring and repetitive. The purpose of making the comparison is to put our modern play-centred nurseries into a broader perspective, and to show what may be lost when play becomes over-emphasized. But how could things be otherwise? How can we broaden children's experiences when they are in nurseries, and compensate them for the loss of much that is meaningful in the adult world?

Some ideas as to how this might be done are suggested by the Children's Community Centre in North London. This centre, as we have already seen, is a community nursery, set up and controlled by parents, and based in a converted terrace house. From the start the parents and workers were concerned that the experiences offered to the children should be less 'institutionalized' than is typically found in other nurseries, and they have actively sought ways to realize this aim. There is, for example, a strong emphasis on *outings*: the workers try and arrange an outing *every day* and all the children are encouraged to go:

> The kids really enjoy trips on public transport and if you're well organized (in small groups) it's not as nervewracking as you might think with a large bunch of under-fives on a tube or bus ... we've been on trips to Kew Gardens, the Science Museum, Big Ben, London Zoo, Kings Cross Station and Heathrow Airport, to name a few ... In addition to big outings there has been endless observation of work on the local building site, visits to the bus station, bank, post office, pet shop, florist, and other local sources of interest ... [8]

Another important feature of the CCC is that the workers have consciously tried to avoid the friendly but detached attitude to the children which is often developed by those working 'professionally' with young children, and have instead sought the more intimate relationships which are characteristic of people closely involved in each other's lives. This does not just mean cuddling the children when they are upset, but involves the adults opening up their own feelings to the children, and letting the children experience them as real people with joys and sorrows of their own.

The CCC also aims to involve children as far as possible in the day-to-day running of the nursery:

> We try to involve them in everything that happens at the

Centre so that they will come to feel that the place is theirs: they come out shopping for some of the food, help to cut up fruit or butter bread for snacks, go to the launderette to do the washing, make rice pudding or jelly for dessert. Some of the older kids are so competent now that they are truly helpful and their labour is really positively employed! We're not just trying to keep them occupied in asking them to lay the tables but believe that they are sharing the work in doing so. Why should one person do all the work for all the kids? Why don't we share the jobs and work for each other instead?[8]

In this respect they are helped by having a relatively small centre (fifteen to twenty children), and being based in a converted house. As in the children's own homes the kitchen becomes an important focus of activities:

The ground floor has the kitchen at the back, opening on to the front room where we have snacks and lunch. At other times the tables are used for small games – Lego, jigsaws, playdough etc. An adult who is preparing food in the kitchen, with or without help from the kids, is within easy talking distance of the tables. The free flow between kitchen and front room means that making meals is not, as in an institution, an isolated activity which produces food as if by magic: it's part of the life of the Centre and at best involves the kids in sharing work with adults and doing something for each other.[8]

The importance which the Children's Community Centre attaches to involving children in 'real-life' situations might not be shared by many nursery staff. These staff might feel that children of this age are too young to be involved in such activities, and that their time would be more valuably spent in freely chosen play. In reply the CCC workers would argue that children of this age *can* make an important contribution to the working of the centre, and that they enjoy doing so. However one should not expect this to happen instantaneously: when the CCC first introduced a meal-time routine which allowed the children to serve themselves, pour their own drinks, clear away the dirty dishes and scrape the plates, they had to undergo a 'chaotic, nightmarish first week' before things settled down. Nor are the CCC children in any way deprived of play experience. Play is an important part of the children's day, and they spend a good deal of time in the usual nursery activities – creative art activities, building bricks, acting roles in the home area, doing puzzles etc. But the Centre children are having other experiences too: sharing the adult world of shops and launderettes, of buses and tubes, of buying and preparing their own food. By being given responsibilities within the CCC itself, the children are being offered a chance to make a positive contribution to their lives – to feel, even if only for a short part of the day, valued and worthwhile instead of small, helpless and dependent on adults.

While the Children's Community Centre involves children in domestic work, nurseries in other parts of the world involve children in different kinds of work. In China, for example, practically all schools have their own plot of land for the children to grow crops on:

The kindergartens (for children aged between three and seven years) are no exception to this, and the small children take their watering, weeding and planting duties very seriously. They are not encouraged to do this simply to see how things grow, but also to experience what working on the land means, so that they can begin to appreciate what a peasant's life is like.[9]

In China it is also common for young children to spend a small amount of time each week in 'productive labour'. A team of eminent American psychologists who visited China recently reported on what this means:

Kindergarten teachers explained that love for manual labour is considered a virtue in Chinese society, and that each kindergarten is called on to organize its own 'factory'. All the kindergarten children take part in some form of manual labour each week, typically for two twenty-minute periods. These periods are not considered demonstrations or exercises, but serious attempts to get children to experience manual labour and to produce useful products.

What do children accomplish? We saw a wide variety of kindergarten factories. Children tested flashlight bulbs, folded cartons in which the bulbs were to be packed for shipment, and inserted the bulbs into the forty or so holes in each carton. Children were given bowls of beans and taught to separate bad beans and stems from good beans ... At another school children assembled and organized materials for a sewing machine factory. Some children tied plastic string onto labels and others opened and stacked small plastic envelopes into which screws or small parts could later be placed. All of these were activities in which the children could be successful and through which they could see that their efforts resulted in products that were useful to themselves or to other people. In one case at least, the children were taken to see the factory where their own products were used.[10]

We are not suggesting that these Chinese ideas are necessarily feasible or in all respects desirable in British nurseries – the conditions in the two countries are obviously poles apart. Rather they show what is possible when a society decides that children should learn about more than simply the world of play.

Hidden values (or what teachers aren't aware of teaching)

These examples of young Chinese children growing crops and experiencing 'productive labour' illustrate an important difference between the Chinese and British education systems. In China teachers and child-care workers are much more explicit about the *values* they are aiming to transmit, and have consciously developed ways of putting these aims into practice. In Britain this happens all too rarely – partly because there is less general agreement on values in our society, and partly because many teachers would regard such a process as 'indoctrination' and foreign to the liberal traditions of British education. Yet the transmission of attitudes and values is so much a part of everyday life in schools that it often goes entirely unnoticed.

The values which teachers are consciously trying to put across may often conflict with the messages which are implicitly contained in their teaching methods. Most nursery teachers, for example, attach a good deal of importance to developing co-operation and sharing between children, and would rate 'fostering social development' highly amongst their aims. Many teachers consciously try and put these aims into practice by encouraging children to share toys, not to grab other children's property, and to take turns. Yet the implicit message contained in the free play method is very much an 'individualistic' rather than a 'co-operative' ethic. Much of the play equipment is designed and set out in a way that encourages children to play separately rather than together. At the clay table, children will usually be given separate lumps of clay on separate boards and encouraged to produce separate models, and in the painting corner individual sheets of paper are fixed to individual easels for individual paintings. Group activities, such as music, dancing and group games, used to be very popular in nurseries thirty or forty years ago, but they have now become much rarer. A recent study by Barbara Tizard and her colleagues of twelve pre-school centres found that four-year-olds spent over half their time playing on their own, rather than with other children, while for three-year-olds the proportion was over two thirds[11].

This process is by no means inevitable. Many of the basic nursery activities *can* be organized and laid out in a way that actively encourages children to play together rather than separately. Paintings can be done on large rolls of paper, big floor puzzles can be used as well as small table puzzles, and there could be more outdoor equipment like see-saws, which require co-ordinated action to make them work, rather than swings and tricycles, which do not. The staff could devise small jobs for the children – carrying large pieces of play equipment or moving tables around for milk – which require children to work together. If a child comes up and asks the teacher for help with her buckles or to put a coat on, the teacher could suggest that another child helps her instead; similarly, if a child hurts himself or is crying for some reason the teacher could suggest other children comfort him rather than doing it herself. These ideas would not be hard to put into practice – and some teachers do this kind of thing already – once the staff had made explicit what they were trying to do for the children.

Sex-role stereotyping

Another area where teachers might be unconsciously influencing young children is in their ideas about sex roles. By the age of three or four years most children have already learnt that society expects different sorts of behaviour from males and females; they know, for example, that daddies do 'real' work while mummies 'just' stay at home and look after children. There are also distinct sex differences in children's play at nursery school or playgroup: girls play more on swings and climbing frames, or with dolls, or in the Wendy house, while boys prefer trucks and tricycles, large building blocks, and miniature cars and garages. Boys are also more aggressive than girls, and spend more time in physical fighting. Some psychologists, such as Corinne Hutt[12], have suggested that these differences in behaviour are largely explained by innate biological differences between the sexes. While these differences cannot be denied, it is not clear how crucial they are in shaping differences in behaviour. What is clear, however, is that there are also massive *cultural* forces at work in our society, which must inevitably shape and influence our attitudes about how boys and girls should behave.

One major source of this sex-role stereotyping is children's picture books. Young children spend a lot of time looking at picture books or being read stories, and books provide an important source of their ideas and expectations about the world. Yet several recent studies have shown that these books contain a considerable bias against females[13, 14]. At its most basic level, there are simply far fewer female characters in children's stories: most books are about boys, men or male animals, and most deal exclusively with male adventures. There are also clear differences in the *kinds* of activity which boys and girls perform in picture books. Boys are much more often depicted in exciting and adventurous roles, usually outside the house, while girls are generally shown to be passive and housebound. When boys and girls do have adventures together, it is usually the boys who lead and the girls who follow, or the boys who have to rescue the girls. A similar bias is found in the adult roles which are portrayed. Again we find that men are usually active and predominate in out-of-doors activities, while women are generally passive and are usually shown indoors, performing service functions for the men and children in their families. One American study found that out of twenty-five females pictured in fifty-eight books, no fewer than twenty-one were wearing aprons, and this figure included a mother cat, a rabbit, a donkey and an alligator[15]!

There are many other ways in which sex-role stereotypes are transmitted to young children – by parents, by nursery teachers, by other children and by television. Indeed, this process is often so deeply ingrained in our attitudes and behaviour that many of us probably do it quite unconsciously. For example a nursery worker may ask for some 'big strong boys' to help her move some heavy chairs; or she may tell a boy that his new shoes look 'good for climbing' while his sister's shoes 'make her look really pretty'; she may suggest that a child gets her father to mend her broken tricycle, or she may ask what her mother cooked her for tea last night. Such remarks may be fairly innocuous in themselves, but repeated many times during the child's first few years they must inevitably have a persistent effect in developing and reinforcing sex-role stereotypes.

Many parents and nursery workers may feel that the formation of sex-role stereotypes is not necessarily a bad thing. What's wrong with treating boys and girls differently anyway? Might it not be important for children to identify strongly with their sex, and to model themselves on other children or adults of the same sex? Might they not be confused if we do not provide stereotypes for them to identify with?

The issues raised by these objections are clearly of great complexity. However, it seems an important general principle that young children should have as many different experiences as possible in their early years, so that they can discover for themselves the activities which they prefer and those which they do not. If certain activities are ruled out because they are not appropriate for their particular sex, then children are inevitably going to be limited in what they can do and be restricted in their development. It is also important to consider the *roles* that boys and girls are being channelled into. In the most stereotyped version, girls are expected to be passive, obedient, domestic and kind, and to service others, while boys are expected to be tough, assertive, confident and adventurous, and to be serviced by others. These roles are not neutral, but convey the underlying attitude that males are superior to females, and can expect to dominate and be serviced by them. Such a bias would be unacceptable if 'males' was replaced by 'whites' and 'females' by 'blacks': why should it be accepted as it stands?

Men in nurseries

One way in which nurseries can challenge sex-role stereotyping is by encouraging more men into working in nurseries. If the children's daily experience is of men changing nappies, cooking meals, comforting babies and developing close caring relationships with young children, they are less likely to adhere to the stereotyped view that these things can be done only by women. At present many children spend their first few years in an almost exclusively female world – both at home and in the nursery. Virtually all nursery staff are female, whether they are in nursery schools, playgroups or day nurseries. In addition, there are many children – for example those who are brought up by women living alone, or whose fathers work long hours or work away from home – who may have very little contact with men outside the nursery, and who may become uncertain or fearful in their relationships with men. Encouraging men to work in nurseries not only helps to break down sex-role stereotypes, but can also provide many children with their first close relationship with a male adult.

Why are there so few men in nurseries? Part of the problem is that, because child-care work has always been done by women, the pay, conditions of work and future prospects are poor compared with what men earn in other jobs. In addition, only a small number of men are at present prepared to break with tradition and take on this kind of work, and those men who do apply may find themselves faced with considerable opposition. One male applicant for a nursery nurse course was strongly discouraged by the local authority training officer:

I really wanted to work with young children but the training officer tried to put me right off doing the course. He said I should become a social worker instead, because I'd stand a better chance of promotion. He said it would be really dull working in a nursery all day, stuck there with all those women and kids.

Such attitudes are by no means universal, and a few local authorities are now actively encouraging men to take up nursery work. The London Borough of Camden explicitly aims to staff some of its newer nurseries with equal numbers of male and female staff, and it has generally been able to find suitable men to fill the places. In at least two of the nurseries care of very small babies has been entrusted to male workers, with very successful results.

It is important however not to underestimate the difficulties which may be experienced by men who take up working with young children. Some parents may be hesitant about leaving their children in the care of a man rather than a woman, and the onus is then on the man to show that their children are in safe and caring hands. Other men may have different problems with parents: for example, a male nursery teacher in a working-class area of London found that a number of parents disapproved of his 'soft' attitude towards the children, which they felt was not becoming of a man. They believed that a male teacher should set firmer standards of behaviour than a female teacher, and wanted him to be more authoritarian with the children. Other men may have difficulties coming to terms with their own feelings about child-care and a man's role in society, however strongly motivated they are to work with children. This is clearly demonstrated in these contributions from two men who worked at the Children's Community Centre:

'Walking past the construction site near the Centre – you have certain feelings about you being with these kids and these guys are doing all this heavy labour . . .'

'Yes, in fact the exchanges that take place [at the site] are sometimes unexpected: I usually feel that they must be thinking "Christ, that guy's got it easy" – that they're about to jeer any minute, and in fact they quite often say things like "I don't envy you that lot."'

Non-sexist books and materials

Another way in which sex-role stereotyping can be challenged is by making staff and parents aware of the stereotyping which is so large a feature of most children's books. While we would not wish to see well-tried favourites banished from the shelves, it would be a good counter-balance to introduce some of the non-sexist books that have recently been produced. Many of them simply contain straightforward children's stories in which males and females are treated equally and where boys and girls share the adventures and exciting roles.

Some nurseries have developed their own stories and songs for transmitting non-sexist ideas. A Women's Liberation Group in Birmingham who started their own playgroup have reproduced a number of these in their pamphlet. One story features a witch called Flying Fred and a giant called Big Bet. Another story tells how some children see a mouse one day at their playgroup. The mouse runs across the floor past one of the children's fathers, who shrieks and jumps on a chair! In the end it is two little girls in the playgroup who devise a clever way of catching the mouse[16].

Although much of the impetus for developing non-sexist materials has come from groups with an explicitly feminist orientation, the issue is now being taken up much more widely. In 1973, the Inner London Education Authority's Standing Committee on Career Opportunities for Women and Girls called for:

... fundamental changes in the choice of material and methods from the nursery schools upwards. We have been informed of a project put into effect in Sweden which seeks to replace early readers in which boys are invariably shown in the dominant roles with girls playing supporting parts. We feel that such a project could, with advantage, be considered here ... all possible emphasis should be given in the preparation of material ... to combat traditional attitudes and to broaden the concept of the roles of women in society.[17]

Intervening in children's play

A third way in which sexism can be challenged in nurseries is by confronting the sex-role stereotyping which often occurs in children's play. A good example of what this might mean in practice is provided by an American nursery teacher called Phyllis Greenleaf. She recalls how she used to react when children were excluded from games simply because of their sex:

> If a group of boys excluded the girls in their dramatic play – chanting 'no girls here, no girls here' ... I would smile, confident that this excluding behaviour was normal to four-year-olds and therefore not harmful. Likewise, if some girls excluded the boys from cooking in the housekeeping corner I felt no need to intervene in their free play ...[18]

At this time Phyllis Greenleaf was actively trying to confront *racist* attitudes in the children's play, and, as she herself admits, would have intervened if a group of white children had chanted 'no blacks here, no blacks here'. She gradually came to realize that she was being inconsistent in her attitudes, and was unintentionally contributing to the children's development of stereo-typed sex roles. This made her want to change the way she was teaching, and she got together with a group of other nursery teachers in Boston to work out ways in which they could confront this kind of stereotyping. Here is an example of how they started to intervene in the children's play:

> Early in the fall, three-year-olds Linda and Joanna were playing house in the outdoor kitchen. Larry, a somewhat shy boy, hesitantly walked into the playhouse to join them. He was instantly stopped by Joanna who asserted confidently 'No, Larry, you can't play here. Boys don't cook'. Linda nodded in agreement. Larry, looking somewhat rejected, began to retreat.
> At this point the teacher said, in a matter of fact way, 'Joanna, I know lots of men who like to cook, and I know many women who don't enjoy cooking.'

The kids looked up at the teacher with puzzled and interested expressions.

'Yes my daddy cooks,' Linda proudly asserted to the other kids.

'You know, I'm a woman and I don't like to cook – at least not all the time. So my husband and I both cook,' the teacher added.

Joanna especially looked baffled. Nevertheless, Larry joined the girls in the cooking. For the moment Joanna accepted this.[18]

We have described here a number of ways in which nursery staff can challenge sex-role stereotyping in young children. Of course, stereotyping and the prejudice that goes with it applies to other groups as well – such as handicapped people and ethnic minority groups, to take just two obvious examples. Nurseries can be involved in combating the racism and fear and ignorance of handicap that is so widespread in our society, and many of the methods being used to tackle sexism are equally relevant in these other areas. For example, nurseries could make a point of employing staff from a wide range of cultural groups; they could use the small but growing number of books where the children do *not* live in stereotyped, white middle-class families, but are sometimes black, or poor, or handicapped, or living with only one parent; and the staff could intervene at appropriate moments in the children's play, explaining why some children are different from others and pointing out that difference does not entail inferiority.

While it is easy enough to suggest approaches which nurseries could adopt, it is much harder to know how well they work in practice. How effective *are* these ideas in changing children's attitudes towards sexual or other stereotypes? Do the children who go to a nursery which strongly emphasizes non-sexism, for example, differ from those who do not? Are their parents more likely than others to favour sexual equality and be aware of, and opposed to, sexism? At present there is virtually no evidence with which to answer these questions, as no systematic evaluation of these nurseries has been carried out. It is possible that the influence of the nursery will be small compared with the opposing influences in the rest of society – particularly for children who spend only a short time each day in the nursery. The answer to this, of course, is not to give up the struggle within the nursery, but to extend it into the world outside.

In this chapter we have looked at a number of alternatives to free play which have been tried out in this country and abroad. Although these innovations differ in many ways, they have one important feature in common: in each case nursery staff have made explicit the concepts, skills, knowledge or values which they want children to acquire, they have devised ways of putting these aims into practice, and in some cases they have tried to evaluate their success in achieving their aims. This in itself marks an important and radical departure from current practice, for it is unusual to find this kind of self-critical discussion and evaluation of aims in nurseries today. Yet apart from the obvious benefits it provides for the children, this way of working can also be stimulating and rewarding for the staff, giving greater meaning and satisfaction to the work, and leading to closer communication between the staff themselves. Moreover, if parents are to become more involved in deciding what their children learn at nurseries – as we argued in Chapter 8 – then the open discussion of educational aims and methods will become not just a desirable but an essential feature of nursery life.

What should the educational aims of nurseries be? Is it more important to develop certain concepts or skills, or provide children with 'real-life' experiences, or to foster particular attitudes and values? How much emphasis should still be given to play? There are no 'right' answers to these and similar questions, for it is up to the staff and parents of each individual nursery to

work out together the aims and goals which they
themselves want to achieve. Nor are ideas discussed in
this chapter in any way incompatible with each other, or
with a certain amount of free play. A nursery could well
have aims in all the areas discussed here – and many
more besides – while still leaving a sizable part of the
day for more traditional play activities: the precise
balance of activities would again be something for
parents and staff to decide for themselves.

10 What is to be done?

What we want to see

Throughout this book we have argued that a good nursery service must be based on three fundamental principles: there must be enough places for all parents who want them; parents must be able to choose the age when their children can start and the hours they attend for each day; and nurseries should aim to meet the needs of all children for play, care and education. We have also argued that parents should be able to take part in decision-making, and have some say over what their children are learning in nurseries. If these principles are to be put into effect, many radical changes are required in the orientation and organization of pre-school services. These include: making one government department, at central and local level, responsible for *all* nursery services, requiring local authorities to ensure enough places in their area for all parents who want them, integrating the training and approaches of all kinds of nursery staff, setting up democratic management structures, developing alternatives to free play, and evolving new kinds of nurseries for giving these ideas concrete realization.

It would be tempting to go on and develop a blueprint of what the ideal nursery service would look like – a standard recipe based on a 'best-buy' type of nursery, to be applied in any place or circumstance. We have resisted this for a number of reasons.

First, there are in fact several types of nursery which could provide the sort of service we want to see. We are particularly enthusiastic about the concept of a 'nursery centre' – based either on the Coram Children's Centre or on the community nursery idea – because these centres represent exciting and radical departures from current practice, and are the nearest we have at present to an ideal nursery of the future. While nursery centres would hopefully form the core of any ideal nursery service, they are clearly not the only way forward. Extended-hour schools, with or without units for under-threes, salaried childminders attached to local authority nurseries, and extended-hour playgroups all have the potential to provide a wide range of hours, take children over and under three, and meet children's needs for play, care and education; all – with the exception of childminders – could allow parents to take part in decision-making and give them a say in what their children were learning. There could also be a future for ordinary playgroups – *provided* they were adequately funded and supervised, and *provided* there were other options open to parents as well. The aim of any 'ideal' nursery service would be to increase parents' choice and encourage variety rather than impose a standard model on everybody – provided everyone has equal access to all the options available.

A second argument against developing a blueprint is that every area of the country has to devise the pattern of services which best suits its particular circumstances. Areas differ greatly in traditions, existing resources and needs: what may be right for Durham could be wrong for Dorset, while the perfect answer to Manchester's needs could be a disaster in Midlothian. Even within one local authority, different services might be required for different districts. Many of the nurseries we have described have developed in urban communities, particularly in London: they may not be appropriate for other areas – particularly rural ones.

A third reason why we cannot develop a detailed blueprint is that there are still fundamental questions to be resolved about *how these services are to be provided.* While the local authority would be responsible for ensuring there were enough nursery services of adequate quality in its area, it would not necessarily have to supply all the services itself. It could do this, but it could also channel funds – from local or central government sources – to *private* nurseries and minders, to nurseries attached to *workplaces,* or to nurseries set up by *voluntary* and *community* groups, so that they were available to all parents free of charge.

What are the advantages and disadvantages of each approach?

Private nurseries and minders. Without state support, private nurseries and childminders cannot provide a service of adequate quality, at a cost that all families can afford, while ensuring proper pay and working conditions for the staff or minders. But should this support be given, whether through tax reliefs, cash benefits or vouchers to parents, or as direct subsidies to private services themselves? The *practical* arguments against it are that a private marker is very difficult to plan for or regulate: the local authotity can have only a limited idea of what is actually going on at a private minder's, and no way of preventing her shutting up shop when she feels like it. This would make it hard for the authority to guarantee to parents that the services in its area were of adequate quality, or even that there were enough places to go round.

Then there is the question of how far private provision is compatible with greater parental involvement and democratic management. Obviously, childminding presents particular problems, but even in nurseries, private ownership may be difficult to reconcile with these aims. There are also *political* arguments against the state supporting the private sector. Even with government financial aid, all families would not in practice have equal access to all private services. The most affluent would always corner the best, or at least the most expensive, and quality would be determined more by parental income and status than by the needs of children and parents.

Attitudes to the state's encouragement of private services – whether in health, welfare or education – must ultimately reflect personal political values. For some it is an attractive proposition; to us, however, it seems an unappetizing recipe for a more unjust and socially divided society.

Workplace nurseries. A second approach is for local authorities, or central government acting through local authorities, to give more support for employers wishing to provide nurseries for their employees. Given the present dearth of nursery places for working mothers this approach has obvious short-term attractions, but in the long term it has more against it than for it. The main objection is the 'tied cottage' nature of these nurseries, which hinders parents from changing jobs when they want to, and means their children are uprooted if they do. It would also mean separating the children of working parents from other children. Finally, most people work some distance from their homes and so workplace nurseries could possibly involve children in long and tiring journeys. On the other hand, such nurseries might enable children and parents to see more of each other during the day, given changes in existing practice which usually discourage such contacts.

Voluntary and community groups. A third approach is for the state to give greatly increased support to voluntary and community initiatives. In practice, this would mean putting existing playgroups on a secure financial footing and helping some to develop a wider range of hours and ages; encouraging local groups to set up and run community nurseries; and ensuring that all playgroups and community nurseries were adequately housed and equipped, as well as being staffed by paid workers, with salary and working conditions similar to those offered in state nurseries. Parents would be actively involved in management and could help in other ways too.

State funding of voluntary initiatives on this scale is virtually unheard-of in Britain, but it is well established in Denmark. The Danish government pays up to 85 per cent of the costs of any school with twelve children or more, provided it meets certain minimum standards[1]. Such a system would open up tremendous opportunities for parent- and community-inspired innovations like the Children's Community Centre, as well as for innovations started by voluntary organizations, like the Coram Children's Centre, and could lead to a constructive dialogue between the state and voluntary sectors, with each learning new ideas from the other. It would give parents a wider choice in what was available to them, and above all would allow them – as in Danish schools – to have a much greater say in what was happening to their children in the nurseries.

There are however drawbacks to this approach. Relying heavily on local initiatives would result in considerable variation from one area to the next. Parents would have far more choice in some areas than in others, and, as in the private sector, this could also slow progress to greater parent control in the *state* sector by creaming off the more articulate and involved parents to the voluntary sector: instead of achieving more democratic management and greater parental involvement in *all* nurseries, we could end up by concentrating these opportunities in *one* group of nurseries only. The end product could too easily become a two-tier and socially divisive system. The most serious objection, however, is that it could be seen by central and local government as a cheap option, and a way of avoiding their own responsibility to provide services. Rather than the state encouraging parent initiatives to enrich and add variety to the services in an area, parents could find that the state was depending on them to

provide the services themselves – without giving them
enough resources to do it properly.

Will it happen? The politics of nurseries

Whichever way it is provided, a nursery service along
the lines we propose would of course cost much more
than the present limited service. In a society with a
gross domestic product of £95,400 million in 1976, and
which in the same year spent £3 billion on tobacco and
£6 billion on alcohol, the question is not whether the
extra cost could be afforded but whether it will be. The
real issue is therefore *political*.

Major steps forward in social policy invariably derive
not from altruism or the dispassionate application of
knowledge, but from political or economic threat or
necessity, as defined by those who hold power. Politically
and economically weak groups, such as pre-school
children and their mothers, are unlikely to pose such a
threat. There has, it is true, been some increase in the
last decade or so in resources going to nurseries. A few
thousand day nursery places have been added, and
nursery education is steadily expanding to meet a
commitment to provide part-time places for all three-
and four-year-olds whose parents want this limited
provision. But neither of these steps, nor the small
sums spent by local authorities on supporting playgroups or childminders, add up to anything like a
nursery service on demand, and government expenditure on nursery services remains modest, running in
1976/7 to about £35 millions* by social services departments on council day nurseries and playgroups [2] and
£153 millions on schooling for under-fives[3]. By

* This is net expenditure, after fees are taken into account. The
figure also refers to England and Wales only, while education expenditure includes Scotland as well: the inclusion of Scotland would
probably add 10–15 per cent to the total for council day nurseries
and playgroups.

comparison, expenditure on primary, secondary and further/higher education in the same period was £1,540 millions, £2,000 millions and £1,930 millions respectively[3]. Throughout this century, any available funds have usually been channelled to secondary and higher education because these have been seen as paying economic dividends – such as a better educated workforce – which nurseries could not equal. The recent limited expansion of nursery education came primarily because it was believed that such early education could have an impact on *later schooling*, and not for any more immediate benefits it might produce.

The relationship between the powerlessness of mothers and children and the inadequacy of services for them is most clearly seen in the response – or lack of it – by successive governments to the needs of working mothers. In the Second World War, the urgent need for women workers led to a rapid increase in day nurseries, from 194 in 1941 to 1,450 only three years later[4]. After the war, the importance (to those in power) of married women in the economy rapidly diminished and it seemed necessary and appropriate for them to return to their pre-war position as housewives and as a peripheral and minor part of the labour force. Day nursery places were run down to pre-war levels, and even though mothers have stubbornly persisted in going out to work, there have been virtually no services provided for them since then. The only exception to this policy occurred in the sixties, when the state needed more nurses and teachers: it is surely significant that these are among the few groups of women workers with substantial public investment in their training – and these women alone were encouraged to use nurseries and go back to work[5]. For all other women, the doctrine of maternal deprivation was called on to justify the lack of nurseries and the need for them to stay at home with their children. This doctrine was used to cover up the real reasons for the general inaction – that the position of women, and particularly mothers, in the labour force is so lowly, and investment in their education and training so limited, that it is uneconomic for the state to introduce adequate and therefore costly employment and child-care measures for their benefit.

What successive governments have in fact done is implicitly to encourage the growth of private child-minding, by providing no alternative provision and by placing a minimum of obstacles in the way; they have, for example, kept the regulation and supervision of minders to a minimum. Private minding has great advantages for governments and employers: it requires little or no investment from either; fees are related to what low-paid workers can afford; and the service expands and contracts with little cost except to minders and mothers. It is, in short, ideally suited to meet the needs of a disadvantaged and weak sector of the labour force; indeed, childminders themselves form part of that sector, sharing the low pay and status, minimal training, poor job prospects and high turnover of the mothers who use them.

Another reason for the low priority given to nursery services is that those who hold political and economic power are predominantly men, with little or no under-standing of the realities of motherhood, and no day-to-day responsibilities themselves for pre-school children. Imagine the reaction of government and employers to a situation where all civil servants, middle managers and professional men with pre-school children suddenly found themselves actually responsible for the daily care of their children. Would they be left to make their own arrangements as best they could? Or be given an out-dated list of local childminders and be left to find one with a vacancy? Or told to choose between a family and a career? Or would nursery services and employment measures suddenly become a major item on the economic and political agenda, an essential feature of the industrial strategy, while company nurseries or child-care allowances joined the company car, BUPA membership and help with school fees as a standard fringe benefit?

The under-developed state of nursery services is not solely a sin of omission, the result of mothers and young children having too little economic and political muscle. As we saw in Chapter 2, many people believe that nursery attendance, and the separation of mother and child that it entails, may be positively harmful; others find the prospect of change in the organization of family life, sex roles and the upbringing of children generally unpalatable. Rather than change, they would prefer to see the 'traditional' model of family life – two parents with mother at home full-time – restored and strengthened. The concept of equal opportunities is ignored or accorded lip service but little else. The depression, isolation and other stresses so widespread among mothers, and the increasing numbers going out to work, are regarded not as a sign of basic weaknesses in their preferred model but as the result of temporary difficulties that can be righted – usually for a fairly modest outlay of public funds and putting few demands on fathers, employers and the providers of services.

This position, with its rejection of a widespread state-supported nursery service, is exemplified in the following excerpt from an interview with Lynda Chalker, then Conservative Party Social Services spokesperson and now a Junior Minister in the Department of Health.

'The Tory Party has always concentrated more on the caring role of women than on their industrial role. We are committed to the concept of equal opportunity but once the right exists in law, the practice must be left to the individual . . .'

[Mrs Chalker] is against the idea that child-care should always be paid for out of the rates. 'If someone is going out to work and has taken a decision to have children as well, the financial responsibility for that child must in toto be theirs.' Nursery centres, recently advocated in the TUC Under Fives Report, make her think of Russian nurseries. Instead, Mrs Chalker favours 'an easing of taxation so that there is a little more in the family coffers to allow people some choice.' [Angela Phillips, the interviewer] pointed out that private day care of decent quality costs £25–£40 per child per week. [Mrs Chalker] said most people could find a service that was cheaper than that and childminders, for example, were considerably cheaper and performed a much needed service.

She can see no prospect of provision for paternity leave, to enable parents to share the burden of child-care more equally. 'It would disrupt industry in a way which perhaps has not been fully thought through by its advocates'...

She would like to see encouragement of more informal community-based arrangements whereby women at home could get occasional breaks from child-care. Did that mean more money for things like 'drop in' playcentres? 'Do local community groups really need more money,' she said, 'or do councils just say we must give it to them?'

'Maybe in years to come, the country will look at the labour market and decide that, perhaps, it would be better for women with children to stay at home'...

The Tories are committed to equal opportunity for women in the workplace. Their policy is distinctive in the sense that they do not see a state-subsidized network of child-care facilities as an essential ingredient of that equal opportunity. For Lynda Chalker there appear to be three possibilities: women who can afford to make private child-care arrangements should be free to do so; others will choose to take time out from paid work to look after their own young children; others again will have to look to volunteers in the local community to provide child-care facilities without government cash.[6]

It should be clear from all that has gone before in this book that we fundamentally disagree with the views expressed above and the attitudes underlying them. However it would be naïve not to accept that such views are widely held – by supporters of all major political parties – and that they act as a powerful brake to any government introducing measures to develop nurseries, change employment practices or otherwise alter the status quo.

Which way from here?

It would be inappropriate to end on a wholly pessimistic note, for there are many hopeful signs that things may be changing. The growth of the women's movement since the late sixties has helped many women to realize and understand their secondary role in society. Mothers in particular have begun to see how the organization of child-care in our society reduces their opportunities in so many areas of life. The raising of women's consciousness in this way has led to heightened political awareness and here lies the first step towards political strength. Many local nursery campaigns have sprung up, fighting for more nursery places, more say for parents in nurseries and better training and conditions for all who work with under-fives; students and staff in various colleges are also pressing for better nursery facilities. Some of these groups, like the Birmingham Women's Liberation Group, have even set up and run their own nurseries. The Leeds Animation Group has produced a short cartoon film – 'We Want Nurseries' – to get the message across, while the London Nursery Campaign has published a handbook for parents and local groups on how to establish and run a community nursery. There are also national campaigns – such as the Campaign for Nursery Education – which are lobbying government to provide more nurseries.

There are signs of a real and growing interest in the needs of working mothers from the trade-union movement. Some local trades councils have been actively engaged in supporting local campaigns, while the TUC has adopted a policy calling for free and flexible nurseries for all parents who want them, as well as more democratic management structures[7]. Reports from the 'Think Tank' [8] and the Equal Opportunities Commission [9] have also urged the need for increased provision for children with working parents, as well as more co-ordination between the providers of services.

Recently, too, Shirley Williams, then the Secretary of State for Education and Science, has spoken of:

the need to establish more fairly the concept of mutual parental responsibilities, fatherhood as well as motherhood. Fathers must be made aware that the job of looking after the family can no longer be left to their wives . . . We can use the margin that current tragically high levels of unemployment gives us to make working hours more flexible, to create more short-day and part-time jobs, to reduce overtime, to allow a margin of time off to both parents which can be used when a member of the family is ill. In other words, work should be adapted not just to individuals but also to families.[10]

In private life more men and women are questioning whether the exercise of traditional sex roles within the nuclear family is the only, or even the best, way of life and parenthood for them. Finally, as we have seen throughout this book, there are many people working in or close to nurseries who are struggling against the restraints of tradition, dogma and bureaucracy, and are actively searching for new ways to provide better nurseries for parents and their children.

All these signs are encouraging and suggest that the potential for change is present, though it will not be realized overnight. Though all these activities and indicators are moving together in a common direction, they do not as yet add up to a major movement requiring urgent political response. The unanswered question at the moment is whether society, and those in positions of power and influence, will attempt to reject or even fight equal opportunities, the evolution of more varied forms of family life and parenthood, the encouragement of men to take a greater part in child-care and the development of the sort of nurseries we have advocated – or whether they will accept these ideas and create new policies to help provide a better life for women, men and children.

Appendix

The table that follows shows, for each local authority in England, Scotland and Wales, rates of provision for different types of nursery provision. It should not however be used without reference to the notes below, which explain in detail its background and limitations.

What are rates of provision? They are the *number of places* provided in different types of provision *per 1,000* children under five in the population. Thus, if an authority has 600 places in day nurseries and a total pre-school population of 30,000, its rate of provision for day nurseries is 20.

The figures given are not however as cut-and-dried as this introduction might suggest. The source used for nursery schools, classes and reception centres [1] gives the number of part-time and full-time *pupils* in nursery schools and classes, rather than *places*. We have therefore assumed that there are two part-time pupils per place, but this makes no allowance for any vacant places, which there probably are in some nursery classes (especially in areas where the demand is for more than part-time provision).

The reception class figures refer to the number of *under-fives* in reception classes – and not the total number of places in these classes, many of which will be occupied by children over five.

The other point to be borne in mind is that some places provide longer periods of care than others. Thus, most playgroup places are for two and a half hours a day, in term-time only, while nearly all day nursery places are available for eight or more hours a day, throughout the year. Similarly, 'minders' include some 70,000 all-day places (plus some 18,000 part-time places). Each day nursery or all-day childminder place therefore provides far more hours of care per year than each playgroup place and therefore accounts for a proportionately larger share of total resources.

How up-to-date are the figures? For English and Welsh authorities, the nursery education and reception class figures are for 31 December 1976, while all day nursery, playgroup and minder figures are for 31 March 1977, the latest date for which statistics were available at the time of writing. For Scottish authorities, education figures refer to September 1976, the remainder to March 1976 [1–3]. Calculations of rates of provision are based on estimates of numbers of children under five at 30 June 1976. There are no published estimates for 1977.

The time-lag between 1976/7 and publication of this book means that the situation in each local authority will have changed somewhat in that period. Changes in population will alter the proportion of children attending nurseries even if the number of places available does not change. Some authorities may have a spurt of new openings for some types of provision, so moving them up the league table, while others may well have closed some places as part of their programme of spending cuts. Having made these qualifications, the table does give a fair indication of patterns of provision, and relative positions and levels of provision are unlikely to change markedly over a short period of time.

What order are the local authorities in? They have been organized according to the type of authority they are. First come the thirty-two London boroughs with those in Inner and Outer London grouped separately (no separate education figures are given for the boroughs in the Inner London Education Authority area since they are not published). Then come metropolitan districts within the six metropolitan counties – Merseyside, South and West Yorkshire, Tyne and Wear, West Midlands, Greater Manchester – followed by the thirty-nine English non-metropolitan counties. Finally, the Welsh and Scottish councils are listed.

How to read the table. Types of provision have been grouped as far as possible according to who provides them. Thus, columns 1–4 include provision made directly by local authorities – council nursery schools and classes, day nurseries and playgroups – and a figure for these types combined. Because reception classes are not primarily for children under five, though an increasing number of these children have been admitted to them in recent years, they are shown separately in column 9. Column 5 covers voluntary and most private play-groups; since the former are by far the most common, this column gives some indication of the contribution of the voluntary sector, which ranges from local parent-run playgroups to playgroups run by large charities such as Save the Children Fund. Finally, columns 6–8 show provision mainly made by private bodies and individuals. 'Day nurseries' (column 6) includes workplace, private and voluntary nurseries providing all-day care – though the voluntary nurseries are very much in the minority. Column 7 covers all-day and part-time minders; some of the latter (who account for 20 per cent of minder places nationally) are in practice individuals running small playgroups in their homes. Column 8 gives the total for columns 6 and 7 combined.

The table does not include places in private schools or places with unregistered childminders.

Two other points should be made. Figures have been rounded up (if 0.5 or over) or down (if 0.4 or less) and an asterisk indicates 0.4 or less: and there are no figures for minders in Newham, because of an apparent error in the reported number.

	1	2	3	4	5
	Provided by local authority				Voluntary/ Private
	Nursery schools/ classes	Day nurseries	Play-groups	Total	Play-groups
Outer London					
Barking	50	15	—	65	100
Barnet	43	13	1	56	135
Bexley	20	4	—	24	170
Brent	42	42	—	84	94
Bromley	4	3	—	7	239
Croydon	16	8	—	25	152
Ealing	39	18	5	62	89
Enfield	25	6	—	31	130
Haringey	64	19	13	95	51
Harrow	26	9	—	35	157
Havering	9	12	—	22	145
Hillingdon	50	14	—	64	133
Hounslow	48	14	—	62	88
Kingston	63	12	—	75	99
Merton	63	15	—	78	107
Newham	77	14	11	102	74
Redbridge	21	8	2	30	247
Richmond	22	15	—	37	214
Sutton	42	5	—	47	148
Waltham Forest	40	19	—	59	141
Inner London	79	40	6	125	102
Camden	—	95	30	—	126
Greenwich	—	13	31	—	104
Hackney	—	37	10	—	68
Hammersmith	—	50	—	—	56
Islington	—	62	—	—	118
Kensington	—	54	—	—	155
Lambeth	—	37	—	—	102
Lewisham	—	17	—	—	104
Southwark	—	41	—	—	104
Tower Hamlets	—	40	—	—	73

6	7	8	9	10	11
Other private provision			LEA	Total	Total
Day nurseries	Minders	Total	Reception classes	Excluding reception classes	Including reception classes
—	24	24	107	190	297
2	18	21	106	212	318
14	37	50	48	244	292
25	68	93	115	270	385
10	40	50	52	296	348
2	35	37	98	213	307
4	56	60	115	211	326
2	32	34	110	195	305
10	33	43	111	189	300
6	51	57	68	249	316
3	18	21	105	187	292
3	14	17	119	214	332
33	31	65	128	214	342
15	76	91	91	265	365
16	38	54	106	238	345
5	?	?	43	?	?
18	27	45	45	322	367
16	65	80	105	332	437
36	34	70	4	265	269
4	23	27	71	227	298
18	47	64	55	291	345
45	27	72	—	—	—
4	45	50	—	—	—
18	58	77	—	—	—
6	46	52	—	—	—
19	35	54	—	—	—
35	37	73	—	—	—
17	49	66	—	—	—
3	57	59	—	—	—
—	44	44	—	—	—
13	35	47	—	—	—

	1	2	3	4	5
	Provided by local authority				*Voluntary/ Private*
	Nursery schools/ classes	Day nurseries	Play- groups	Total	Play- groups

Inner London – cont.

Wandsworth	—	29	—	—	107
Westminster	—	60	8	—	64

Merseyside

Knowsley	22	29	—	50	49
Liverpool	73	29	—	102	81
St Helens	29	5	—	34	103
Sefton	46	14	—	60	87
Wirral	32	10	—	41	102

South Yorkshire

Barnsley	78	—	—	78	80
Doncaster	65	—	—	65	60
Rotherham	75	—	—	75	69
Sheffield	56	7	—	64	104

West Yorkshire

Bradford	61	14	—	75	71
Calderdale	70	12	—	81	105
Kirklees	34	9	—	43	92
Leeds	33	9	—	43	106
Wakefield	64	4	—	68	69

Tyne & Wear

Gateshead	37	7	1	45	100
Newcastle	72	14	6	92	107
N. Tyneside	54	3	1	59	73
S. Tyneside	60	20	—	79	55
Sunderland	44	8	—	53	79

6	7	8	9	10	11
Other private provision			*LEA*	*Total*	*Total*
Day nurseries	Minders	Total	Reception classes	Excluding reception classes	Including reception classes
24	64	87	—	—	—
55	29	84	—	—	—
—	*	*	66	100	166
22	9	31	131	214	345
—	17	17	134	154	288
13	22	35	130	182	310
4	25	29	112	172	284
—	11	11	75	169	244
3	15	18	145	143	288
—	5	5	83	149	232
—	11	11	83	179	262
5	28	34	86	179	265
2	15	17	137	203	341
2	21	23	70	158	228
19	33	53	90	202	292
—	6	6	95	144	239
1	8	9	138	154	291
13	18	31	133	230	363
5	7	13	142	145	287
25	8	33	141	167	309
2	5	7	144	139	283

	1	2	3	4	5
	Provided by local authority				*Voluntary/ Private*
	Nursery schools/ classes	Day nurseries	Play- groups	Total	Play- groups

West Midlands

Birmingham	65	19	—	84	95
Coventry	37	19	—	56	98
Dudley	50	—	1	51	74
Sandwell	59	6	2	68	59
Solihull	32	5	—	37	100
Walsall	74	7	—	81	50
Wolverhampton	68	7	—	74	83

Greater Manchester

Bolton	77	13	—	90	79
Bury	23	8	—	31	101
Manchester	175	37	—	212	57
Oldham	51	14	1	66	88
Rochdale	51	16	—	68	68
Salford	84	16	—	100	63
Stockport	26	9	—	35	123
Tameside	41	29	2	73	59
Trafford	20	26	—	46	102
Wigan	28	9	—	37	63

Non-metropolitan counties

Avon	34	9	—	43	140
Bedfordshire	46	7	—	53	133
Berkshire	42	2	—	44	133
Buckinghamshire	22	1	—	23	171
Cambridgeshire	25	5	—	30	117
Cheshire	32	7	*	40	97
Cleveland	58	10	7	76	91
Cornwall	20	—	—	20	163
Cumbria	37	4	—	41	136

6	7	8	9	10	11
Other private provision			*LEA*	*Total*	*Total*
Day nurseries	Minders	Total	Reception classes	Excluding reception classes	Including reception classes
13	25	37	63	216	278
4	38	41	132	195	328
6	12	18	35	143	178
2	14	16	133	143	276
—	29	29	159	166	325
7	18	25	118	157	275
—	9	9	66	166	232
2	17	18	140	186	326
—	20	20	130	151	281
9	12	21	84	290	375
8	30	38	133	192	326
11	25	36	139	171	311
7	15	22	141	186	327
7	23	30	132	188	320
3	15	18	126	149	276
10	61	71	21	219	241
—	18	18	131	117	248
8	18	26	69	208	278
17	33	50	35	236	271
6	28	34	25	212	236
5	36	41	30	235	265
8	47	54	97	200	298
3	21	24	81	160	242
20	5	25	88	191	279
1	9	11	90	193	283
5	5	10	126	187	313

	1	2	3	4	5
	Provided by local authority				*Voluntary/ Private*
	Nursery schools/ classes	Day nurseries	Play-groups	Total	Play-groups

Non-metropolitan counties – cont.

	1	2	3	4	5
Derbyshire	43	7	—	50	104
Devon	13	2	—	15	158
Dorset	9	3	—	12	168
Durham	51	4	—	55	93
East Sussex	12	5	—	17	150
Essex	10	3	—	13	151
Gloucestershire	—	2	*	3	159
Hampshire	8	4	—	12	186
Hereford & Worcester	7	1	*	9	141
Hertfordshire	55	6	—	61	128
Humberside	39	2	1	42	95
I. of Wight	10	—	—	10	157
Kent	8	*	—	8	137
Lancashire	30	16	2	48	85
Leicestershire	54	9	2	65	126
Lincolnshire	14	2	1	17	135
Norfolk	9	1	—	11	136
N. Yorkshire	29	4	2	34	140
Northamptonshire	18	2	—	20	137
Northumberland	23	2	6	30	102
Nottinghamshire	55	9	1	64	100
Oxfordshire	28	3	—	31	152
Salop	18	—	—	18	133
Somerset	7	3	—	10	155
Staffordshire	54	4	—	58	106
Suffolk	16	2	—	18	135
Surrey	22	4	—	26	174
Warwickshire	28	—	*	29	140
West Sussex	7	—	—	7	172
Wiltshire	1	—	—	1	130

6	7	8	9	10	11
Other private provision			*LEA*	*Total*	*Total*
Day nurseries	Minders	Total	Reception classes	Excluding reception classes	Including reception classes
*	15	15	77	169	247
3	13	17	58	189	248
13	41	54	35	234	268
—	6	6	135	153	289
19	19	38	81	206	287
6	32	38	47	202	249
10	33	43	69	205	274
7	49	57	30	254	285
6	21	27	72	177	249
12	30	42	83	231	314
9	12	21	71	158	229
—	14	14	132	180	313
18	48	66	36	211	246
3	26	29	114	162	277
4	44	48	19	239	258
3	18	21	118	174	292
5	26	31	83	178	261
21	17	37	66	211	277
20	44	64	89	221	309
3	12	16	148	148	296
11	10	20	45	184	230
10	30	40	17	223	240
4	51	55	41	205	246
2	37	40	84	204	288
2	38	40	65	204	269
4	29	33	56	186	242
7	47	54	36	254	290
6	33	39	101	208	309
14	45	60	30	239	268
7	22	29	70	160	231

	1	2	3	4	5
	Provided by local authority				Voluntary/ Private
	Nursery schools/ classes	Day nurseries	Play- groups	Total	Play- groups
Wales					
Clwyd	50	—	—	50	122
Dyfed	54	—	—	54	105
Gwent	61	2	—	63	73
Gwynedd	183	—	—	183	129
Mid Glamorgan	143	—	4	147	58
Powys	78	—	—	78	95
S. Glamorgan	48	1	—	49	115
W. Glamorgan	120	—	4	124	49
Scotland					
Borders	20	—	2	22	218
Central	26	19	—	64	128
Dumfries & Galloway	14	—	—	14	128
Fife	62	—	1	63	139
Grampian	42	10	16	68	121
Highland	6	—	—	6	161
Lothian	66	18	6	90	153
Orkney	27	—	—	27	254
Shetland	—	—	—	—	343
Strathclyde	36	8	3	47	106
Tayside	43	21	1	65	141
Western Isles	27	—	—	27	121

6	7	8	9	10	11
Other private provision			*LEA*	*Total*	*Total*
Day nurseries	Minders	Total	Reception classes	Excluding reception classes	Including reception classes
5	8	13	144	185	330
1	13	14	142	173	315
2	7	9	148	144	292
—	8	8	66	319	385
3	7	10	118	215	334
2	8	10	148	182	330
21	12	33	117	197	315
2	5	7	134	180	314
7	4	11	37	251	288
—	3	3	29	195	225
—	—	—	39	142	180
3	8	12	—	213	214
1	2	3	34	192	225
—	—	—	19	168	186
1	5	5	8	247	256
—	—	—	3	281	284
—	1	1	39	344	383
1	1	3	34	155	189
—	9	9	4	215	220
—	—	—	38	148	186

References

1. The case for nurseries – a better deal for mothers . . .

1 Bone, M. (1977), *Pre-School Children and Their Need for Day Care*, HMSO, London.

2 Osborn, A. (1975), *The Day Care of Children under Five in the City of Westminster*, Westminster Social Services Dept, London.

3 Hannon, P. (1977), *The Belfield Pre-School Survey*, Belfield Community Council, Rochdale.

4 Greenwich Programme Planning Section (1972), *Day Care and Play for Under-5s in Greenwich*, London Borough of Greenwich, London.

5 Watts, J. (1976), *Pre-School Education and the Family*, unpublished report, University of Aberdeen Institute of Education.

6 Bernal, J. (1973), 'Night waking in infants during the first 14 months', *Developmental Medicine and Child Neurology*, 15, 760.

7 Richman, N., Stevenson, J. E., and Graham, P. J. (1975), 'Prevalence of behaviour problems in 3-year-old children: an epidemiological study in a London Borough', *Journal of Child Psychology and Psychiatry*, 16, 277.

8 Oakley, A. (1974), *The Sociology of Housework*, Martin Robertson, London.

9 Bax, M., Moss, P., and Plewis, I. (1979), *Pre-School Families and Services*, unpublished report, Thomas

Coram Research Unit, London University Institute of Education.

10 Ginsberg, S. (1976), 'Women, work and conflict', in Fonda, N., and Moss, P. (eds.), *Mothers in Employment*, Brunel University, Uxbridge.

11 Boulton, M. (forthcoming), *Women's Attitudes to Being Mothers and Looking After Children*, doctoral thesis, University of London.

12 Bernard, J. (1975), *The Future of Motherhood*, Penguin Books, Baltimore.

13 Brown, G., and Harris, T. O. (1978), *Social Origins of Depression: A Study of Psychiatric Disorder in Women*, Tavistock, London.

14 Richman, N. (1978), 'Depression in mothers of young children', *Journal of the Royal Society of Medicine*, 71, 489.

15 Brown, G. W., Bhrolcaain, M. N., and Harris, T. (1975), 'Social class and psychiatric disturbance among women in an urban population', *Sociology*, 9, 225.

16 Office of Population Censuses and Surveys (1979), *General Household Survey, 1977*, HMSO, London.

17 Unpublished data from 'Child Health and Education in the Seventies' study, Bristol University Department of Child Health.

18 Department of Employment (1977), 'New projections of future labour force', *DE Gazette*, 6, 587.

19 Kamerman, S. (1978), *Work and Family in Industrialised Societies*, paper prepared for the Rockefeller Conference on 'Women, Family and Work', 21–22 September 1978.

20 Finegan, T. A. (1975), 'Participation of married women in the labour force', in Lloyd, C. B. (ed.), *Sex, Discrimination and the Division of Labour*, Columbia University Press, New York.

21 Hunt, A., Fox, J., and Morgan, M. (1974), *Families and Their Needs*, HMSO, London.

22 Department of Employment (1977), *New Survey of Earnings, 1976: Volume F*, HMSO, London.

23 Unpublished analysis of 1974 FES data by Dept of Health and Social Security (SR3).

24 Hunt, A. (1978), *Management Attitudes and Practices towards Women at Work*, HMSO, London.

25 Polachek, S. W. (1975), 'Discontinuous labour force participation and its effect on women's market earnings', in Lloyd, C. B. (ed.), *Sex, Discrimination and the Division of Labour*, Columbia University Press, New York.

2. . . . *and a better deal for children too*

1 Brown, G. W., and Davidson, S. (1978), 'Social class, psychiatric disorder of mother and accident to children', *The Lancet*, I, 378.

2 Rutter, M. (1966), *Children of Sick Patients – an Environmental and Psychiatric Study*, OUP, London.

3 Weissman, M., and Paykel, S. (1976), *The Depressed Woman: A Study of Social Relationships*, University of Chicago Press, Chicago.

4 Richman, N. (1976), 'Depression in mothers of pre-school children', *Journal of Child Psychology and Psychiatry*, 17, 75.

5 Morton, J. (1976), 'When a flat is home', *New Society*, 36, 307.

6 Bone, M. (1977), *Pre-School Children and Their Need for Day Care*, HMSO, London.

7 Bax, M., Moss, P., and Plewis, I. (1979), *Pre-School Families and Services*, unpublished report, Thomas Coram Research Unit, London University Institute of Education.

8 Watts, J. (1976), *Pre-School Education and the Family*, unpublished report, University of Aberdeen Institute of Education.

9 Tizard, B. (1977), *Parent Involvement in Nursery*

Education, Report for 1976–77, unpublished report, Thomas Coram Research Unit, London University Institute of Education.

10 Garber, H., and Heber, F. R. (1977), 'The Milwaukee Project: indications of the effectiveness of early intervention in preventing mental retardation', in Mittler, P. (ed.), *Research to Practise in Mental Retardation*, Vol. 1, University Park Press, Baltimore.

11 Tizard, J., Moss, P., and Perry, J. (1976), *All Our Children*, Temple Smith, London.

12 Hunt, J. McV. (1961), *Intelligence and Experience*, Ronald Press, New York.

13 Bloom, B. S. (1964), *Stability and Change in Human Characteristics*, John Wiley, London.

14 Clarke, A. M., and Clarke, A. D. B. (1976), 'Overview and implications', in Clarke, A. M., and Clarke, A. D. B. (eds.), *Early Experience: Myth and Evidence*, Open Books, London.

15 Ministry of Health (1945), Circular 221/45.

16 Ministry of Health (1968), Circular 37/68.

17 Bowlby, J. (1951), *Maternal Care and Child Health*, World Health Organization, Geneva.

18 Bowlby, J. (1973), *Attachment and Loss, Vol. II: Separation*, Hogarth Press, London.

19 World Health Organization Expert Committee on Mental Health (1951), *Report on the Second Session*, WHO, Geneva.

20 Schaffer, M. R., and Emerson, P. E. (1964), 'The development of social attachment in infancy', *Monograph of the Society for Research in Child Development*, vol. 29, no. 94.

21 Schaffer, M. R. (1977), *Mothering*, Fontana/Open Books, London.

22 Blehar, M. (1974), 'Anxious attachment and defensive reactions associated with day care', *Child Development*, 45, 683.

23 Brookhart, J., and Hock, E. (1976), 'The effects of

experimental context and experimental background on infants' behaviour towards their mothers and a stranger', *Child Development*, 47, 333.

24 Doyle, A. (1975), 'Infant development in day care', *Developmental Psychology*, 11, 655.

25 Roopnarine, J. L., and Lamb, M. E. (1978), 'The effects of day care on attachment and exploratory behaviour in a strange situation', *Merill Palmer Quarterly*, 24, 85.

26 Caldwell, B., Wright, C., Hanig, A., and Tannenbaum, J. (1970), 'Infant day care and attachment', *American Journal of Ortho-psychiatry*, 40, 397.

27 Farran, D., and Ramey, C. T. (1976), *Social Interaction Behaviour of High-Risk Children with Their Mothers*, paper presented at the meeting of the American Association on Mental Deficiency, Chicago.

28 Ricciuti, H. N. (1974), 'Fear and the development of social attachments in the first year of life', in Lewis, M., and Rosenblum, L. (eds.), *Origins of Fear*, John Wiley, New York.

29 Willis, A. G., and Ricciuti, H. N. (1974), *Longitudinal Observations of Infants' Daily Arrivals at a Day Care Centre*, technical report from the Cornell Research Programme in Early Development and Education.

30 Kagan, J., Kearsley, R., and Zelazo, P. (1976), *The Effects of Infant Day Care on Psychological Attachment*, paper presented at the meeting of the American Association of Science, Boston.

31 Loda, F., Glezen, P., and Clyde, W. (1972), 'Respiratory disease in group day care', *Pediatrics*, 49, 428.

32 Strangert, K. (1976), 'Respiratory illness in preschool children with different forms of day care', *Pediatrics*, 57, 191.

33 Belsky, J., and Steinberg, L. D. (1978), 'The effects of day care: a critical review', *Child Development*, 49, 929–49.

3. The opposition case – some objections to nurseries

1 Whitbread, N. (1972), *The Evolution of the Nursery-Infant School*, Routledge and Kegan Paul, London.

2 Gathorne-Hardy, J. (1972), *The Rise and Fall of the British Nanny*, Hodder and Stoughton, London.

3 Board of Education (1905), *Report of Children under Five Years of Age in Public Elementary Schools by Women Inspectors*, Parliamentary Papers, 1905.

4 Women's Co-operative Guild (1917), *Maternity*, Women's Co-operative Guild, Harmondsworth.

5 Spring-Rice, M. (1939), *Working-Class Wives*, Penguin Books, London.

6 Royal Commission on Population (1949), *Report* (Cmnd, 7695), HMSO, London.

7 Bax, M., Moss, P., and Plewis, I. (1979), *Pre-School Families and Services*, unpublished report, Thomas Coram Research Unit, London University Institute of Education.

8 Wallston, B. (1973), 'The effects of maternal employment on children', *Journal of Child Psychology and Psychiatry*, 14, 81–93.

9 Rutter, M. (1972), *Maternal Deprivation Re-assessed*, Penguin Books, Harmondsworth.

10 Jobling, M. (1973), *Children of Working Mothers*, Highlight No. 2, National Children's Bureau, London.

11 Kamerman, S. (1978), *Work and Family in Industrialised Societies*, paper prepared for the Rockefeller Conference on 'Women, Family and Work', 21–22 September 1978.

12 Ferge, Z. (1976), 'The relations between paid and unpaid working women', *Labour and Society*, April 1976.

13 McLean, U. (1977), 'Helping to hold the baby – Hungarian style', *Morning Star*, 24 April 1977.

14 Land, H. (1977), *Who Cares for the Family*, paper given at the annual conference of the Social Administration Association, July 1978.

15 Central Office of Statistics (1977), *Statistical Pocket Book of Hungary, 1977*, Central Office of Statistics, Budapest.

16 *Sunday Express*, 2 October 1977.

17 Central Statistical Office (1978), *Social Trends 9*, HMSO, London.

18 Cook, A. (1975), *The Working Mother*, New York State School of Industrial and Labor Relations, Ithaca.

19 Young, M., and Willmott, P. (1973), *The Symmetrical Family*, Routledge and Kegan Paul, London.

20 National Board for Prices and Incomes (1970), *Hours of Work, Overtime and Shiftworking*, Report No. 161, HMSO, London.

21 Department of Employment (1977), *New Survey of Earnings, 1976: Volume F*, HMSO, London.

22 Cohen, G. (1977), 'Absentee husbands in spiralist families: the myth of the symmetrical family', *Journal of Marriage and the Family*, 39, 595–604.

23 Office of Population Censuses and Surveys (1978), *One-Parent Families, 1971 and 1976*, OPCS, London.

24 Swedish Ministry of Health and Social Affairs (1977), *Parental Insurance in Sweden – Some Data*, Ministry of Health and Social Affairs International Secretariat, Stockholm.

25 Melsted, L. (1979), 'Election Year, '79: Swedish family policy', *Current Sweden*, 225, Swedish Institute, Stockholm.

26 Rosengren, B. (1976), 'More time for the children: a survey of recent developments in the care of young children', *Current Sweden*, 131, Swedish Institute, Stockholm.

4. What's what in the nursery world

 1 Department of Health and Social Security (1978), *Staff of Local Authority Social Services Departments at 30/9/76*, DHSS, London.

2 Department of Health and Social Security (1979), *Children's Day Care Facilities at 31 March 1977, England,* DHSS, London.

3 Welsh Office (1978), *Activities of Social Services Departments, Year Ended 31 March 1977,* Welsh Office, Cardiff.

4 Department of Education and Science (1978), *Statistics of Education 1977, Vol. 1,* HMSO, London.

5 Department of Health and Social Security (1976), 'Day care provision for the under-fives', in *Low Cost Day Care Provision for the Under-Fives,* DHSS, London.

6 Parry, M., and Archer, H. (1974), *Pre-School Education,* Macmillan, London.

7 Osborn, A. (1976), *The Day Care of Children under Five in the City of Westminster,* Westminster Social Services Dept, London.

8 Department of the Environment and the Welsh Office (1978), *Local Government Financial Statistics: England and Wales, 1976/77,* HMSO, London.

9 Department of Education and Science (1973), Circular 2173, *Nursery Education.*

10 Pre-School Playgroups Association (1978), *Facts and Figures, 1977,* PPA, London.

11 Bone, M. (1977), *Pre-School Children and the Need for Day-Care,* HMSO, London.

12 Pre-School Playgroups Association (1977), *Facts and Figures, 1976,* PPA, London.

13 Inner London Pre-School Playgroups Association (1977), *Playgroups: A Shared Experience,* ILPPA, London.

14 Local Authorities Association (1977), *Under Fives,* Local Authorities Association, London.

15 Department of Education and Science (1977), *Statistics of Education, 1976,* Vol. 1, HMSO, London.

16 Mayall, B., and Petrie, P. (1977), *Mother, Minder and Child,* London University Institute of Education, London.

17 Day, C. (1975), *Company Day Nurseries*, Institute of Personnel Management, London.

5. The present system – a badly fitting puzzle

1 Bone, M. (1977), *Pre-School Children and the Need for Day-Care*, HMSO, London.
2 *Spare Rib*, April 1977.
3 Department of Health and Social Security and Department of Education and Science (1978), Joint Circular, 25 January 1978, *Co-ordination of Services for Children under 5*.
4 Owen, D. (1976), Foreword, in *Low Cost Day Care Provision for the Under-Fives*, DHSS, London.
5 Bax, M., Moss, P., and Plewis, I. (1979), *Pre-School Families and Services*, unpublished report, Thomas Coram Research Unit, London University Institute of Education.
6 Department of Education and Science (1976), 'Nursery education: current provision and policy', in *Low Cost Day Care Provision for the Under-Fives*, DHSS, London.
7 Hunt, A. (1968), *Survey of Women's Employment*, Government Social Survey, London.

6. New approaches to old problems

1 Mottershead, P. (1978), *A Survey of Child Care for Pre-School Children with Working Parents*, Equal Opportunities Commission, Manchester.
2 Moss, P. (1978), *Alternative Models of Group Child-Care for Pre-School Children with Working Parents*, Equal Opportunities Commission, Manchester.
3 Knight, D. (1977), 'Second-rate day nurseries', *Contact*, July 1977.
4 Department of Health and Social Security and Department of Education and Science (1976),

Joint Circular, 9 March 1976, *Co-ordination of Local Authority Services for Children under 5.*

5 Department of Health and Social Security and Department of Education and Science (1978), Joint Circular, 25 January 1978, *Co-ordination of Services for Children under 5.*

6 Thomas Coram Foundation (1976), *The Children's Centre*, Thomas Coram Foundation, London.

7 Children's Community Centre (1974), *Our Experiences of Collective Child Care*, Children's Community Centre, London.

7. *Childminding – has it a part to play?*

1 Central Policy Review Staff (1978), *Services for Young Children with Working Mothers*, HMSO, London.

2 Jackson, B. (1976), 'Childminding: a breakthrough point in the cycle of deprivation', in *Low Cost Day Care Provision for the Under-Fives*, DHSS, London.

3 Trades Union Congress (1977), *The Under-Fives: The Report of a TUC Working Party*, TUC, London.

4 Jackson, B. (1973), 'The childminders', *New Society*, 29 November 1973.

5 Van Der Eyken, W. (1977), *The Pre-School Years* (4th edition), Penguin Books, Harmondsworth.

6 Mayall, B., and Petrie, P. (1977), *Mother, Minder and Child*, NFER, Slough.

7 Nurseries and Child-Minders Regulation Act, 1948, amended in the Health Services and Public Health Act, 1968.

8 Department of Health and Social Security (1976), 'Day care provision for the under-fives', in *Low Cost Day Care Provision for the Under-Fives*, DHSS, London.

9 Parry, M., and Archer, H. (1974), *Pre-School Education*, Macmillan, London.

10 Community Relations Commission (1975), *Who Minds?*, CRC, London.

11 Kamerman, S., and Kahn, A. (1979), paper presented to conference on 'Alternative Policies for the Care of Children under Age 3', Copenhagen, 18–19 June 1979.

12 Department of Health and Social Security and Department of Education and Science (1978), Joint Circular, 9 March 1976, *Co-ordination of Services for Children under 5*.

13 Wardell, R. D. (1977), 'Day fostering in Humberside', *Social Work Service*, May 1977.

14 Macauley, N. (1977), *Information Sheet*, Department of Social Work, Edinburgh Division, Lothian Regional Council.

15 Willmott, P., and Challis, L. (1977), *The Groveway Project: An Experiment in Salaried Childminding*, Department of the Environment, London.

8. But what about the parents?

1 Pinkerton, G. (1978), 'Where do you come in at the nursery?', *Nursery World*, 19 October 1978.

2 Tizard, B. (1977), 'No common ground', *Times Educational Supplement*, 27 May 1977.

3 National Union of Teachers (1977), *The Needs of the Under-Fives*, NUT, London.

4 Tizard, B. (1978), 'Carry on communicating', *Times Educational Supplement*, 3 February 1978.

5 Committee into the Management and Government of Schools (1977), *Report: A New Partnership for Our Schools*, HMSO, London.

6 *Times Educational Supplement*, 23 September 1977.

7 *Times Educational Supplement*, 30 September 1977.

8 Ministry of Consumer Affairs and Government Administration (1977), *Kindergartens in Norway*, Ministry of Consumer Affairs, Oslo.

9 Peters, D. (1978), 'Parents into the mainstream', *Times Educational Supplement*, 30 September 1977.

10 Watts, J. (1976), *Pre-School Education and the Family*, unpublished report, University of Aberdeen Institute of Education.

11 Pre-School Playgroups Association (1977), *Facts and Figures, 1976*, PPA, London.

12 Pre-School Playgroups Association (1978), *Facts and Figures, 1977*, PPA, London.

13 Lucas, J., and McKennel, V. (1974), *The Penguin Book of Playgroups*, Penguin Books, Harmondsworth.

14 Children's Community Centre (1974), *Our Experiences of Collective Child Care*, Children's Community Centre, London.

9. Early education – there's more to it than play

1 Board of Education (1905), *Report of Children under Five Years of Age in Public Elementary Schools by Women Inspectors*, Parliamentary Papers, 1905.

2 Smith, P. (1978), 'Play is only one way to learn', *New Society*, 27 July 1978.

3 Tough, J. (1977), *The Development of Meaning*, George Allen and Unwin, London.

4 Tough, J. (1976), *Listening to Children Talking*, Ward Lock Educational, London.

5 Tough, J. (1977), *Talking and Learning*, Ward Lock Educational, London.

6 March, L. (1973), *Swimming under Five*, W. Heffer and Sons, London.

7 'The White Rabbit' (1978), 'Who's deprived?', *Humpty Dumpty*, 9.

8 Children's Community Centre (1974), *Our Experiences of Collective Child Care*, Children's Community Centre, London.

9 Marger, S. (1977), 'The theory and practice of childcare in China', in Socialist Child-Care Collective

(eds.), *Changing Child-Care*, Writers and Readers Publishing Co-operative, London.

10 Kessien, W. (ed.), *Childhood in China*, Yale University Press, New Haven.

11 Tizard, B., Philips, J., and Plewis, I. (1976), 'Play in pre-school centres – I. Play measures and their relation to age, sex and IQ', *Journal of Child Psychology and Psychiatry*, 17, 251.

12 Hutt, C. (1972), *Males and Females*, Penguin Books, Harmondsworth.

13 Weitzman, L. et al. (1976), 'Sex-role socialisation in picture books for pre-school children', in Children's Rights Workshop (eds.), *Sexism in Children's Books*, Writers and Readers Publishing Co-operative, London.

14 Czaplinski, S. (1976), 'Sexism in award-winning picture books', in Children's Rights Workshop (eds.), *Sexism in Children's Books*, Writers and Readers Publishing Co-operative, London.

15 Nilsen, A. P. (1970), *Women in Children's Literature*, paper prepared for Modern Language Association workshop on 'Children's Literature', New York.

16 Birmingham Women's Liberation Group (1975), *Out of the Pumpkin Shell*, Flat Earth Press, Birmingham.

17 Quoted in Children's Rights Workshop (eds.) (1976), *Sexism in Children's Books*, Writers and Readers Publishing Co-operative, London.

18 Greenleaf, P. (1972), *Liberating Young Children from Sex Roles*, New England Free Press, Somerville, Mass.

10. What is to be done?

1 Newell, P. (1978), 'Time for a change?', *Times Educational Supplement*, 29 September 1978.

2 Department of the Environment and the Welsh Office (1978), *Local Government Financial Statistics : England and Wales, 1976/77*, HMSO, London.

3 Central Statistical Office (1978), *Social Trends 9*, HMSO, London.

4 Ferguson, S., and Fitzgerald, H. (1954), *Studies in the Social Services*, HMSO, London.

5 Tizard, J., Moss, P., and Perry, J. (1976), *All Our Children*, Temple Smith, London.

6 *Guardian*, 17 October 1978.

7 Trades Union Congress (1978), *The Under-Fives : The Report of a TUC Working Party*, TUC, London.

8 Central Policy Review Staff (1978), *Services for Young Children with Working Mothers*, HMSO, London.

9 Equal Opportunities Commission (1978), *I Want to Work, but What About the Kids*, Equal Opportunities Commission, Manchester.

10 *The Times*, 1978.

Appendix

1 Central Policy Review Staff (1978), *Services for Young Children with Working Mothers*, HMSO, London.

2 Department of Health and Social Security (1979), *Children's Day Care Facilities at 31 March 1977, England*, DHSS, London.

3 Welsh Office (1978), *Activities of Social Services Departments, Year ended 31 March 1977*, Welsh Office, Cardiff.

Index

More About Penguins and Pelicans

Penguinews, which appears every month, contains details of all the new books issued by Penguins as they are published. It is supplemented by our stocklist, which includes almost 5,000 titles.

A specimen copy of *Penguinews* will be sent to you free on request. Please write to Dept EP, Penguin Books Ltd, Harmondsworth, Middlesex, for your copy.

In the U.S.A.: For a complete list of books available from Penguins in the United States write to Dept CS, Penguin Books, 625 Madison Avenue, New York, New York 10022.

In Canada: For a complete list of books available from Penguins in Canada write to Penguin Books Canada Ltd, 2801 John Street, Markham, Ontario L3R 1B4.

In Australia: For a complete list of books available from Penguins in Australia write to the Marketing Department, Penguin Books Australia Ltd, P.O. Box 257, Ringwood, Victoria 3134.

Penguins for Parents

Baby & Child
Penelope Leach

'A first-rate handbook of children and is, in my view, to be wholly recommended to anyone expecting a baby or who has one already. It stands head and shoulders above anything else of the same type that is available at the moment. It is clear, easy to understand, well-written and excellently informed . . . I know I will look it up again and again' – Mary Kenny in the *Spectator*

Toddlers and Parents
T. Berry Brazelton

Bewildered, anxious, amused, exhausted by your toddler? Each chapter in this indispensable guide focuses on a special problem: working parents, single parents, large families, disturbed families, hyperactive children, toddler rivalry, and the use of day nurseries, playgroups and minders. Interspersed with the descriptions are reassuring, practical analyses of the toddler's psychological motivation and sympathetic, constructive comments on the parents' reactions.

Helping Your Handicapped Child
A Step-by-Step Guide to Everyday Problems
Janet Carr

A practical book designed for anyone who has, or who works with, mentally handicapped children. Based on the teaching method of behaviour modification, it tells you how to see what your child can or cannot do, and why; how to break down into manageable steps what you want to teach, and how to guide and encourage as you go.

Children in their Primary Schools
Henry Pluckrose

In this introduction to the many methods which abound
in English primary schools, Henry Pluckrose discusses
both the content of the curriculum and the philosophy
which underlies it. He points out the relative merits of rigid
and freer time-tables, and shows us how play and work
are equally essential, can be equally educative, and in many
cases are actually interchangeable. He also explores the
current problems and looks ahead to the changes we can
expect in the next ten years.

Clever Children in Comprehensive Schools
Auriol Stevens

Do you wilfully sacrifice bright children for political
principles if you send them to a comprehensive school?
In this sane and well-balanced assessment of comprehensive
and selective school methods, the education correspondent
of the *Observer* gives the facts – about mixed ability
teaching, about the minimum size for a comprehensive with a
good sixth form, about the challenge of research versus
the slog of disciplined work, about provision for science
and language teaching. She is sensitive both to the dilemma
that faces parents as well as to the problems met by
teachers who strive to fulfil the varied needs of their pupils.

The Public School Phenomenon
Jonathan Gathorne-Hardy

In 1736 Dr Heath of Eton retired to bed for a week with
strained muscles after giving seventy boys ten strokes each;
only twenty years ago eight hundred Cheltenham girls
were required to lift their skirts on a midwinter parade to
check that they were wearing regulation knickers. Today
British public schools are a source of sharp controversy.
Should they be abolished? What effects (sexual and
otherwise) do they have on the characters of their pupils?
Do they accentuate class differences? Mr Gathorne-Hardy
clarifies many of these questions in his unique,
comprehensive and entertaining history.

'A massive fund of information, intelligence, bright ideas
and considerable humour' – C. P. Snow